African American Foodways

African American Foodways

EXPLORATIONS OF HISTORY AND CULTURE

Edited by Anne L. Bower

University of Illinois Press
Urbana and Chicago

∞ This book is printed on acid-free paper.

Library of Congress Cataloging-in-Publication Data
African American foodways : explorations of history and culture /
edited by Anne L. Bower.
p.   cm. — (The food series)
Includes bibliographical references and index.
ISBN-13: 978-0-252-03185-4 (cloth : alk. paper)
ISBN-10: 0-252-03185-7 (cloth : alk. paper)
1. African American cookery.
I. Bower, Anne.
TX715.A2428   2007
641.59'296073—dc22   2006100933

For Ursula,
who is just beginning to taste the world

Contents

Acknowledgments

Graduate school did not prepare me for the complexities of foodways scholarship. Whatever expertise I've gathered in the field and thus brought to the task of editing this book comes, rather, from scholars and foodies whose work I've read and, in some cases, with whom I've worked over the years. To all those whose knowledge has been shared with me through books and articles, at conferences, culinary historian meetings (in Chicago, Houston, and elsewhere), and via emails and telephone conversations I therefore send out a generalized but sincere expression of gratitude. I must, however, give credit to those who directly inspired *African American Foodways*. Bruce Kraig and Andrew Smith first spoke to me about editing this book, and my friend and colleague Thomas Piontek offered ideas and feedback on my writing. At the University of Illinois Press, director and editor-in-chief Willis Regier's interest in the project never flagged despite many delays, and Mary Giles's sharp eyes helped craft our finished product most effectively. I also thank the individual contributors to the volume; without their ideas, patience, and good spirits this book could never have happened. Finally, I am grateful for my amazing and growing family for sharing my food enthusiasms and experimentations via conversation, reading, and, of course, all the good meals we've cooked and eaten together.

Introduction: Watching *Soul Food*
Anne L. Bower

A steaming pot of greens flavored with pieces of smoky meat, a pile of fluffy biscuits or a bubbling peach cobbler, chicken fried to irresistible crispness or stewed with dumplings, creamy, spicy sweet potato pie — these are some of the dishes people picture when African American food or its supposed equivalent, soul food, is mentioned. The history and cultural traditions behind and around this food are all too often forgotten, however. My hope is that the seven essays in *African American Foodways: Explorations of History and Culture* will help readers see how explorations of food history and its intersections with other historical developments yield important understanding of African American culture. As the essays and the careful documentation that accompanies them demonstrate, soul food is just a *part* of the huge topic we call African American foodways.

George Tillman's *Soul Food* (1997) uses particular food and foodways to take us into the lives of a modern Chicago family.[1] Although entertaining and heartwarming, the movie presents only a partial glance at the ways in which African American food impacts how people know themselves and their world. Analyses, explorations, and histories such as those provided in *African American Foodways* help put a narrative like *Soul Food* into a larger, more realistic, and more complex framework.

In Tillman's film Sunday dinner is a ritual that brings a sometimes fractious African American family together. Writer-director Tillman explains that in his own family, such dinners had a unifying force: "All my aunts and uncles, plus ministers and, sometimes, even homeless people would come over for my grandmother's food." He came to understand that his grandmother was providing much more than a delicious meal and a time for the family to gather. "There was always a lot going on!" he states provocatively.[2]

As the film opens the camera presents a collage of family photos while the song "Mama, I Love You" plays. The song is a paean to women's central role in holding African American culture together. Intercut with the photo collection, which gives a sense of the Joseph family's long history, is a bright shot of the laden dinner table and another of the family gathered around that table.[3] This table will play a central role in the film, surrounded by ten or more people when all is well, hosting just a few to represent the family's disintegration when its matriarch is no longer in control, and empty at the nadir of the family's unity. Once the movie's narrative begins, Tillman uses a voice-over by schoolboy Ahmad (Brandon Hammond) to introduce a familiar, reassuring, and somewhat stereotypical concept. Ahmad says that his grandmother, Big Mama Jo (Irma P. Hall) "stops arguments" with her green beans, fried chicken, and other traditional foods. Big Mama is the matriarch who makes sure that Sunday dinner brings her family together each week. As Ahmad explains, "During slavery times we didn't have a lot to celebrate, so cooking became how we expressed our love for each other." He has learned that these weekly meals are about "more than just eating," and it is he who, after his grandmother's death, maneuvers the family back together for another Sunday dinner.

As the essays in *African American Foodways* demonstrate, there's always "more than just eating," involved in trying to understand the origins and meanings of African American food. Of course, when it comes to food, each essayist, and each reader, too, feels the influence of family and local community and of such factors as where we grew up and where we live now along with particular values about nutrition, ecology, or economics. For this reason, *African American Foodways* provides more than one essay on the history of African American foods, more than one essay that discusses that ubiquitous "sign" of soul food—fried chicken. Freud told us that sometimes a cigar is just a cigar, and maybe there are times when a piece of fried chicken is just a piece of fried chicken. For those concerned with the study of African American food, however, it is important to note that social and economic influences, changing women's roles, culinary history, health concerns, race, and class issues are also part of the meal.

In *Soul Food*, the dishes that show up on Big Mama's table for her family (and movie viewers) to savor include fried chicken and/or chicken and dumplings, deep-fried catfish, macaroni and cheese, string beans, collard greens, black-eyed peas with ham hocks, peach cobbler, and sweet corn bread.[4] Chitterlings are mentioned, shown in passing, but never discussed. Those doing the cooking are the women—Big Mama and her three daughters. Of the daughters only one is given consistent praise as a cook: Ahmad's mother, Maxine. Terri, an ambitious lawyer and the family's financial anchor, is teased for being a bad cook; Bird, the youngest, who has started her own beauty shop, has mixed success in the kitchen. Occasionally a man helps out, but he is usually sent off to watch football if enough women's hands are available.

The production of a family's emotional stability, as well as the making of food such as greens, corn bread, and fried catfish, have traditionally been associated with women. The matriarchal role exemplified by Big Mama includes the production of meals that hold families and communities together, the oral communication of food traditions and history that can nourish the body and the soul, and the emotional labor of helping family members with disagreements and problems. Mama Jo's powers are intuitive and experiential, based on long years of solving family conflicts and performing domestic work, whether for pay or at home. Her knowledge has been gathered not from books but from life and from the stories others have told her. One daughter wonders how she knows how much of an ingredient to add without measuring; Big Mama's recipes are all in her head. It is a question Mama Jo doesn't answer; she knows, as a casual gesture demonstrates, through experience. She's asked, too, why ham hocks are added to vegetables and briefly explains that hocks were often the only meat people had during slavery days. The implied although never discussed assumption is that knowing one's history and passing it along—with words and with food—is a way of maintaining personal and community identity. At another point Mama Jo defines soul food as "cooking from the heart."

The presumption that cooking is a way for a woman to express her heart—her love for family—feeds into gender stereotypes that for the most part the film enforces. In his directorial commentary, available on the DVD version of the film, Tillman explains that he grew up with six aunts and a strong grandmother and wanted to focus on the matriarch and her central role and then on how a family deals with the loss of that central maternal figure. The one woman in the film who doesn't cook—Big Mama's daughter, Terri, the successful lawyer—has been divorced once, becomes estranged from her husband during the course of the story, has no children, and is often portrayed as heartless and cold. The idea that women who don't participate in cooking and other domestic duties lack heart, perhaps a true evocation of an opinion that Tillman's matriarch and her family share, needs undoing.

A number of the essays within *African American Foodways* look at the many ways African American women have expressed heart. For some, holding onto cookery traditions and sharing them with families and communities do play a central role. For others, however, heart is just as well expressed through nondomestic activities such as businesses (including catering), the professions (including the arts, teaching, scholarship), and leadership roles in the community.

Tillman's bigger-than-life maternal figure can be read as a mere stereotype, a Mammy or Aunt Jemima. This stereotype, as Alice A. Deck defines her, is "a very large, dark earth mother who represents fecundity, self-sufficiency, and endless succor [;] exists to do nothing but prepare and serve food, along with a hearty helping of her homespun wisdom about life [; and] works best not from printed recipes but from a memory that links her to previous generations of slave women and black earth mothers." Further, this figure, with "large breasts, muscular arms, and wide hips," is an "idealized representation of an autonomous black woman" who needs "no other to complete her, yet many others in her orbit can be completed by her."[5] Although this definition seems to fit Mama Jo it quickly becomes apparent that she cannot entirely "complete" the lives of others; most have problems (romantic, financial, and personal) beyond her ken or capacity. She also has her own difficulties and weaknesses, the effects of diabetes among them. Because she has not taken her medication nor followed a regulated diet, circulation to one leg has become blocked, and the leg must eventually be amputated. During the course of the film she is hospitalized and eventually dies.

As the stereotype of the mythical mother figure breaks apart some useful although difficult questions emerge for thoughtful viewers: How can the strength embodied by a woman like Big Mama and her grand food traditions continue today in ways that are healthy but still hold to tradition and foster family closeness?[6] How can women like Big Mama's three daughters sustain their heritage in the face of so many temptations, demands, and difficulties? Must the challenge of holding a black family together continue to be pictured as mostly a woman's job?

Big Mama's sickness and death raise these issues and more—some of which are central to the essays in *African American Foodways*. How could Mama Jo have found a way to change her diet enough to improve her health and yet receive the same satisfaction from her own cooking and eating, the same joy in providing tradition for her large family?[7] Statistics demonstrate that the incidence of diabetes is higher in African Americans than in whites and worse for African American women than men. Women's family and community roles may adversely affect their health in the case of this disease. Sandra A. Black believes that "certain sociocultural factors, such as the role that women play in the family, may affect women's vulnerability to diabetes. Women are often the keepers of culture, the family members who pass on cultural practices, such as what foods are served for holiday celebrations or what activities family members are encouraged to engage in. This responsibility to maintain cultural practices and pass them on to younger generations can make it difficult for a mother or grandmother to successfully make lifestyle changes."[8]

Perhaps if Big Mama had been raised knowing more about the varieties of foods prepared by her African ancestors as well as her African American ones (including their herbal medicines), she would have practiced a healthier lifestyle. Then one factor in diabetes, diet, could have improved even if her circumstances didn't. This kind of exploration is not part of Tillman's film. But even if a woman like Mama Joe made the kinds of dietary changes reported to affect diabetes and hypertension, would those changes alone make enough of a difference? What about the stress factors affecting minorities? What about attitudes a person of color might hold toward health care providers and systems that practice subtle or overt discrimination? And what about economic pressures?[9] These, too, are topics never raised in the movie but ones important to exploring African American foodways today, whether the explorers are restaurateurs, cookbook authors, foodways scholars, or people involved with health care. Consequently, discussions of social, economic, and political inequities and their effects on African American history, culture, and foodways enter strongly into a number of the essays in African American Foodways.

African American food involves a fusion of African, Caribbean, South American, and other influences, few of which enter Tillman's movie. The women in Soul Food may occasionally battle over who makes a particular dish the best, but in general they celebrate the resourcefulness of their southern ancestors in using what came to hand to prepare nourishing and delicious dishes. As was common among many black Americans until recently, the characters in the movie do not dwell on their African ancestry but take their food history back only to the nineteenth century.

More recent students of culinary history, while taking into account the assumptions at the heart of this movie's depiction of the relationship between African Americans and their best-known foods, take a wider view of food heritage and related cultural history, a view the essays in African American Foodways reflect. Discussing the complicated origins of African and African American dishes, looking into the material and symbolic power of these foods, and exploring rituals and stereotypes associated with the food are all part of this book. Like the movie, however, the essays collected here place women's roles as preservers of food traditions at the heart of African American community survival.

In Soul Food the person who returns the family to its Sunday dinner tradition after Big Mama's death and relates the family's history is not a woman. It's the young boy, Ahmad. Young as he is, Ahmad manages to manipulate his conflicted relatives and family friends into gathering again around the Sunday dinner table. His voice-over confides to the audience that this meal is "a way we share our joys and sorrows—something the old folks say is missing from today's families." He doesn't cook the food although he lends a hand. Does Ahmad's role—attempting to hold the family together—portend social change in gender roles? Is Tillman among those working to help (African American) men accept more domestic responsibilities? Or is Tillman doing something much more conventional, something that sustains a gender assumption from the past—portraying men as those best able to take public responsibility for creating and telling history? Based on the character portrayals in the movie and the director's commentary, Tillman seems to be doing all these things. As he reiterates, he is nostalgic for the Sunday dinners he knew as a child and believes that cultural traditions such as those Sunday dinners will help sustain strong families and communities.[10]

All who have contributed to *African American Foodways* share some aspect of this belief in the power of food to signify much more than calories. Our perspectives are shaped by varied disciplines, but our expansive ways of understanding foodways allow us to see women of the past as historians as well as cooks and food as a major component of culture and not just what's for supper.

We are, of course, indebted to others who have studied and written about African American history, culture, and food traditions. In that last category, we've benefited from publications, ranging from Verta Mae Grosvenor's *Vibration Cooking; or, The Travel Notes of a Geechee Girl* (1970) to the equally valuable *The African Heritage Cookbook* (1971) in which Helen Mendes explored the West African roots of heritage cookery. In more recent years a number of African American cookbooks, such as those by Heidi Cusick, Jessica Harris, and Diane Spivey, have continued to provide useful combinations of recipes and culinary scholarship, and Karen Hess's *The Carolina Rice Kitchen: The African Connection* (1992) brought a deeper understanding of the economics and social history surrounding African American lives and cooking in the past.[11]

What has also inspired us are developments in food studies that began in the late 1980s and early 1990s with an ever-increasing production of journals, books, and academic courses, even degree programs in food studies.[12] Books like Laura Shapiro's *Perfection Salad: Women and Cooking at the Turn of the Century*, Linda Keller Brown's and Kay Mussell's essay collection *Ethnic and Regional Foodways in the United States: The Performance of Group Identity*, and Deane W. Curtin and Lisa M. Heldke's *Cooking, Eating, Thinking: Transformative Philosphies of Food* are three academic markers of this change. There are, of course, others; I only list these as examples. As the variety of essays in *African American Foodways* makes clear, studying food often provides new insight into our disciplines. We've gone beyond the old saw "we are what we eat" to realize that we are also what we don't eat and that our present lives are influenced deeply by what our ancestors did or didn't eat.

How odd that at the very time food is finally being studied as an integral part of culture, as important to our sense of identity and community as legal systems, literary texts, or national histories, there are so many people, regardless of race, age, ethnicity, and often class, who eat many meals without actually participating in food preparation. Fast-food (eaten in place or taken home), frozen or otherwise processed foods packaged for quick preparation, and snack foods neatly wrapped in plastic or foil abound. A Gallup study done in the mid-1980s indicated that, even then, 50 percent of Americans ate "frozen, packaged, or take-out meals" at dinnertime, and I'm sure that percentage has increased.[13] Is part of our study of food because of nostalgia — like that expressed by George Tillman — for the spiritual, aesthetic, nutritional, and familial values we associate with old-fashioned family dinners?

Soul Food's idealized representation of Sunday dinners takes on a mythological force. Everything is prepared from scratch, everything is available in abundance (the table is crowded with huge quantities of food, more than the people present could possibly consume), and Big Mama has a gardening tradition that her children and grandchildren will carry on; the film ends with a scene of assorted family members harvesting tomatoes and corn against the backdrop of Big Mama's house. I call the food symbolization mythological because it is so unquestioned, so static in its idealization and representation. No one says, "I'd rather not put fat meat in the collards." No one talks about what chitterlings are or wonders what ancestors ate back in Africa, before slavery. No one in the film mentions that much of what white Americans claim as southern food was invented by their ancestors, cooks working in slave masters' kitchens. No one says, "This chicken is delicious, but I hate the way whites still make jokes about us and fried chicken." None of the women says, "Let's make the men cook tonight."[14] And no one alters the recipes or suggests that foodways are always evolving.

Tillman does not question soul food itself.[15] The family members in the film are pressured by divorce, jail, sickness, death, birth, career change, and more, and the traditional foods that Big Mama has cooked — and her children will continue to cook — provide stability and a sense of home. Although it may sometimes carry those messages for those of us contributing to African American Foodways, our vision of African American food and what it means grows and evolves. And yet at the very same time a term like soul food continues to be a powerful way to signify something African Americans share throughout and beyond the United States. As the food journalist Donna Pierce sees it, this food heritage is one of the few elements that can still bring black people in the United States together, no matter what their line of work, level of education, or place of birth.[16] This importance and power of soul food will endure, of course, even though many people, unlike Tillman's movie family, will change how they cook these dishes. Some individuals won't buy fresh collard greens and spend time chopping them but will use frozen greens, pre-washed and chopped, or take them already cooked and seasoned from a can. Or, they might buy fried chicken at KFC or a local equivalent, lace black-eyed peas with smoked turkey instead of ham hocks, or consider curries and enchiladas as acceptable additions to the soul food table.

The intent of the present volume is not only to broaden understanding and appreciation of what African American food traditions have come to "mean" but also to explore intersections of foodways with history and culture. To ignore the powerful ways food and food customs have shaped group and individual identities and the economic, political, and social organization of society makes no sense. Food, it turns out, is an excellent locus for the study of group dynamics—how different populations exclude, include, reject, accept, and otherwise influence each other. In the case of Africans and African Americans, the study of foodways enlarges respect for the way a people, so egregiously oppressed, have miraculously managed to hold on to certain traditions from their West African origins yet have adapted and evolved various customs (food is just one example, after all), contributing hugely to this strange patchwork we call American society.

The book's subtitle, "Explorations of History and Culture," should indicate that much work remains in the field of African American foodways, whether focusing on culinary history, the social sciences, literature and the arts, health, economics and business, or popular culture. My hope is that this volume will spur other research into African American food itself and assist new understanding of foodways' importance as a field.

The first section of *African American Foodways* focuses on the history of African American food, as understood from different disciplinary perspectives. First comes Robert L. Hall's carefully documented essay about the long and complicated past of African food history. Hall uses both old and new source materials to detail the interrelationships between African foods and agricultural practices and the Atlantic slave trade, opening the complexity of how African American foodways came to be. Following Hall's historical analysis is William C. Whit's sociological study "Soul Food as Cultural Creation," which is organized around different aspects of foodways, from procuring food through cooking it and then disposing of the waste. For Whit, African American foodways constitute a stellar example of culture—something created, evolving, learned, and shared—an important adaptive response to the world. Next, Anne Yentsch, an archeologist and anthropologist, considers the transfer of culture in particular southern locations; one of her interests is how foodways of West Africa have affected cooking and eating customs that many today term *southern*. Yentsch provides extensive information about both pre– and post–Civil War foodways of blacks in the southern United States, incorporating social and class factors in most useful ways.

Part 2 contains four essays that deal with some of the ways African American food has been represented and the power of those representations. This section begins with Doris Witt's exploration of "intersections" between African American literary history and culinary studies, historically as well as currently, in a productive combination of the "high culture" of literature and the only recently recognized study of culinary history. Psyche Williams-Forson investigates the power of a food often associated with African Americans. In "Chickens and Chains: Using African American Foodways to Understand Black Identities" she demonstrates that food-linked stereotypes can powerfully affect contemporary culture and daily lives; knowing more about foodways history may be one way to undo stereotypes and prejudice. Rafia Zafar moves the discussion to an analysis of the rhetorical strategies used by the African American authors of one nineteenth-century and two early-twentieth-century cookbooks. Her "Recipes for Respect: Black Hospitality Entrepreneurs before World War I" helps us understand how these cookbook writers turned the supposedly simple task of writing recipe books into acts of personal agency. Closing out Part 2, in "Recipes for History: The National Council of Negro Women's Five Historical Cookbooks" I discuss five cookbooks and argue that each, in its own distinctive way, preserves and evolves what we understand as African American food and history. The authors of these cookbooks are actually historians, and their books can be understood as contributing to African American group identity formation.

⌐⌐

Preserving and evolving—it seems to me those are key terms when talking about ways to maintain African American food traditions and the history associated with them. Because my background is in literature, these dual acts resonate with what I see happening in literary studies. Henry Louis Gates, speaking of literary canons, has stated that we each form a personal canon based on the literature to which we're exposed but that "a canon, as it has functioned in every literary tradition, has served as the commonplace book of our *shared* culture."[17] I agree with his idea that we need to hold on to some critical or seminal texts, although ideas about which to select will vary. Yet focusing repeatedly on one set of honored texts can lead to the reification of literature. Such a canon must be constantly supplemented. Perhaps, we could consider soul food as the culinary canon of African American culture—the "commonplace book" of eating. But any canon, if it becomes rigid or stultified, ceases to reflect a culture's creativity, flexibility, and conflicts.

And so, to reflect that evolving and preserving ethos, I offer, even though it's unconventional to do so in the introduction to a collection of essays, a recipe for a dish I tasted in Chicago during the cooking demonstration portion of the Chicago Culinary Historians' June 2001 "Grits and Greens" conference on African American food. I've chosen this particular recipe because it exemplifies—in terms of food—an argument that the cultural critic Stuart Hall has made concerning all forms of ethnic and racial heritage. When looking at aspects of tradition that have helped a community endure, Hall explains, we have to see that "the question of tradition itself has to be conceptually rephrased." In order to keep traditions viable rather than essentialized or stereotyped, those traditions must undergo a "reworking [that] transmits the capacity to be both the same and different, both located in a tradition and yet not constrained by it."[18] Innovative recipes can do for soul food what jazz does for great old standards—hold onto tradition but give that tradition new relevance and vitality. Such innovative recipes also remind us that many African and African American dishes were "fusion" foods long before that term became fashionable.[19]

Kocoa Scott-Winbush, a Chicago cookbook author, television and radio presenter, and food event coordinator, doesn't call herself a cook of soul food; rather, she prepares "creative cuisine for soul nourishment." Her dishes blend methods and ingredients from all parts of the world and confirm that new combinations and ingredients only add to soul food's vitality. What follows is my transcription of one of her creations, based on watching her prepare the dish and on a handout she provided at the Chicago event.[20] I have used it as a first course or appetizer for five or six people, putting one or two crêpes on each small plate. With larger portions it becomes the main course.

Chicken and Collard Green Crêpes with Béchamel Sauce

1. Prepare 12–16 crêpes, using any basic crêpe recipe. Then preheat oven to 350 degrees.
2. For the filling, combine well:
> 3 cups cooked chicken, cut into small chunks
> 1 cup cooked or canned mushrooms, drained well
> 1 cup cooked collard greens, all liquid squeezed out
> Salt and pepper to taste
3. Prepare the béchamel sauce:
> ½ stick butter
> 4 tablespoons flour
> 2 cups milk, warmed slightly
> Salt and pepper to taste
> Small pinch of nutmeg

In a medium saucepan, melt the butter completely and then add flour. Whisk the flour into the butter thoroughly and continue whisking for five to six minutes over a low flame (do not brown) to cook away any flour taste. Add milk slowly while whisking, to prevent lumps from forming. If necessary, add more milk to achieve the consistency of thin porridge or pudding. Season with salt, pepper, and nutmeg. Let cool slightly before using.

4. Assemble the crêpes:

Use one-twelfth to one-sixteenth of the filling for each; place filling on crêpe, and roll securely. Place them seam side down in a lightly buttered casserole dish. At this point you can bake them (covered with aluminum foil) for thirty minutes and then serve with the warm sauce. You can also refrigerate the crêpes for up to two days, then heat, sauce, and serve. Or, freeze them for up to a week, defrost, and heat and serve with the béchamel sauce or a variant—a smooth cheese sauce. Add grated cheddar, to taste, and enough milk to achieve the consistency you prefer.

NOTES

1. *Soul Food*, with Vanessa Williams, Irma P. Hall, Vivica Fox, Nia Long, and Brandon Hammond. Directed by George Tillman Jr. Twentieth-Century Fox Studios, 1997.

2. "*Soul Food*: The Movie," Twentieth-Century Fox, *www.soul-food.com/movie.html*, accessed 14 May 2002.

3. I missed this film when it was in theaters, and the first time I watched it was on a

video-taped version, which has a completely different beginning than the DVD version. The video begins with mixed shots of the music video for "We're Not Making Love No More" intermingled with shots of characters from the drama intercut with many food-related images, including platters of fried chicken, a couple flirting as they eat, and a couple enjoying cooking together.

4. Psyche Williams-Forson, in "We Still Dying to Get Some Soul Food?" a presentation at the Mid-Atlantic Popular Culture–American Culture Assn. meeting in Pittsburgh (Nov. 2, 2002), pointed out that the foods served at Big Mama's table are particular to her family's Mississippi origins. Had the Josephs been from Louisiana, rice would have been present and collards probably would not. What constitutes "soul food" to one group may not be exactly the same as it is to another group.

5. Alice A. Deck, "'Now Then—Who Said Biscuits?': The Black Woman Cook as Fetish in American Advertising, 1905–1953," in *Kitchen Culture in America*, edited by Sherrie A. Inness (Philadelphia: University of Pennsylvania Press, 2001), 69, 70.

6. In his director's commentary Tillman explains that his grandmother died during the time he was making the film. His other comments also make clear that the issue of creating and maintaining strong families, with or without a matriarchal presence, was very much on his mind throughout the film's evolution.

7. Recent recipes in cookbooks, magazines, on cooking shows, and on Web sites have provided lower-fat alternatives to traditional soul food preparation methods. For example, *Ebony* magazine has been conducting sessions to guide preparation of healthier food for black reunions.

8. Sandra A. Black, "Diabetes, Diversity, and Disparity: What Do We Do with the Evidence?" *American Journal of Public Health* 92 (April 2002): online at http://www.ajph.org/cgi/content/full/92/4/543#F1, accessed June 10, 2002.

9. Black provides a table showing risk factors affecting the development of diabetes; among these she includes economic pressures, attitudes, education, psychological factors, stress, and coping. Both subtle and overt discrimination practiced by health-care systems and providers have been discussed as major contributors to differential rates of disease, diabetes included, among whites and minorities ("Racial Inequalities in Health Care," *Talk of the Nation*, National Public Radio, March 12, 2002).

10. Another effect of using the child's point of view is that the adult artist's responsibility for his depictions, in terms of the "burden of representation placed on black artists," can be somewhat avoided. Ahmad cannot analyze his grandmother's sickness, his relatives, and his mother's patterns of behavior. Williams-Forson, "We Still Dying to Get Some Soul Food?"

11. The titles of Cusick's, Harris's, and Spivey's books are, respectively, *Soul and Spice: African Cooking in the Americas* (San Francisco: Chronicle, 1995); *The Welcome Table: African-American Heritage Cooking* (New York: Simon and Schuster, 1995); and *The Peppers, Cracklings, and Knots of Wool Cookbook* (Albany: SUNY Press, 1999).

12. Both New York University and Boston University offer degrees in food studies, and more recently Dillard University, a historically black private institution in New Orleans, has created an endowed chair in black culinary studies and culture after receiving a $1 million donation from Ray Charles two years before his death. In making his gift, Charles described "traditions of food preparation in the black community that were really a kind of art, that his family had been part of" explained Michael Lomax,

president of Dillard University at the time the gift was made. Mimi Read, "A Gift to Black Cuisine, from Ray Charles," *New York Times*, Feb. 23, 2005, F5.

13. Joan Acocella, "American Pie: The Culinary Canon, from Ketchup to Cuisine Moralisée," *The New Yorker*, Dec. 6, 1999, 148–54, 162–65. In *Food Politics: How the Food Industry Influences Nutrition and Health* (Berkeley: University of California Press, 2002), Marion Nestle reports that "half of all meals are consumed outside the home, a quarter of them as fast food" (19). She does not provide figures for what percentage of supposedly home-cooked meals are actually canned or pre-packaged foods merely heated up by their consumers.

14. In fairness to Tillman, we do see men cooking on two occasions in the film. Kenny, Maxine's husband, is shown helping Maxine prepare the Sunday dinner Ahmad has maneuvered everyone to attend. Once other women arrive, however, he is shooed out of the kitchen. At an earlier point in the movie we see that Miles, husband of the successful lawyer Terri, has made a special dinner for her—a salad and what appears to be pasta.

15. Another important point when discussing soul food is to realize that it does not represent the totality of African American food traditions. J. Martin Favor maintains that most scholars of African American culture have emphasized folk roots, which means that the ways of rural, southern, poor African Americans have been taken as emblematic of all black culture. Such a focus can essentialize black culture, leaving out as it does the many contributions and conventions of middle-class African Americans and people of color who have immigrated to the United States from the Caribbean and from Africa and other parts of the world. Favor does not discuss foodways, but his point applies as well to analysis of culinary arts as part of African American culture. Favor, *Authentic Blackness: The Folk in the New Negro Renaissance* (Durham: Duke University Press, 1999), 3–9.

16. Telephone interview with Donna Pierce, May 1, 2002.

17. Henry Louis Gates Jr., "The Master's Pieces: On Canon Formation and the African-American Tradition," in *Loose Canons: Notes on the Culture Wars* (New York: Oxford University Press, 1992), 21, emphasis added.

18. Stuart Hall, "Subjects in History: Making Diasporic Identities," in *The House That Race Built: Black Americans, U.S. Terrain*, edited by Wahneema Lubiano (New York: Pantheon Books, 1997), 293–94.

19. Donna R. Gabaccia, in *We Are What We Eat: Ethnic Food and the Making of Americans* (Cambridge: Harvard University Press, 1998), notes that even in the Colonial period, fusion foods (what she calls "Colonial Creoles") were being created, with different regions providing opportunities for different mixtures of food traditions and materials. Slaves brought to the Colonies had already begun this process in West Africa, adapting "their eating to New World crops before they left home" (18).

20. Permission for use of this recipe has been granted by Kocoa Scott-Winbush.

PART 1

The History of
African American Food

1

Food Crops, Medicinal Plants, and the Atlantic Slave Trade

Robert L. Hall

Imagine sitting down to a spicy meal of gumbo (an okra dish), chicken garnished with peanuts (goobers), black-eyed peas or pigeon peas and rice, and a cold glass of cola, all topped off with a slice of yam pie or watermelon. When Americans of any hue consume such a meal they are ingesting tastes of Africa that constitute a fusion of foodstuffs originating from every part of the globe. What Alfred W. Crosby Jr. called the "Columbian exchange" is only the most recent phase of food crop exchanges that have been occurring between Africa and other parts of the world for hundreds, if not thousands, of years. Indeed, because it focuses almost exclusively on the period since 1492 Crosby's concept may not be broad enough, for at least two other exchanges contributed to the cuisines of Africa that developed by the time of the Atlantic slave trade. The Malay trade across the Indian Ocean involved the introduction to Africa of cowpeas, bananas, plantains, and, possibly, coconuts, and contacts with the Mediterranean world before 1400 CE via trans-Saharan trade resulted in the introduction to sub-Saharan Africa of Asian rice, cardamom, and, possibly, okra. The continuity, vitality, and creative adaptations of particular culinary traditions in the Americas testify to the richness of African cultures and the resourcefulness of those Africans who were coerced to come yet brought that richness with them and imparted it to host societies.

Clearly, there are many reasons to investigate the foodways of Africa. Biological and sociological studies look to foodways studies to help understand the relationship among diet, morbidity, and mortality in the African regions that supplied America's slaves. Thus Kenneth F. Kiple believes that "we need to know what the peoples of these regions ate, and what they did not eat."[1] As Philip D. Curtin has pointed out, "the [Atlantic] slave trade constituted a movement of people along these new lines of communication, but two other demographically important migrations took place along these same lines — the migration of diseases and the migration of food crops."[2] This essay, by focusing on the various links between diet and the transatlantic slave trade, contributes toward that effort to discover what Africans ate in the various regions that supplied captive laborers for the Western Hemisphere. In addition, I seek to understand the development of African American foodways and the influence of Africans' foodways on the development of American culinary history. Thus it is critical to discover what food crops and culinary habits were (or could have been) transported into the New World with the human cargo of the Atlantic trade.

Sidney Mintz suggests that "one way to discover what happened to African culinary, folkloric, and musical traditions in the American South is by examining so-called southern (white) culture. How 'African' *all* Americans are is conventionally hidden by the assumption that, under conditions of oppression, acculturation is a one-way street."[3] That insight is supported by the earlier work of Mary Tolford Wilson, who described provocatively what she called "peaceful integration," the adoption of slaves' food by the slave-owning class. She concentrated on four food crops — peanuts, okra, cowpeas (especially black-eyed peas), and sesame — that were either indigenous to Africa or introduced into North America by Africans.[4] The work of scholars like Mintz and Wilson points to the usefulness of studying the foodways of Africans to gain insight not only into the origins of African American food but also into much of what we call "southern" American cuisine.

I have organized the majority of my discussion into three broad categories: first, food crops originally domesticated in Africa; second, crops indigenous to other continents that reached Africa both before and after Columbus's voyages to the Western Hemisphere; and, third, food from a variety of sources that became part of African and African American cuisine, partly because of the slave trade.

African Agricultural Origins and Dispersals

Africans in several regions of the continent played significant roles in developing agriculture, domesticating plants, and dispersing food plants and culinary styles to other parts of the world.[5] The world's major tropical food crops may be divided into three broad categories: noncereal energy crops (cassava, sweet potatoes, yams, and bananas); cereals (including rice, maize, sorghum, and the millets); and legumes (including the groundnut, the common bean, soybeans, and chickpeas). From the first group I will focus on the yam, which Merrick Posnansky described as "perhaps the most important indigenous food crop in West Africa." This starchy, tuberous root is a staple crop for more than 40 percent of the population of West Africa and eaten by many more as a secondary food. Furthermore, more than two-thirds of the world's yams are grown in the area between the Ivory Coast and the Cameroon. According to Oliver Davies, the process of vegeculture based on the domestication of yams native to Africa south of the Sahara Desert may have been established as early as 5000–4000 BCE.[6]

The incidence of yam cultivation and consumption within Africa was not without far-reaching political and religious ramifications. One characteristic of the yam is the certainty of yield, which, according to Posnansky, "led to high population densities and the necessity for both a political superstructure to coordinate their activities and a religious superstructure to ensure [their] successful continuity."[7] In his *Mission from Cape Coast to Ashantee* (London, 1819) Thomas Edward Bowditch gave an elaborate account of a yam festival. Another observer noted that among the Ewe of Aloi, Togo, the ceremony of the yam festival consists of offering palm-wine libations and three portions of cooked yams, part of which have been mixed with palm oil. In addition, a sheep and some fowls are presented to Mawu (God), and prayers are offered for as good a harvest in the coming year. Only after such ceremonies have been performed are the lineage head and entire group permitted to eat the new yams.[8]

Although his discussion of yam yields is neither specific nor substantiated, Posnansky's emphasis is the certainty, or reliability, of yield and not necessarily the amount of yield. Indeed, Pierre Gourou has estimated that with a yield of fifteen hundredweight per acre, yam yields fall between those of millet (five hundredweight per acre) and cassava (thirty-two hundredweight per acre). Because yams do not constitute an agricultural system or complex in themselves, their cultivation alone cannot account for the high population densities and cultural forms to which Posnansky alludes. In his more satisfying examination of the gradual domestication of yams in West Africa, D. G. Coursey suggests that a process described as "protoculture" involving "the removal of wild plants to more convenient, accessible, or advantageous locations in or near settlements" developed in West Africa nearly five thousand years ago. Then, about four thousand years ago, Neolithic grain-crop cultivators influenced by Southwest Asian cultural patterns began to move away from the dessicating Sahara belt and interact with yam "protoculturalists." The "cross-fertilization of ideas" that took place led "to the development of a yam-based agriculture in something approaching the present form."[9]

Only one of the four major varieties of yams cultivated in West Africa, *Dioscorea alata* (the greater yam), is an exclusively Asian variety, and in most regions of West Africa it is the fourth most popular species. It probably reached West Africa from Asia as part of ships' victuals during the post-Columbian period but could also have been introduced earlier via the Malay trade in the Indian Ocean basin. During the period of European colonization of the Western Hemisphere *Dioscorea alata* was transplanted from Africa to Haiti, where it became a central item in the diet of Haitian slaves. The crop eventually spread throughout the tropical New World, where it became a standard food of black peasants.[10] *Dioscorea bulbifera* is a species of yam commonly indigenous to both Africa and Asia. The predominant and favored varieties in West Africa are *Dioscorea cayenensis*, a forest-zone species, and *D. rotundata* (the white guinea yam), neither of which are Asian varieties.

Discussing the Gambia, William Smith, who traveled to Africa in the 1730s, wrote, "Their chief Roots are Yams and Potatoes." Similarly, Smith found that among the abundant foodstuffs of Cape Coast, "Their best Roots are Yams and Potatoes." During an expedition to the Niger Delta area of what is now Nigeria in the 1850s, the emigrationist Robert Campbell saw the Egbas (part of the Yoruba people) consume the dish *fufu*, which consists of cooked yams beaten with water in a wooden mortar.[11] In a somewhat forced argument, Oliver Davies suggests that the nearly universal preference for yams in a pounded form rather than boiled or fried is a culturally induced relic of earlier efforts to reduce toxicity.[12] Although wild yams are well known for being poisonous, some edible wild varieties do not seem to require the elaborate detoxification procedures.

Etymology contributes insights not only into the possible origins of certain domesticated crops but also into the probable paths of their diffusion. The yam provides a case in point. The probable derivation of the term *yam* is the Portuguese *inhame* or the Spanish *iñame*. These words probably derived from one or more West African languages. They are akin to the Wolof terms *nyam* or *nyami*, the latter a verb meaning "to eat." There is a phrase in the Gullah dialect spoken in the Sea Islands off Georgia and South Carolina, *nyam ye vittles*, which means "eat your food."[13]

Whether of the Asian or the indigenous African varieties, yams were frequently put on slave ships as provisions for slaves during the Middle Passage, particularly when the involuntary African passengers were known to have come from yam-eating societies. Prominent among Africans who preferred yams were slaves shipped from the port of Calabar in what is now Nigeria. "The Calabar slaves," wrote James Barbot, "value this root above any other food, as being used to it in their own country." The records of such slave ships as the *Arthur* (1678), the *Elizabeth* (1754), the *Friend* (1768), and the *Othello* (1768–69) indicate that significant quantities of yams were provisioned along with lesser quantities of plantains, limes, pepper, palm oil, and "gobbagobs" (goobers or peanuts). Not only did yams "take up so much room," as John Barbot (the uncle of James) observed, but also on longer voyages they sometimes rotted before they could be consumed. A large number of yams had to be loaded—more than a hundred thousand for a cargo of five hundred slaves, or about two hundred yams per person, according to one estimate by John Barbot.[14]

The production of many food crops indigenous to Africa, particularly yams, could lend itself to plantation-style slave labor in Africa. During the late eighteenth and early nineteenth centuries plantations employing slave labor dominated the economy of the Futa Jallon region of Senegambia. During his visit to the area in 1820 René Caillié found in Gneretemile "an ouronde, or slave village, surrounded by good plantations of bananas, cotton, cassavas and yams. . . . [Near] Maraca . . . we found ourselves in a sandy plain, containing several small slave villages." At the plantation of Popoco located about two days' travel from the capital of Timbo, Caillié saw "between one hundred and fifty and two hundred slaves, who are employed in agriculture." They cultivated cassava, yams, peanuts, rice, and millet. Further evidence for the importance of yams to African populations comes from a particular technique that one leader tried. Oluyole, the *basorun* (military ruler) of the city of Ibadan from 1837 to 1847, conducted successful experiments in the construction of yam mounds. Seeking to grow yams sufficiently large to constitute a single load in themselves (more than forty kilograms each), he commanded slaves, mostly Hausa and Muslim, to erect massive compost heaps of weeds, banana and plantain stalks, and earth. Once yam seedlings were planted on the tops of these mounds, their roots would grow downward to fill them.[15]

Next I turn to the cereal category of major foodstuffs. Roland Portères and

George P. Murdock argue that cereal cultivation of the savanna (or grasslands) predated the vegeculture of the tropical rain forest. Murdock also believes that there were centers in the West African savanna where agriculture was developed independently by Africans. Although challenging Murdock's localization of this pioneering effort in the nuclear Mande area near the headwaters of the River Niger, H. G. Baker concludes, "It does seem that there is great botanical evidence of a long agricultural history in Africa and that peoples of the Sudan Zone were among the leaders in African agricultural development." He lists thirteen "likely African domesticates."[16]

There is little doubt that farming economies have a long history on the African continent. Evidence of grain cultivation at Fayum dates to at least 4000 BCE. Certain types of millet, sorghum, and rice were probably domesticated in Africa and have been cultivated there since antiquity.[17] African groups began to experiment with wild grasses from which they domesticated the millets—sorghum, pennisetum, and eleusine—by about the third millennium BCE. Sesame was also developed on the southern *sahel* ("shore") of the Sahara Desert and had diffused to Sumer before 2350 BCE.[18]

In *West African Food in the Middle Ages, According to Arabic Sources,* Tadeusz Lewicki indicates that the millets and sorghums were dominant staple crops in Africa at least a thousand years ago. The millets are among the oldest groups of cereal crops grown in Africa south of the Sahara Desert. There is some confusion of nomenclature because "millet" and "sorghum" are sometimes used synonymously. Nehemiah Levtzion and J. F. P. Hopkins, in their translation of early Arabic sources for West African history, arbitrarily rendered the Arabic *dukhn* as millet and *dhura* as sorghum. In the *Mukhtasar Kitab al-Buldan,* published in 290 Anno Hegirae (or about 903 CE), Ibn al-Faqih described the food of the medieval kingdom of Ghana: "The food of the people there consists of sorghum (*dhura*), which they call *dukhn* 'millet' and of cowpeas (*lubiya*)." When introduced into the New World, this grain-yielding plant, widely grown for food in North and West Africa, was known as guinea corn.[19] Also known as *durra*, this crop is designated *Zorghum vulgate* by botanists.[20]

Most of the people of Central Africa were also peasant farmers who raised small livestock and cultivated millet and bananas. They were cultivating these crops in 1482 when the first contacts with the Portuguese began.[21] The three major varieties of the millets are sorghum, *Pennisetum* (or bulrush or pearl millet), and *Eleusine corocana.* In 1749–50 Michel Adanson, a French traveler in Gambia, observed that "the higher grounds were covered with millet; and there also the indigo and cotton plants displayed a most lovely verdure."[22]

There is a curious connection between African-cultivated grain crops and the Atlantic slave trade. In his study of the British slave trade to Spanish America between 1700 and 1739, Colin Palmer found that the rhythm of agricultural cycles on the African side of the Atlantic had something to do with the seasonal availability of captives for export. "African traders were least likely to sell their slaves during planting and harvesting periods. The captives were evidently being employed in agrarian tasks and were only parted with when their labor was no longer required." This was so at Gajaaga, Senegambia, "where slave owners used their slaves to plant millet prior to selling them to the French."[23]

As for rice, Roland Portères has argued that wet rice of the species *Oryza glaberrima* was first domesticated on the middle Niger about 1500 BCE, with a secondary cradle between the Sine-Salum and the Cassamance Rivers. It was cultivated at Jenné-Jeno by 50 CE. Fossilized food remains unearthed by archaeologists at Jenné-Jeno, the oldest known Iron Age city in Africa south of the Sahara, reveal a mixed diet that included rice. The bones, grain fragments, and utensils found at the site showed that between 100 and 1200 CE "everyone in this part of town dined nutritiously on catfish, perch, rice, beef, and presumably milk." According to the McIntoshes, annual silt-bearing floods of the Niger River yielded huge surpluses of rice, making it one of Jenné's major exports.[24]

Such scholars as Peter H. Wood, Judith A. Carney, Karen Hess, and John Michael Vlach argue that South Carolina's early economic success owed a great deal to the contributions of black slaves and their agricultural knowledge—especially in the area of rice cultivation.[25] Rice had a profound impact upon colonial South Carolina and Georgia. That buyers of slaves both in Africa and Carolina were aware of the ethnic backgrounds of enslaved Africans has been demonstrated by Darold D. Wax, Peter H. Wood, and Daniel C. Littlefield as well as in the work of Ulrich B. Phillips.[26]

Among the "background factors" very much in demand in the rice-growing districts of North America was experience in wet rice cultivation. This is suggested, for instance, by a notice in the July 11, 1785, *Evening Gazette* (Charleston) announcing the arrival of a Danish ship bearing "a choice cargo of Windward and Gold Coast Negroes, who have been accustomed to the planting of rice." As Wood has pointed out, "literally hundreds of black immigrants were more familiar with the planting, hoeing, processing, and cooking of rice than were the European settlers who purchased them." Although the type of rice that became a staple crop in colonial South Carolina was probably the Asian variety, *Oryza sativa*, rather than the African domesticate *O. glaberrima*, the agricultural know-how for cultivating it was contributed by African slaves, many of whom had probably grown both species of rice before arriving in North America. Blacks who inhabit the Sea Islands and the coastal lowlands of Georgia and South Carolina have been called Gullahs or Geechees. Janie Gilliard Moore gives a food-related folk definition of Geechees as "the people who eat rice daily for dinner."[27] The fanners, storage baskets, and rice mortars that survive and continue to be made in coastal South Carolina today by the lineal descendants of Africans imported into South Carolina are symbols of the African-derived technology and know-how that enabled rice to flourish in the United States.[28]

Another indigenous plant important to Africans for a variety of uses was the oil palm tree. As will be seen in further discussion of provisioning of slave ships for the transatlantic voyage, palm oil was widely recommended for a variety of uses by those familiar with the trade. Derivatives of the indigenous African oil palm *Elaeis guineensis* were used for cosmetic, medicinal, or nutritional purposes. The former slave Olaudah Equiano, who claimed to have been born in Igbo country in 1745, described several uses of the plant: "They are totally unaquainted with strong or spiritous liquors and their principle beverage is palm wine. This is got from a tree of that name by tapping it at the top and fastening a large gourd to it, and sometimes one tree will yield three or four gallons in a night. When just drawn it is of a most delicious sweetness, but in a few days it acquires a tartish and more spiritous flavour, though I never saw anyone intoxicated by it. The same tree also produces nuts and oil."[29]

European travelers such as Andrew Battell and William Smith commented on the making of palm wine. Battell (1565–1614), an English sailor seized by the Portuguese from a British privateer in South American waters and imprisoned in Luanda (Central Africa) where he lived with the Jaga people for twenty-one months, described how the Jagas (or Gagas) gathered palm wine:

> These Gagas delight in no country, but where there is great store of Pal-mares, or groves of palms. For they delight greatly in the wine and in the fruit of the palm, which serveth to eat and to make oil. And they draw their wine contrary to the Imbondos. These palm trees are six or seven fathoms high, and have no leaves but in the tip; and they have a device to go up to the top of the tree, and lay no hands on it, and they draw the wine in the top of the tree in a bottle.
>
> But these Gagas cut the palm-trees down by the root, which lie ten days before they will give wine. And then they make a square hole in the top and heart of the tree, and take out of the hole every morning a quart, and at night a quart. So that every tree giveth two quarts of wine a day for the space of six and twenty days, and then it drieth up.[30]

Describing the Gambia area during the 1740s, William Smith wrote, "For Nature likewise affords them two or three Sorts of pleasant strong Wines, with no other Trouble than that of boring a small Hole in a Palm-Tree, and hanging a Callabash under the Droppings of it, which sometimes will fill one to three Quarts in a Day."[31]

There was also a non-nutrient use for palm oil that no consideration of the slave trade can omit—rubbing slaves down before sale to make them look sleek and young. So cunning were the "cabrashiers," said Thomas Phillips, captain of the *Hannibal* during its slaving voyage in 1693, that "they shave them all close before we see them, so that let them be never so old we can see no grey hairs in their heads or beards; and then having liquored them well and sleeked with palm oil, 'tis no easy matter to know an old one from a middle-aged one, but by the teeths decay."[32]

Food Crops from Other Continents

Crops indigenous to other continents reached Africa both before and after Columbus's voyages to the Western Hemisphere. Such Asian crops as bananas and Asian varieties of yams, rice, and cowpeas had become staples in parts of Africa well before Columbus's voyages to the Americas. American-domesticated crops such as maize and manioc (cassava) became widespread in Africa following those voyages.[33] The accelerated development of forest people seems to have been made possible when several Asian plants, most notably the water yam (*Dioscorea alata*), cocoyam or taro (*Colocasia esculentum*), plantain (*Musa sapientum var. paradisiaca*), banana (*Musa sapientum*), and Asian varieties of rice (notably *Oryza sativa*) were introduced. Plantains were "the subject of festivals among the Mini of Okoroba [in present-day Nigeria], and used for rituals in Nembe [also in present-day Nigeria]." Through trade, certain areas of the freshwater Niger Delta supplied much of the vegetable diet (mainly plantains and cocoyams [or taro]) in the salt-water areas of the Eastern Delta in precontact times. After the early 1500s the preexisting long-distance, north to south trade routes became conduits not only for slaves bound for the Americas but also for "the foodstuffs to feed them on the river and during the Atlantic crossing."[34]

We do not understand fully the details of how and when the plants of Indonesia and other parts of Southeast Asia reached West Africa, but we do know that Indonesian mariners visited the coasts of East Africa from at least a century or two BCE to about the end of the first millennium CE. The Malaysian plants that the mariners left behind on the mainland of East Africa proved signally important to the agricultural development of many societies in equatorial forest regions.[35] Such Asian crops as banana and taro (coco yam or eddoes) spread rapidly through the forest areas, eventually reaching West Africa. The banana, the fruit of a herbaceous plant, is endemic to the rain forests of Southeast Asia and may have been cultivated there as far back as 1000 BCE.[36] N. W. Simmonds estimated that the banana, a tropical noncereal energy plant of the genus *Musa*, arrived early enough from Southeast Asia (probably from Indonesia rather than from India) to diffuse to Buganda and produce twenty-three original somatic mutants, a process that might have taken between 1,500 and 2,000 years. The word *banana* derives from a usage in a West African language, possibly Wolof.

Al-Masudi visited Madagascar during the tenth century CE and found East Africans eating bananas and coconuts, both plants of Asian origin.[37] According to Jacob Egharevba, coconuts were first introduced into the city of Benin by Joao Afonso d'Aveiro, a Portuguese traveler who arrived in 1485, but the ultimate origin of coconuts is much disputed. From the point of view of the Americas, coconuts are an Africanism. The Portuguese found bananas in West Africa when they began their voyages of African exploration in the fifteenth century and took them to the Canary Islands. Given that little credible evidence of bananas in the New World before Columbus exists, the introduction of bananas from the Canary Islands to Haiti in 1516 seems to mark their entry into the Western Hemisphere. Many Asian domesticates now cultivated in Africa may have been introduced from Indonesia via Madagascar during the first three centuries CE, but as Thurstan Shaw has stated, "Just how these Asiatic cultigens spread from the East African coast must be a very interesting story, but we know little about it at the moment."[38]

The beginnings of European expansion, especially the exploration and colonization of the New World, brought to Africa new food imports from the Americas (notably maize and cassava but also the peanut) and the East that were added to the acquired tastes of populations in Atlantic Africa.[39] One of the most important crops introduced into Africa from the Americas was maize, which is first documented in the regions of Africa of most direct interest to the Portuguese during the late fifteenth and early sixteenth centuries. Roland Portères maintained that maize was introduced independently by the Spanish from the Caribbean to the Mediterranean basin and Egypt and by the Portuguese from Brazil to the Guinea coast. Some of the timing and the impact of these new food plants can be grasped through oral tradition. David Birmingham's paraphrase of "local folklore" reflects the first contact of the Portuguese with the Kongo-Angola coastline at Luanda in the 1480s: "The white men arrived in ships with wings which shone in the sun like knives; they brought maize and cassava and groundnuts and tobacco."[40] The oral tradition remembered by the Pende people who fled from Angola to avoid Portuguese domination near the end of the seventeenth century is paraphrased more extensively by Birmingham:

> They say that the white men arrived in ships with wings which shone in the sun like knives. They spat fire at the Mbundu and forced their king, the Ngola, to flee from the coast and abandon his salt pans and his banana plantations. Some of the bolder Mbundu remained behind and sold eggs and chickens to the white men in return for cloth and beads. When the white men came again they brought maize and cassava and groundnuts and tobacco and knives and hoes. In order that the new crops should succeed it was necessary to say a prayer of which the words are still remembered. The tradition concludes by saying that "from that time until our day the Whites brought us nothing but wars and miseries."[41]

Some scholars, like M. D. W. Jeffreys, have argued that there was a variety of maize in Africa before Columbus's voyages to the Western Hemisphere and that the Portuguese took it to Portugal from Africa. Jeffreys believed that Arabs traversed the Atlantic Ocean around 1000 CE, brought back American maize, and introduced it into Africa. References to Arabs sailing across the Atlantic are found in Chinese sources dated around 1178.[42] Jeffreys's view, however, does not reflect the general consensus among students of maize. According to the oral traditions of the Bushongo people of South Central Congo, maize was first introduced to them in the 1600s. Also in the 1600s Olfert Dapper noted an abundance of maize on the Gold Coast. James C. McCann states in his excellent *Maize and Grace: Africa's Encounter with a New World Crop, 1500–2000* that there is "little documentary evidence" of who introduced maize into Africa, how they did it, or how African farmers responded to it. The search for the initial introduction of maize into Africa goes on, but its far-reaching impact, even to the present, is undeniable.[43] From the New World also came peanuts, papaya, guava, avocado, pineapple, and manioc (cassava).[44]

Linguistic evidence from southern Nigeria divides plant names into three groups: those cultivated before Asiatic introductions (including raffia palm, oil palm, African yams, and kola nuts); the Asiatic introductions; and the latest arrivals from the Americas such as maize and cassava. Williamson has found that in the Niger Delta of southern Nigeria the names by which cassava, rice, oranges, limes, and coconuts are known are all derived from Portuguese, which suggests that Portuguese naval squadrons, with their far-flung contacts, were among the chief agents of importation.[45] The Portuguese also planted groves of lemons, limes, and oranges along the Atlantic Coast. According to J. M. Gray, oranges and limes (along with pawpaw and groundnuts) were introduced into the Gambia area by the Portuguese. The groundnut (*Arachis hypogaea*) originated in Bolivia and, when introduced into Africa by European voyagers, probably took its place in African diets in the same niche occupied by longstanding indigenous varieties of peanutlike plants such as the Bambara groundnut.[46] Although native to South America, the peanut was probably introduced into North America via enslaved Africans transported into colonial Virginia.[47]

Cassava, like maize, was a relative latecomer to Africa. E. J. Alagoa believes that "cassava was apparently introduced to the Niger Delta by the Portuguese through Warri and Benin." According to him, the plant name was recorded at Warri by John Barbot in the late 1600s: "magnoc bushes, which they call *Mandi-hoka* in their language; of which they make *cassaba*, or *Farinha de Pao*, that is in Portuguese, wood-meal, which is the bread they commonly feed on."[48] Stephen H. Hymer suggested that the introduction into precolonial Ghana of new staple crops from the Americas by the Portuguese, particularly maize and cassava, resulted in a "revolution in land use [that] played an important role in making possible a denser settlement in forest areas."[49]

Kenneth F. Kiple, who has made substantial contributions to the biological history of the African diaspora, states, "The American crops in turn stimulated the growth of West African populations, many of which, unhappily and ironically, were drained off by the African diaspora to the hemisphere that had supplied the plants to begin with." Elaborating on this cruel irony, Crosby speculates that before 1850, "the increased food production [maize, manioc, and other American plants] enabled the slave trade to go on as long as it did without pumping the black well of Africa dry. The Atlantic slave traders drew many, perhaps most, of their cargoes from the rain forest areas, precisely those areas where American crops enabled heavier settlements than before."

Although the statements by Kiple and Crosby may be somewhat difficult to document exactly, very similar statements have been made by such influential historians as Philip D. Curtin, who observed, mainly about maize and manioc:

> If other factors affecting population size had remained constant, the predictable result would have been population growth wherever these crops replaced less efficient cultigens. Since this process took place over very large areas, it seems possible and even probable that population growth resulting from new food crops exceeded population losses through the slave trade. Whatever population loss may have followed the introduction of new diseases would have

been temporary, while more efficient food crops tend to make possible a permanently higher level of population. It is even possible that, for sub-saharan Africa as a whole, the net demographic effect of the three Atlantic migrations was population growth, not decline. Only further research in demographic and epidemiological history can give a firm answer.[50]

Foods from a Variety of Sources

A large window into the variety of foods from all over the world that contributed to the development of African American and American cuisine is provided by focusing once again on the provisions carried in the holds of slave ships during the Middle Passage.[51] By the early 1700s, having learned from experience, both the Royal African and the South Sea companies paid close attention to the feeding of their African captives during the voyage. Experience taught that although some European foods were acceptable, Africans fared better when fed their customary food. Thus in 1705 the Royal African Company's factors at Whydah recommended corn, yams, malagueta pepper, and palm oil as items suitable for the slaves' diet. In 1707 the Royal African Company agents at Cape Coast were advised to supplement supplies of beans taken on in London with fifty chests of corn, forty pounds of malagueta peppers, twenty pounds of palm oil, two bushels of salt, and twenty gallons of rum for each hundred slaves. In 1723, when the South Sea Company paid the Royal African Company to "slave" one of its ships, the contract specified the following provisions to be laid in for 340 African slaves: 14 bushels of salt, 280 chests of corn, 170 pounds of malagueta pepper, and 70 gallons of palm oil.[52] Such provisions are typical of the items loaded on the slavers.

Alexander Falconbridge observed that each group of Africans preferred "the produce of their native soil." In his pamphlet published in 1788, Falconbridge said, "In their own country, the Negroes in general live on animal food and fish, with roots, yams, and Indian corn. The horse beans and rice, with which they are fed aboard ship, are chiefly taken from Europe. The latter, indeed, is sometimes purchased on the coast, being far superior to any other."[53] Implying a link between robustness of diet and robustness of body and mind, Falconbridge also commented that "the Gold Coast Negroes scarcely ever refuse any food that is offered them, and they generally eat larger quantities of whatever is placed before them, than any other species of Negroes, whom they likewise excel in strength of body and mind."[54]

Thus, depending partly upon the African country from whence the captives came, a morning meal during the Middle Passage might consist of imported or locally cultivated Indian corn, or rice or yams. Evening meals sometimes consisted of foods to which the captives had been accustomed in Africa—usually either yams or rice—and such provisions from Europe as dried beans, peas, wheat, shelled barley, and biscuits. That African women prepared much of the food during the voyage is suggested by an entry from the journal of the ship *Mary* for Monday, June 20, 1796: "The Women Cleaning Rice and Grinding corn for corn cakes."[55] All of these items were usually mixed with a sauce of meat or fish or with palm oil, a constant and widely sought element in many traditional African cuisines. Once survivors of the Middle Passage reached plantation America, the meals they consumed in the fields commonly consisted of boiled yams, eddoes (taros), okra, callaloo, and plantain, all seasoned generously with cayenne pepper and salt.

Despite the stereotypical identification of African Americans with watermelon, there is a kernel of truth to the linkage between the people's and the food's African origins. Geographers and botanists generally agree that the watermelon plant was first domesticated in West Africa and that it constitutes one of Africa's several original contributions to the world's storehouse of foodstuffs. It remains unclear precisely when and how African-domesticated watermelon came to be cultivated and consumed in North America, but by the early 1730s Virginians of both races had grown quite fond of it.[56] According to the Englishman William Hugh Grove, who visited Virginia in 1732, the Virginians he knew "chiefly Esteem the Water Melon, which is green, as bigg as a Pump[k]in, smoothe, not furrowed. They Eat it as an apple, but in my opinion [it is] too flatt and Waterish. They say [eating] it hurts no one, even in fever." Anne Ritson's eventual love for the African fruit was reflected in one of her poems:

> The water melon most they love,
> I never could the fruit approve;
> It was so very light and sweet,
> It did not seem as fit to eat,
> Melting so quickly in the mouth,
> Like syllabub and trifle froth;
> Yet during autumn's sultry air,
> Its coolness was delicious fare.[57]

Charles W. Joyner argues in *Down by the Riverside*, his widely acclaimed study of slave folklife in the Waccamaw district of South Carolina, that "if material ingredients of slave foodways were merely ordinary plantation foodstuffs, their preparation and spicing and their symbolic meaning were governed by African culinary grammars." Thus Joyner stresses "the role of condiments and seasonings in slave food." Although the work of Kenneth F. Kiple and Virginia H. King has underscored the critical importance of diet, nutrition, and genetic background for the physical survival of Africans in the New World, Joyner is correct to insist that "food played a role in slave culture beyond mere sustenance. . . . It had immense cultural and ideological significance: the choice of particular foods and particular means of preparation involved issues of crucial importance to the slaves' sense of identity. Slave cooks not only maintained cultural continuity with West African cuisine but also adapted the African tradition creatively to the necessities and opportunities of a new culinary environment."[58]

As Edward S. Ayensu, the former chair of the Department of Botany at the Smithsonian Institution, has indicated, the contributions of black Americans "that have been least publicized were those that concern the plants brought to the Americas by Black Slaves from the Old World or those native American plants that they adapted for their use and made popular." Various writers have attempted to list Africa's contributions to the diets of New World populations. Romeo B. Garrett mentioned black-eyed peas, watermelon, okra, and cola drinks. When the German traveler Heinrich Barth visited the northern Nigerian town of Kano in 1851 he found enormous quantities of kola nuts (*Cola nitida*) in the town's central market. When chewed, kola nuts quench thirst and act as a stimulant, much the same as coffee or tea. Used as a hospitality dish in parts of West Africa, kola nuts were a major item of trade among such people as the Hausa of northern Nigeria. Extracts from the kola nut eventually became one of the ingredients of a drink that has become known as Coca-Cola and is now considered as American as apple pie. John Michael Vlach included rice, guinea corn (also known as great millet or sorghum), guinea grass, and guinea squash (*Panicum jumentarum*).[59]

Longer lists exist. Michel Laguerre's "A Sample of African Plants Brought to the Caribbean by Slave Ships" includes eleven plants.[60] William Ed Grimé's now somewhat outdated yet still interesting *Ethno-Botany of the Black Americans* (1979) identified seventeen plants introduced by slaves, giving their scientific names, their common names, and their principal uses (table 1).

In the most extensive listing of all, Judith A. Carney identifies three areas of sub-Saharan Africa where "agricultural domestication unfolded." The three regions and examples of the domesticated plants that Carney traced to each appear in table 2.

Table 1. Food and Medicinal Plants of Africa

Botanical Name	Common Name(s)	Use(s)
Abelmoschus esculentus	okra, guimgombo[a]	food
Arachis hypogaea	groundnut, peanut, goober pinder, pinda gub-a-gubs[b]	food, household
Blighia sapida	ackee, aka, akee	food
Cajanus cajan	Angola pea, pigeon pea	food
Cannabis sativa	diamba, marijuana, riamba	relaxation, medicinal
Cassia italica	senna, Jamaican senna	medicinal
Cola acuminata	bichy tree, cocu	medicinal, food
Cucumis anguria	maroon cucumber, West Indian gherkin	food
Dioscorea alata	yam bacara	food
Dioscorea cayenensis	yellow yam	food
Elaeis guineensis	African oil palm	food, medicinal
Monodora myristica	Dunal, calabash nutmeg	food
Phaseolus lunatus[c]	broad bean	food
Sesamum indicum	bene, benne, Eastern foxglove	food
Sorghum vulgare varo	guinea corn, saccharatum guinea wheat	food
Tephrosia sinapou[d]	Surinam poison	traps and poison
Vigna unguiculata	black-eyed pea, cowpeas	food

Source: William Ed Grimé, *Ethno-Botany of the Black Americans* (Algoniac, Mich.: Reference Publications, 1970).

[a]*Quimbombo* is okra stew in a version of the Oba's ear story, a tale told in Havana, Cuba. See William Bascom, "Oba's Ear: A Yoruba Myth in Cuba and Brazil," in *African Folklore in the New World,* edited by Daniel J. Crowley (Austin: University of Texas Press, 1977), 4–5. *Gumbo* is a Bantu name for okra (*Webster's New World Dictionary of the English Language,* 2d college ed. (repr. Louisville: World Publishing, 1977), 2489.

[b]*Pinder* or *pinda* and *guba* (*gooba* or *goober*) are identical in sound and meaning to words used by societies in Angola. The tracing of the origin and development of a word and its meaning (etymology) is a significant part of the process of reconstructing the histories of American ethnic groups and their cultural interactions. Let us take the word *goober,* for example. The plant signified by that term, *Arachis hypogaea,* is believed to be of South American origins. The plant had reached the African continent early during the era of transatlantic slave trading and was later introduced into North America via Africa during later phases of the trade. *Goober* is "a variation of the Congolese word *nguba.*" *Morris Dictionary of Word and Phrase Origins* (New York, 1977), 252.

[c]The translation of *Phaseolus lunatus* as the broad bean is better understood as the New World lima bean. Perhaps, as an anonymous reader of this essay has pointed out, Grimé meant chickpeas or fava beans.

[d]For a good eyewitness account of how *Tephrosia toxicaria* (sinapou) is still used for "chemical fishing" by the Djuka of Surinam see S. Allen Counter and David L. Evans, *I Sought My Brother: An Afro-American Reunion* (Cambridge: MIT Press, 1981), 159–61. The bush-dwelling Djuka call the plant *neku.* The plant, found in both Africa and South America, stuns fish by temporarily blocking their breathing apparatus but has no toxic effects on humans who might later consume the fish.

Table 2. Selected Domesticated Plants of Sub-Saharan Africa
(by Region)

1. East African savannah (Sudan to the highlands of Ethiopia and Uganda:
    Coffee
    Sorghum
    Tef
    Finger millet
    Castor bean
    Ensente

2. West African savannah (Atlantic Coast inland to Lake Chad, including
    the floodplain of the inland delta of the Niger River in Mali):
    Pearl millet
    Fonio
    Bottle gourd
    Shea butter tree
    Baobab
    Watermelon
    African rice (*Oryza glaberrima*)

3. Tropical rainforest region of West and Central Africa (from Nigeria and
    Cameroon southeast to the Congo Basin):
    White guinea yams
    Yellow guinea yams
    Oil palm
    Tamarind
    Sesame
    Okra
    Cowpeas (black-eyed peas)
    Pigeon pea

Source: Judith A. Carney, "African Rice in the Columbian Exchange,"
Journal of African History 42 (2001): 378.

Because a significant part of "the African culinary grammar" alluded to
but not elaborated upon in detail by Joyner resides in the condiments and
seasonings used to prepare foods, some space must be devoted to the topic
of pepper. The Windward Coast of Africa between Cape Mount and Assini
(roughly present-day Liberia and Ivory Coast) was particularly noteworthy for
its malagueta pepper. The malagueta pepper—derived from the small, brown,
spicy berry of the wild tree known to botanists as *Amomis caryophyllata*—was
used to prepare both food and beverages. Malagueta pepper is known by many
names, including African pepper, British pepper, paradise grain, and guinea
pepper. The parts of Africa from which malagueta pepper was obtained were
known as the Grain Coast during the era of the Atlantic slave trade.

Many African traditional dishes are characterized by "hot" seasoning with either red pepper (cayenne), malagueta pepper, or both. During the 1820s the slaver Captain Théophilus Conneau was served an inviting "palavra sauce" by a wife of one of his landlords among the "Bager people." "I inquired the nature of the ingredients," wrote Conneau, "and was told by my trade man it was wild hog. This . . . was highly flavored with red and malagueta pepper, and with the seasoning of eight hours fasting; it was devoured by me with the gastronomic appetite of an alderman." A "Mandingo stew" that Conneau consumed on December 5, 1827, contained "mutton minced with roasted ground nuts (or peanuts) and rolled up into a shape of forced-meat balls, which when stewed up with milk, butter and a little malaguetta pepper, is a rich dish if eaten with rice *en pilau.* Monsieur Fortoni of Paris might not be ashamed to present a dish of it to his aristocratic gastronomers of the Boulevard des Italiens."[61]

Malagueta pepper was also thought to have medicinal value in preventing dysentery and stomach disorders, major scourges of the Middle Passage. Records of the Royal African Company and other sources indicate that some agents in the slave trade tried to discern what treatments for illnesses the Africans themselves used, especially for disorders prevalent during the Middle Passage. A 1672 report on the trade of the Royal African Company stated that "ships staying a day or more they trade on the Grain and Quaqua coast for Guineygrains or Mallagruetts, which is physic for Negroes." The entry in the journal of the *Arthur* for Sunday April 21, 1678, recorded the death of "one Negro man" and the statement that "some more wee have sick and though wee have noe Docktor yett wee doe the Best wee Cann for them giveinge them Brandy and Malagetta: there is nothinge wantinge to them." In 1699 the Royal African Company factors at River Sherbro were instructed to "keep friendship with some natives that understand the best remedies for their distempers." William Bosman said of the Gold Coast area that the "chief medicaments" were lime, malagueta pepper, cardamon (an East Indian spice), several varieties of herb, and the roots, branches, and gums of trees.[62]

Along the coast of what is now Liberia, the toponym *Cess*, often identified with that coast, derives from the Portuguese *cesto*, which refers to the pannier or large basket in which the malagueta pepper was brought for sale. A final illustration of the ubiquity of malagueta pepper in the slave trade and of its perceived medicinal value comes from Thomas Phillips's account of the voyage of the *Hannibal* in 1694. "The reason of our buying this pepper," he wrote "is to give our negroes in their messes to keep them from the flux and dry belyach, which they are very incident to."[63]

The malagueta pepper is only one of numerous medicinal plants brought to the New World from "Guinea."[64] Leaves from the plant known commonly as guinea mint are made into a tea to treat such complaints as indigestion and flatulence. Another plant, the pungent and bitter tasting guinea-hen weed, known scientifically as *Petiveria alliacea*, is believed to have been brought from Guinea by slaves and is now widely distributed in tropical America, especially Jamaica.[65]

Conclusion

Black Americans and other African-derived populations in the Western Hemisphere recognize that most of the food products discussed here were inextricably linked to slavery. Either they served to increase the African population and thus support the overseas slave trade (as with maize and manioc introduced from the Americas), were used cosmetically to make slaves look young and sleek for sale (rubbing with palm oil), were fed to slaves as provisions during the infamous Middle Passage (yams, peanuts, and rice), were provided to keep slaves healthy during that voyage (citrus fruit and malagueta peppers), or became plantation products that required or used slave labor in the New World (as in the case of rice). The often perversely ironic links between the spread of certain foodstuffs and African bondage in the Western Hemisphere makes for a good deal of ambivalence about African cultural influences among Native American, Euro-American, and African American populations. Joseph G. Brand, Morley R. Kare, and Michael Naim argue that "food habits are one of the last characteristics of a cultural group to disappear as the culture changes."[66] Part of the task of this chapter has been to assess the validity of such a notion with regard to the impact of the Atlantic slave trade on the food habits of various groups of Africans forcefully transported to the Western Hemisphere between 1501 and 1865. As occurred with Africans holding onto aspects of their religions, oral traditions, musical and dance behavior, and even material culture despite the traumas of initial capture, so, too, they held onto much of their African culinary past.[67] Of course, they did have to adapt and change their foodways creatively as they encountered new nutritional, disease, and work environments. In this creative adaptation and innovation the African newcomers not only transformed themselves into New World African Americans but also became vitally important agents in shaping the culinary tastes and a host of other customs of European Americans and Native Americans in the entire hemisphere. Nowhere in the United States is this more evident than in the consumption patterns and food preparation techniques found in the southern states, where the descendants of Africans were concentrated during the antebellum period and for many years after.

NOTES

I wish to acknowledge financial assistance from the following sources that facilitated work on this and related projects between 1985 and 2000: the Graduate School of the University of Maryland Baltimore County, the Smithsonian Institution, Northeastern University, and the American Council of Learned Societies. Thanks also to the following individuals, who, in addition to the editor of this volume and the anonymous readers for the University of Illinois Press, read and commented on the manuscript at various stages: Willie B. Lamousé-Smith, Victor C. Uchendu, Craig Reynolds, Chezia Brenda Thompson, George Brandon, and Jacqueline A. Goggin.

1. Kenneth F. Kiple, "Future Studies of the Biological Past of the Black," *Social Science History* 10 (Winter 1986): 503. See also Kenneth F. Kiple and Virginia Himmelsteib King, *Another Dimension to the Black Diaspora: Diet Disease, and Racism* (New York: Cambridge University Press, 1981), and Kenneth F. Kiple, *The Caribbean Slave: A Biological History* (New York: Cambridge University Press, 1984).

2. Philip D. Curtin, *The Atlantic Slave Trade* (Madison: University of Wisconsin Press, 1969), 270.

3. Sidney Mintz, "History and Anthroplogy," in *Race and Slavery in the Western Hemisphere*, edited by Stanley Engerman and Eugene D. Genovese (Princeton: Princeton University Press, 1975), 483–84n18. See also Mintz's suggestion that such topics as women's work, slave food, diet, and nutrition are subjects in which "the skills of anthropology and history might be usefully combined." Sidney Mintz, "Time, Sugar, and Sweetness," *Marxist Perspectives* 2 (Winter 1979–80): 57. This essay is part of an effort to combine the skills and approaches of these two disciplines in a large study of the impact of the Atlantic slave trade on North American culture. A useful addition to the literature is Anne Elizabeth Yentsch's chapter, "West African Women, Foods, and Cultural Values," in Yentsch, *A Chesapeake Family and Their Slaves: A Study in Historical Archaeology* (New York: Cambridge University Press, 1994), 196–215.

4. Mary Tolford Wilson, "Peaceful Integration: The Owner's Adoption of His Slaves' Food," *Journal of Negro History* 49 (April 1964): 116–27.

5. Richard B. Sheridan, "Africa and the Caribbean in the Atlantic Slave Trade," *American Historical Review* 77 (Feb. 1972): 16n6.

6. Merrick Posnansky, "Yams and the Origin of West African Agriculture," *Odu*, no. 1 (April 1969): 101; Oliver Davies, "The Neolithic Revolution in Ghana," *Transactions of the Historical Society of Ghana* 4 (1962): 14–20; Oliver Davies, *West Africa before the Europeans: Archaeology and Prehistory* (London: Methuen, 1967), 147–55, 205–22. More recently, experimental evidence has been brought to bear in identifying factors involved in the domestication of African yams. See V. E. Chikwendu and C. E. A. Okezie, "Factors Responsible for the Ennoblement of African Yams: Inferences from Experiments in Yam Domestication," in *Foraging and Farming: The Evolution of Plant Exploration*, edited by David R. Harris and Gordon C. Hillman (Boston: Unwin Hyman, 1989), 344–57.

7. Posnansky, "Yams and the Origin of West African Agriculture," 106.

8. Ibid., 106; Thomas Edward Bowditch, *Mission from Cape Coast to Ashantee* (London: John Murray, 1819), 31–40, 358–69, 449–52; D. G. Coursey and Cecelia K. Coursey, "The New Yam Festivals of West Africa," *Anthropos* 66 (1971): 444–84; Emea O. Arua, "Yam Ceremonies and the Values of Ohafia Culture," *Africa* 51, no. 2 (1981): 694–705; Richard Mohr, "Das Yamfest Bei Den Ewe von Aloi Togo." *Anthropos* 57 (1962): 172–82. For other discussions of yam festivals in various parts of West Africa see V. Rahm, "La Cote d'Ivoire, centre de recherches tropicales," *Acta Tropica* 11 (1954): 222–95, and Togbe Afede Asor II, "Ho Yam Festival," *The Ghanaian*, no. 4 (Oct. 1958): 15, 48.

9. Pierre Gourou, *The Tropical World, Its Social and Economic Conditions and Its Future Status*, translated by Edward Dalrymple Laborde (London: Longmans, 1953), 39; D. G. Coursey, "The Origins and Domestication of Yams in Africa," in *Origins of African Plant Domestication*, edited by Jack R. Harlan, Jan M. J. de Wet, and Ann B. L. Stemler (The Hague: Mouton, 1976), 402.

10. Benjamin Núñez, *Dictionary of Afro-Latin American Civilization* (Westport: Greenwood Press, 1980), 490. According to M. J. T. Norman, C. J. Pearson, and P. G. E. Searle, "During the slave trade both *D. alata* and *D. rotundata* were taken from West Africa to the Caribbean" (*The Ecology of Tropical Food Crops* [New York: Cambridge University Press, 1984], 259). *D. cayenensis* was derived from *D. latifolia*, which, according to Chevalier, was domesticated in West Africa. D. G. Coursey, *Yams* (London: Longmans, 1967); Auguste Chevalier, "De quelques *Dioscorea* d'afrique equatoriales toxiques dont plusieurs variétés sont alimentaires," *Revue de Botanique Appliquée et Agriculture Tropicale* 32 (1952): 14–19. The origins and evolution of Old World yams are discussed in J. Alexander and D. G. Coursey, "The Origins of Yam Cultivation," in *The Domestication and Exploitation of Plants and Animals*, edited by P. J. Ucko and G. W. Dimbleby (Chicago: Aldine-Atherton, 1969), 405–25; D. G. Coursey, "Yams (*Dioscorea spp*). (*Dioscoreaceae*)," in *Evolution of Crop Plants*, edited by N. W. Simmonds (New York: Longmans, 1976), 70–74; and D. G. Coursey, "The Origins and Domestication of Yams in Africa," in *Origins of African Plant Domestication*, edited by H. R. Harland, J. M. J. de Wet, and Ann B. L. Stemler (The Hague: Mouton, 1976), 383–408.

11. William Smith, *A New Voyage to Guinea* (1744, repr. London: Frank Cass, 1967), 28, and Robert Campbell, *A Pligrimage to My Motherland: An Account of a Journey among the Egbas and Yorubas of Central Africa in 1859–60* reprinted in *Search for a Place: Black Separatism and Africa, 1860*, introduction by Howard Bell (Ann Arbor: University of Michigan Press, 1969), 182. On the use of yams among the Yoruba see also William R. Bascom, "Some Yoruba Ways with Yams," in *The Anthropologists' Cookbook*, edited by Jessica Kuper (London: Routledge, Kegan Paul, 1977).

12. Oliver Davies, "The Origins of Agriculture in West Africa," *Current Anthropology* 9, no. 5 (1968): 480. For a description of the preparation methods for a variety called *Mbao-Mng'oko* in parts of Tanzania, see E. B. Mhoro and K. Mtotomwema, "Mbao-Mng'Oko: A Wild Edible Yam," *Tanzania Notes and Records*, nos. 88 and 89 (1982): 109–11. An anonymous reader of this manuscript has pointed out that toxicity may not be the actual reason for pounding foods into fufu but rather a taste for the resulting smooth texture. Once transported to the Americas, where, as slaves, West Africans would have had no time to prepare fufu, they may have used okra as an ingredient that would lend the same "mouth feel" to dishes.

13. *Random House Dictionary of the English Language,* 1652. The linguist David Dalby suggested that the words *yam* and *banana* derive from the names for those food crops in the Wolof language. Dalby, "Americanisms That May Once Have Been Africanisms," *The Times* (London), July 19, 1969, 9. See also I. H. Burkill, "The Contact of the Portuguese with African Food Plants which Gave Such Words as 'Yam' to European Languages," *Proceedings of the Linnean Society* 150 (1938): 84–95. There is also a noun, *yambi,* in Gullah that means "sweet potato." In Mende, according to the linguist Lorenzo D. Turner, *yambi* refers to the wild yam. Turner, "Problems Confronting the Investigator of Gullah," *Publications of the American Dialect Society* no. 9 (1948): 74–84, reprinted in *Mother Wit from the Laughing Barrell: Readings in the Interpretation of Afro-American Folklore,* edited by Alan Dundes (Englewood Cliffs: Prentice-Hall, 1973), 127–35.

14. James Barbot and John Casseneuve, "An Abstract of a Voyage to Congo River or Zair, and to Cabinde, in the Year 1700," and John Barbot, "A Supplement to the Description of the Coasts of North and South Guinea, in Churchill's *Voyages,* Vol. 5," both reprinted in *Documents Illustrative of the History of the Slave Trade to America,* edited by Elizabeth Donnan, 4 vols. (Washington: Carnegie Institution of Washington, 1930–35), 1: 463 and 2: 14–15.

15. René Caillié, *Travels through Central Africa to Timbucto and Across the Great Desert to Morocco, Performed in the Years 1824–28* (London: H. Colburn and R. Bentley, 1830), 1:190, 1:192; E. Adeniyi Oroge, "The Institution of Slavery in Yorubaland with Particular Reference to the Nineteenth Century," Ph.D. diss., University of Birmingham, 1971, 160. See also Kólá Akínlàdé, *Oluyole the Basorun: What Great Men Do* (Ibadan: Board Publications, 1987).

16. Roland Portères, "Berceaux agricoles sur le continent Africain," *Journal of African History* 3 (1962): 195–210; George Peter Murdock, *Africa: Its Peoples and Their Culture History* (New York: McGraw-Hill, 1959), 64–76; H. G. Baker, "Comments on the Thesis That There Was a Major Centre of Plant Domestication Near the Headwaters of the River Niger," *Journal of African History* 3 (1962): 229–33. A more recent statement on African cereals is found in Jack R. Harlan, "The Tropical African Cereals," in *Foraging and Farming: The Evolution of Plant Exploitation,* edited by David R. Harris and Gordon C. Hillman (Boston: Unwin Hyman, 1989).

17. See, for example, E. Miege, "Les cereales en Afrique du Nord, le maïs et le sorgho," *Revue de Botanique Appliquée et Agriculture Tropicale* 31 (1951): 137–58, and P. Viguier, "Les sorghos a grain et leur culture au Soudain Française," *Revue de Botanique Appliquée et Agriculture Tropicale* 25 (1945): 163–230.

18. There is no firm consensus among botanists about the precise geographical origin of sesame (*Sesamum indicum*). Portères believed that sesame was domesticated between Lake Chad and Ethiopia, "Berceaux agricoles primaires sur le continent Africain." Purseglove included sesame among the "other important crops which originate in tropical Africa, but for which it is impossible to define the area of domestication with any certainty although eastern Africa is likely for some of them." "The Origins and Migrations of Crops in Tropical Africa," in *Origins of African Plant Domestication,* edited by Jack R. Harlan, Jan M. J. De Wet, and Ann B. L. Stemler (The Hague: Mouton, 1976), 294. Although domestication probably occurred in Africa, possibly, but not necessarily in the Western Sudan, some botanists have suggested that domestication of sesame may

have happened in Asia. N. M. Nayar and K. L. Mehra argue that sesame may have been first cultivated either in Asia or Africa, or in both independently. See "Sesame: Its Uses, Botany, Cytogenetics, and Origin," *Economic Botany* 24 (1970): 20–31; see also Nayer, "Sesame," in *Evolution of Crop Plants*, edited by N. W. Simmonds (London: Longmans, 1976), 25.

19. It remains unclear precisely when and how sorghum was introduced into the Western Hemisphere and, more specifically, to the United States. Melissa Pasanen, "Sorghum Syrup," *The Art of Eating*, no. 53 (Spring 2000): 25.

20. Tadeusz Lewicki, *West African Foods in the Middle Ages, According to Arabic Sources* (1963 [in Polish], repr. New York: Cambridge University Press, 1974); Ibn al-Faqih, *Mukhtasar Kitab al-Buldan* (290 anno hegirae/903 CE.), reprinted in *Corpus of Early Arabic Sources for West African History*, translated and edited by Nehemiah H. Levtzion and J. F. P. Hopkins (New York: Cambridge University Press, 1981), 28; Núñez, *Dictionary of Afro-Latin American Civilization*, 221.

21. The Portuguese mariner Diogo Cão landed near the mouth of the Zaire (Congo) River in 1482. Ernst George Revenstein, "The Voyages of Diogo Cão and Bartolomeu Dias, 1482–88," *Geographical Journal* 7 (1900): 628–29.

22. Michel Adanson, *A Voyage to Senegal, the Isle of Goree and the River Gambia* (London: Nourse, 1759), 151, quoted in Daniel C. Littlefield, *Rice and Slaves: Ethnicity and the Slave Trade in Colonial South Carolina* (Baton Rouge: Louisiana State University Press, 1981), 76.

23. Colin Palmer, *Human Cargoes: The British Slave Trade to Spanish America, 1700–1739* (Urbana: University of Illinois Press, 1981), 28. On Gajaaga, Senegambia, Palmer cites Philip D. Curtin, *Economic Change in Precolonial Africa* (Madison: University of Wisconsin Press, 1975), 170, 176.

24. Portères, "Berceaux agricoles." On Jenné-Jeno, see Susan Keech McIntosh and Roderick J. McIntosh, "West African Prehistory," *American Scientist* 69 (Nov.–Dec. 1981): 608–9; see also R. J. McIntosh and S. K. McIntosh, "The Inland Niger Delta before the Empire of Mali: Evidence from Jenné-Jeno," *Journal of African History* 22 (1981): 1–22, and "Finding West Africa's Oldest City," *National Geographic* 162 (Sept. 1982): 410.

25. John Michael Vlach, *The Afro-American Tradition in Decorative Arts* (Cleveland: Cleveland Museum of Art, 1978). See also Karen Hess, *The Carolina Rice Kitchen: The African Connection* (Columbia: University of South Carolina Press, 1992) and a series of articles by Judith A. Carney, including "From Hands to Tutors: African Expertise in the South Carolina Rice Economy," *Agricultural History* 67, no. 3 (1993): 1–30; "Landscapes of Technology Transfer: Rice Cultivation and African Continuities," *Technology and Clture* 37, no. 1 (1996): 5–35; "The Role of African Rice and Slaves in the History of Rice Cultivation in the Americas," *Human Ecology* 26 (Dec. 1998): 525–45; "Rice Milling, Gender, and Slave Labour in Colonial South Carolina," *Past and Present* 153 (1996): 108–34; "The African Antecedents of Uncle Ben in U.S. Rice History," *Journal of Historical Geography* 29 (2003): 1–21; and Carney's provocative *Black Rice: The African Origins of Rice Cultivation in the Americas* (Cambridge: Harvard University Press, 2001). Another useful source is A. Carpenter's "The History of Rice in Africa," in *Rice in Africa*, edited by I. W. Buddenhagen and J. G. Persley (London: Academic Press, 1979).

26. Darold D. Wax, "Preference for Slaves in Colonial America," *Journal of Negro*

History 58 (Oct. 1973): 371–401; Peter H. Wood, *Black Majority: Negroes in Colonial South Carolina from 1670 through the Stono Rebellion* (New York: W. W. Norton, 1974); Littlefield, *Rice and Slaves*; Ulrich Bonnell Phillips, *American Negro Slavery: A Survey of the Supply, Employment and Control of Negro Labor as Determined by the Plantation Regime* (1918, repr. Baton Rouge: Louisiana State University Press, 1969), 42.

27. Wood, *Black Majority*, 61; Janie Gilliard Moore, "Africanisms among Blacks of the Sea Islands," *Journal of Black Studies* 10 (June 1980): 480. The foodways of the Gullah have received much attention. Perhaps some of the most interesting are discussed in Josephine Beoku-Betts, "'She Make Funny Flat Cake She Call Saraka': Gullah Women and Food Practices under Slavery," in *Working Toward Freedom: Slave Society and Domestic Economy in the American South*, edited by Larry E. Hudson Jr. (Rochester: University of Rochester Press, 1994), 211–31, and "We Got Our Way of Cooking Things," *Gender and Society* 9 (1995): 535–55.

28. Peter H. Wood, "'It Was a Negro Taught Them': A New Look at African Labor in Early South Carolina," *Journal of Asian and African Studies* 9 (1974): 159–79; Robert E. Purdue Jr., "African Baskets in South Carolina," *Economic Botany* 22 (1968): 289–92.

29. Olaudah Equiano (Gustavus Vassa), *Equiano's Travels: His Autobiography; the Interesting Narrative of Olaudah Equiano, or Gustavus Vassa the African*, abridged and edited by Paul Edwards (London: Heinemann, 1967), 5. See also S. Hofstra, "The Social Significance of the Oil Palm in the Life of the Mendi," *Internationales Archiv fur Ethnographie* 34, nos. 5–6 (1937): 105–18.

30. Andrew Battell, *The Strange Adventure of Andrew Battell of Leigh in Angola and the Adjoining Regions*, edited by E. G. Ravenstein (London: Hakluyt Society, 1901), 19–35, reprinted in *African History: Text and Readings*, edited by Robert O. Collins (New York: Random House, 1971), quotations on 383.

31. Smith, *A Voyage to Guinea*, 30–31.

32. Capt. Thomas Phillips Journal, printed in John Churchill's *Collections of Voyages and Travel*, vol. 6 (London: Henry Linton and John Osborn, 1746), reprinted in George Francis Dow, *Slave Ships and Slaving* (Salem, Mass.: Marine Research Society, 1927), 61. For the interconnections between the palm oil trade and the slave trade, see J. N. Oriji, "A Study of the Slave and Palm Produce Trade amongst the Ngwa-Igbo of Southwestern Nigeria," *Cahiers d'Études Africaines* 23 (1983): 311–28; David Northrup, "The Compatibility of the Slave and Palm Oil Trades in the Bight of Biafra," *Journal of African History* 17 (1976): 353–64; and Patrick Manning, "Slaves, Palm Oil, and Political Power on the West African Coast," *African Historical Studies* 2 (1969): 279–88.

33. Marvin P. Miracle, *Maize in Tropical Africa* (Madison: University of Wisconsin Press, 1966); William O. Jones, *Manioc in Africa* (Stanford: Stanford University Press, 1959).

34. E. J. Alagoa, "Long Distance Trade and States in the Niger Delta," *Journal of African History* 11 (1970): 322 (first and second quotations). For a detailed treatment of the introduction and diffusion of cassava cultivation and consumption, see Achim von Oppen, "Cassava: 'Lazy Man's Food'? Indigenous Agricultural Innovation and Dietary Change in Northwestern Zambia (ca. 1650–1970)," *Food and Foodways* 5, no. 1 (1991): 15–38. See also Kay Williamson, "Some Food Plant Names in the Niger Delta," *International Journal of American Linguistics* 36 (1970): 1556–67.

35. For a description of the general historical situation along the East African coast

before the arrival of the Portuguese in 1498, see Gervase Mathew, "The East African Coast until the Coming of the Portuguese," in *History of East Africa*, edited by Roland Oliver and Gervase Mathew (New York: Oxford University Press, 1963), 1: 94–127.

36. Virginia Scott Jenkins, *Bananas: An American History* (Washington: Smithsonian Institution Press, 2000).

37. E. Jefferson Murphy, *History of African Civilization* (New York: Crowell, 1972), 89; Ivan R. Dale, "The Indian Origins of Some African Cultivated Plants and African Cattle," *Uganda Journal* 19 (1955): 62–72. The *Random House Dictionary of the English Language* lists the derivation of "banana" as < Spanish < Portuguese < West African native name. The linguist David Dalby indicates that the term is used in Wolof: "Americanisms That May Once Have Been Africanisms," *The Times* (London), July 19, 1969, 9. Also see C. P. Blakney, "On 'Banana' and 'Iron'": Linguistic Footprints in African History," *Hartford Studies in Linguistics* no. 13 (1963): 124, and Al-Mas'udi, *Les prairies d'or*, edited by C. Barbier de Meynard and P. de Courteille (Paris: Imprimerie impériale, 1861–77), 1: 334, 3: 7, 11, 29.

38. Jacob Egharevba, *A Short History of Benin*, 3d ed. (Ibadan: Ibadan University Press, 1960), 2; Thurstan Shaw, "Early Crops in Africa: A Review of the Evidence," in *Origins of African Plant Domestication*, edited by Jack R. Harlan, Jan M. J. de Wet, and Ann B. L. Stemler (The Hague: Mouton, 1976), 137. See also Richard Gray, "A Report on the Conference: Third Conference on African History and Archaeology," *Journal of African History* 3 (1962): 175–91. More recent archaeological surveys of Africa, such as David W. Phillipson's *African Archaeology* (New York: Cambridge University Press, 1993), refer to bananas as having been "brought . . . across the Indian Ocean" and "introduced from Indonesia" (118, 224). Graham Connah refers to a number of plants being cultivated on the East African coast by about 1900 as having been "introduced to East Africa from India and South-East Asia at some unknown date before the arrival of the Portuguese on this coast." *African Civilizations: An Archaeological Perspective*, 2d ed. (New York: Cambridge University Press, 2001), 188. They do not, however, add much to the little that is known about how the Asiatic cultigens spread within Africa from the East African coast.

39. Stanley B. Alpern, "The European Introduction of Crops into West Africa in Precolonial Times," *History in Africa* 19 (1992): 24–31.

40. Roland Portères, "L'introduction du maïs en Afrique," *Journal d'Agriculture Tropicale et de Botanique Appliquée* 6 (1959): 84–105; David Birmingham, "Central Africa and the Atlantic Slave Trade," in *The Middle Age of African History*, edited by Roland Oliver (New York: Oxford University Press, 1967), 58 (a discussion of crops grown and other economic pursuits).

41. David Birmingham, *The Portuguese Conquest of Angola* (London: Oxford University Press, 1965), 8. The source that Birmingham cites is G. L. Haveaux, *La tradition historique des Bapende orientaux* (Brussels: Academie Royale des Sciences d'Outre-Mer, 1954).

42. M. D. W. Jeffreys, "Maize in West Africa," *Man* 247 (1963): 194; Jeffreys, "How Ancient Is West African Maize?" *Africa* 33 (1963): 115–31; Jeffreys, "Pre-Columbian Maize in Africa," *Nature* 172 (1953): 965–66. Jeffreys has asserted that Arabs crossed the Atlantic around 1000 CE. ("Pre-Columbian Negroes in America," *Scientia* [July–Aug. 1953], 1–16). For a summary of what is found in Chinese sources, see Hui-Lan Li, "A

Case for Pre-Columbia Transatlantic Travel by Arab Ships," *Harvard Journal of Asiatic Studies* 23 (1960–61): 114–26.

43. Marvin P. Miracle, "The Introduction and Spread of Maize in Africa," *Journal of African History* 6 (1965): 39–55; Miracle, *Maize in Tropical Africa*; Olfert Dapper, *Naukeurige Beschrijvinge der Afrikaensche Gewesten van Egypten, Barbaryen, Libyen, Biledulgerid, Negroslant, Guinea, Ethiopien, Abbyssinie: Getrokkenuit Verscheyde Hedendaegse Lantbeschrijvers en Geschriften van Bereisde Onderzoekers Dier Landen* (Amsterdam: Wolfgang, Weesekerge, Boom and Van Someren, 1686), translated into French as *Description de l'Afrique*; James C. McCann, *Maize and Grace: Africa's Encounter with a New World Crop, 1500–2000* (Cambridge: Harvard University Press, 2005), see especially 23–38.

44. Hubert B. Ross, "The Diffusion of the Manioc Plant from South America to Africa: An Essay in Ethnobotanical Culture History," Ph.D. diss., Yale University, 1954.

45. Kay Williamson, "Some Food Plant Names in the Niger Delta," *International Journal of American Linguistics* 36 (1970): 1556–67; E. J. Alagoa, "Long Distance Trade and States in the Niger Delta," *Journal of African History* 11 (1970): 322. For a detailed treatment of the introduction and diffusion of cassava cultivation and consumption see von Oppen, "Cassava: 'The Lazy Man's Food'?"

46. I thank Andrew Smith for informing me that a Bolivian origin for the peanut "had been determined in the 1970s and that subsequent research had concurred" and that "there does not seem to be any controversy over this." Personal communication, July 1, 2000. Smith referred me to the following: C. A. Krapovickas, "The Origin, Variability, and Spread of the Groundnut (*Arachis hypogaea*)," translated by J. Smartt, in *The Domestication and Exploitation of Animals and Plants*, edited by Peter J. Ucko and G. W. Dimbleby (Chicago: Aldine-Atherton, 1969), 431–32; W. C. Gregory, C. A. Krapovickas, and M. P. Gregory, "Structures, Variation, Evolution, and Classification in Arachis," in *Advances in Legume Science*, edited by R. J. Summerfield and A. H. Bunting (London: Royal Botanic Gardens, Kew, 1980), 469–81; and Johnny C. Wynne and Terry Coffelt, "Genetics of Arachis Hypogaea L.," in *Peanut Science and Technology*, edited by Harold K. Pattee and Clyde T. Young (Yoakum, Tex.: American Peanut Research and Education Society, 1982), 51.

47. A. F. Hill, *Economic Botany* (New York: McGraw-Hill, 1937), 359.

48. E. J. Alagoa, "Long-Distance Trade and States in the Niger Delta," *Journal of African History* 11 (1970): 328; John Barbot, *Description of North and South Guinea* (Paris, 1732), 377; see also Jones, *Manioc in Africa*.

49. Stephen H. Hymer, "Economic Forms in Pre-Colonial Ghana," *Journal of Economic History* 30 (March 1970): 41.

50. Kenneth F. Kiple, *The Caribbean Slave: A Biological History* (New York: Cambridge University Press, 1984), 188; Alfred F. Crosby Jr., *The Columbian Exchange* (Westport: Greenwood Press, 1972), 188; Philip D. Curtin, *The Atlantic Slave Trade: A Census* (Madison: University of Wisconsin Press, 1969), 270–71.

51. Herbert S. Klein devotes nearly a page and a half to provisioning for the voyage in *The Atlantic Slave Trade* (New York: Cambridge University Press, 1999), 93–94.

52. Palmer, *Human Cargoes*, 50; PRO T70/52, 100, cited in Palmer, *Human Cargoes*, 58.

53. Alexander Falconbridge, *An Account of the Slave Trade on the Coast of Africa* (1788, repr. New York: AMS Press, 1973), 21–22.

54. Falconbridge, *An Account*, 22.

55. Journal of the ship *Mary*, June 20, 1796. The ship sailed from Providence, Rhode Island, on November 22, 1795, intending to secure a cargo of slaves in Africa and carry them to Georgia, one of the few states where the overseas slave trade was still legal (Georgia did not abolish the trade until 1798). The journal was found by William Warren Sweet, a University of Chicago historian, in the possession of James Bridges of Greencastle, Indiana, and was transcribed by Irene H. Quay. Excerpts from the transcript were published in *Documents Illustrative of the History of the Slave Trade to America*, ed. Donnan, 3: 363–71.

56. Mark Wagner, "The Introduction and Early Use of African Plants in the New World," *Tennessee Archaeologist* 6 (1981): 112–23.

57. Anne Ritson, *A Poetical Picture of America, Being Observations Made during a Residence of Several Years, at Alexandria and Norfolk, in Virginia; Illustrative of the Manners and Customs of the Inhabitants Interspersed with Anecdotes Arising from a General Intercourse with Society in That Country, from the Year 1799 to 1807. By a Lady* (1809). The stanza was quoted in "Virginia in 1732: The Travel Journal of William Hugh Grove," edited by Gregory A. Stiverson and Patrick H. Butler III, *Virginia Magazine of History and Biography* 85 (1977): 35n80.

58. Charles W. Joyner, *Down by the Riverside: Slave Folklife in a South Carolina Slave Community* (Urbana: University of Illinois Press, 1984), 239, 106.

59. Edward S. Ayensu, preface to William Ed Grimé, *Ethno-Botany of the Black Americans* (Algoniac, Mich.: Reference Publications, 1970), xi; Romeo B. Garrett, "African Survivals in American Culture," *Journal of Negro History* 51 (1966): 239–45; Heinrich Barth, *Travels and Discoveries in North and Central Africa*, 3 vols. (New York: Harper and Brothers, 1857), 1: 513–14; Richard W. Hull, *African Cities and Towns before European Conquest* (New York: Norton, 1976), 16; Paul E. Lovejoy, "Kola in the History of West Africa," *Cahiers d'Études Africaines* 20 (1980): 97–134; Lovejoy, *Caravans of Kola: The Hausa Kola Trade, 1700–1900* (Zaria: Ahmadu Bello University Press, 1980); E. J. Kahn Jr., "Coca-Cola," in *Encyclopedia of Southern Culture*, edited by Charles Reagan Wilson and William Ferris (Chapel Hill: University of North Carolina Press, 1989), 739; Vlach, *The Afro-American Tradition in Decorative Arts*, 8. For further discussion of the significance of the kola nut in trade and society in West Africa, see T. A. Russell, "The Kola of Nigeria and the Cameroons," *Tropical Agriculture* 32, no. 3 (1955): 210–40; Abner Cohen, "The Politics of the Kola Trade," *Africa* 36 (1966): 18–36; Lars Sundstrom, "The Cola Nut, Functions in West African Social Life," *Studia Ethnographiica Upsaliensia* 26, no. 2 (1966): 135–49; and B. A. Agiri, "The Yoruba and the Pre-Colonial Kola Trade," *Odu: A Journal of West African Studies*, new series, no. 12 (July 1975): 55–68.

60. Michel Laguerre, *Afro-Caribbean Folk Medicine* (South Hadley, Mass.: Bergin and Garvey, 1987), appendix 1, 91.

61. Théophilus Conneau, *Twenty Years a Slaver*. The original edition of this work was first published in 1854 through the editorial assistance of a Baltimore-based author, Brante Mayer. Its original title was *Captain Canot; or, Twenty Years of an African Slaver*.

During the 1960s or early 1970s, the original manuscript prepared by Conneau and a group of correspondence between him and Mayer surfaced in a Washington, D.C., bookshop. This is the version published by Howard S. Mott, Inc., in 1976, under the title A Slaver's Log Book; or, Twenty Years' Residence in Africa, with an introduction by Mabel M. Smythe. The quotation appears on page 117 of the Mott edition. Variation occurs in the literature concerning how to render the slaver's names, whether Theodore, Théophile, Theophilus, Théophilus, Conneau, or Canot. The best effort to trace the history of the composition and publication of the various editions is Bruce L. Mouser, "Théophilus Conneau: The Saga of a Tale," History in Africa 6 (1979): 97–107.

62. Records of the Royal African Company, PRO T70/51, 17: Calendar of State Papers, Colonial Series, America and West Indies, 1661–1668, Preserved in Her Majesty's Public Record Office and Calendar of State Papers, Colonial Series, America and West Indies, 1669–1674, Preserved in Her Majesty's Public Record Office, both edited by W. Noel Sainsbury (Valduz [Lichtenstein]: Kraus Reprint, 1964), 5: 266, and 5: 412–13; journal of the Arthur, Dec. 6, 1677–May 25, 1678, reprinted in Donnan, ed., Documents Illustrative of the History of the Slave Trade to America, 1: 231. Donnan cites T70:1213 record group in the British Public Record Office.

63. A. Texeira da Mota, Toponimos de Origem Portuguesa na Costa Ocidental de Africa (Bissau, 1950), 233–38; Thomas Phillips, Voyage of the Hannibal in Churchill's Voyages, reprinted in Donnan, Documents, 1: 394.

64. Julia F. Morton, "The Calabash (Crescentia cuijete) in Folk Medicine," Economic Botany 22 (1968): 272–80; Susan McLure, "Parallel Usage of Medicinal Plants by Africans the Their Descendants," Eonomic Botany 36 (1982): 291–301; see also Edward S. Ayensu, Medicinal Plants of West Africa (Algonac, Mich.: Reference Publications, 1978); Bep Oliver-Bever, Medicinal Plants in Tropical West Africa (New York: Cambridge University Press, 1986).

65. Núñez, Dictionary, 222. A growing body of research has looked at Africa as a source for cultural expressions found in the American context, including such things as African folk medicine in colonial Virginia. No attempt has been made in this essay to discuss medicinal uses of plants extensively.

66. Joseph G. Brand, Morley R. Kare, and Michael Naim, "Restraints in Accepting New Foods: Relationships among Taste, Acceptability, and Digestion," in Nutrition, Food, and Man: An Interdisciplinary Perspective, edited by Paul G. Pearson and J. Richard Greenwell (Tucson: University of Arizona Press, 1980), 105.

67. For a more recent description of what she calls "An African Atlantic Culinary Journey," see Jessica B. Harris, "Same Boat, Different Stops: An African Atlantic Culinary Journey," in African Roots/American Cultures: Africa in the Creation of the Americas, edited by Sheila S. Walker (New York: Rowan and Littlefield, 2001), 169–82. Harris has produced a number of culturally and historically informed cookbooks, including The Welcome Table (New York: Simon and Schuster, 1995).

2

Soul Food as Cultural Creation

William C. Whit

In all social science there is probably no more problematic term than *culture*. Some refer to it exclusively as the high culture of music and art whereas others define it as only the generalized belief system of a society. It has also been defined more broadly as the sum of all that human beings do and have done. No definition stands as definitive. Thus, for the purposes of this essay it is necessary that I begin by stating the elements I consider relevant to culture before explaining why I see soul food as constitutive of, and an exemplary performance of, culture. I also explore soul food as a cultural manifestation, relying on a consolidation of others' sociological and historical research.

My working definition of culture includes that it is something learned and shared. It is generally (but not exclusively) confined to human beings. In addition, and importantly, culture originates as an attempt to come to terms with an environment's physical and social aspects. As a system of human interactions, however, culture does more than reflect adaptation. Rather, it is an adaptive response. That term denotes both an active, creative human involvement and a dialectical interplay between human actor and environment.

Once created, cultural formations take on a life of their own and tend to persist. Because cultural creation is ongoing, however, the elements of a given cultural formation continually interact with changing environments and human creativity, resulting in an endless process of human activity and cultural creation. As Tony Whitehead sums up much of this concept, "Culture is part of a larger ecological system, which is historically created, intergenerationally reproduced and moderated, and *functions to allow humans to meet basic biological needs in ways that blunt the impact of deleterious environmental agents and exploit agents that sustain life and culture.*"[1]

Although sociologists have often overlooked the importance of food, an increased awareness of the cultural significance of food has developed since the mid-1980s. As a biological product that is culturally appropriated, food can offer a microcosm of how cultures and subcultures operate. More specifically, by examining the production, collection, storage, distribution, preparation, consumption, and disposal of food, students can see reflected the macrocosmic element of the society in which the food is embedded. As Anne Murcott has observed, "Eating has . . . a moral and symbolic quality. When someone chooses to avoid eating flesh . . . they are making statements about themselves."[2]

Within most societies we find subgroups. Thus, in the United States there exists a variety of immigrants who carry on as ethnic groups in large part through continuing to prepare food and eat it as did ancestors in their countries of origin. Such familiar American institutions as Italian and Chinese restaurants provide evidence of ethnic cuisines that, often in forms adapted to the dominant culture's taste, have long been part of the mainstream culture's food.

More recently, the increased power and influence of African Americans have enabled their own cuisine, dubbed "soul food" in the 1960s, to appear in restaurants of African American entrepreneurs in both ghetto and mainstream areas. (Of course, long before the name was coined unique foods were part of the African American culture and played a strong part in the evolution of southern whites' food culture through the influence of slave cooks.) The increased visibility of soul food synthesizes a number of national cultural influences into a contemporary fusion cuisine. As Helen Mendes states, "Food, like art, music, and literature is an authentic expression of a people's culture. Throughout the history of African-Americans, food has provided more than physical sustenance. It has provided one of the few vehicles through which Blacks have been able to preserve their African heritage."[3]

As a subject within the larger category of so-called ethnic food, soul food is unique. Contrary to the stereotype of Africans having no culture, the existence and continual creation of soul food demonstrates a creation (or series of creations) composed of a variety of elements from Africa, the Americas, and many European sources. Pamela Kittler and Kathryn Sucher aptly note that "black foods offer a unique glimpse into the way that a cuisine develops."[4]

This analysis will include many of the African, American, and European influences on the production, collection (harvest), storage and preservation, distribution, preparation, consumption, and disposal of foods, and my discussion will be constructed around these categories. Throughout, I stress the relative autonomy of food as a cultural creation and the degree to which ongoing cultural re-creation has modified elements within soul food culture.

Production and Procurement

Virtually all Africans who came to the United States, whether before or after the formation of the Republic, came from what were food-growing societies to primarily the southern states, where they were reemployed in agriculture. Although they were initially on a par with white indentured servants, newer immigrants were forced into slavery, and slaveholders used their knowledge of agriculture, especially in growing rice. From Africa, the immigrants brought biological entities and traditions of food utilization that were new to America. Although the original source of some of the following food items may be debated (some are indigenous to Africa, and others were introduced into Africa from the Americas, the Caribbean, Europe, and Asia), it is generally accepted that the following came across the Atlantic with slaves in one way or another: rice, yams, millet, cowpeas, black-eyed peas, sesame seeds, sorghum (guinea corn), oranges, avocados, various bananas and plantains, okra, spinach, mustard greens, eggplant, cassava, maize, some squashes, sweet potatoes, peanuts, chiles, coconuts, and a variety of roots and tubers.[5]

Within the negotiated order of slavery most slaves cultivated private gardens, which Judith Carney describes as "botanical gardens of the dispossessed, the marginal, those who struggled to hold onto their cultural identity under dehumanized conditions." The gardens provided both slaves and masters with a source of cash; slaves might sell their produce, along with chickens, meat, and eggs, to planters.[6] Although there is no statistical accounting of the percentage of slaves that maintained private gardens, doing so made logical sense. Gardens were a free source of additional nutrition for a slave owner's "investment" and must have provided slaves with a source of satisfaction in creating and owning something of their own. As a legacy of this practice, gardening continues to be pervasive in most predominantly African American communities.

Veta Tucker, a director of the African American Studies Program at Grand Valley State University, has stated that private slave gardens were common throughout slavery. As Lucia Stanton writes, "Every slave household at Monticello had a poultry yard and most raised their own vegetables." Stanton makes clear that these gardens were tended after slaves had already put in arduous labor during long workdays.[7] A typical Sunday is revealed in the household account of one of Thomas Jefferson's granddaughters; slaves came with their produce to stock the Monticello kitchen and took home dimes and half-bits in exchange. Some probably obtained passes so they could take their products to Charlottesville for sale as well.[8]

Most important to the nature of soul food is the African tradition of using spices to make food more interesting. The hot malagueta or guinea pepper is the most dominant spice, but other peppers include *pili-pili* and the red pimento, both of which are capsicum peppers of American origin. These were used with European salt, when available, and with onion, garlic, and lemon juice to transform the blandness of basic grains.[9]

In addition, Africans were familiar with pigs, which Europeans brought to America, though Muslim slaves were forbidden to eat pork. They approached it with a traditional African and preindustrial cultural tradition, using the entire food entity. Stomachs, ears, feet, intestines, brains (primarily in head cheese), ribs, back fat, and hocks all assumed prominent roles in what came to be called soul food. Before the Industrial Revolution, people in many countries used similar practices and consumed all parts of an animal.

Unlike many white southerners, slaves had a strong tradition of eating a lot of cooked greens—those from the tops of beets, for example, and wild food such as dandelions. Slaves were resourceful in preparing vegetable sustenance from many other nutritious leafy vegetables, among them chard, collard greens, kale, mustard greens, and purslane.[10] Native American slaves introduced other greens, such as marsh marigold, milkweed, and pokeweed, and these, too, became part of the vegetable sustenance of slaves. Soaking up water in which vegetables had been boiled with corn bread was a common practice. The pot likker contained some vitamins and many minerals leached from the greens by boiling.

Many Africans were from societies that grew rice, and how to do that, as Judith Carney notes, was knowledge that proved extremely useful in the Carolinas. Whites actively sought African knowledge of rice growing, and slaves used that knowledge in the bargaining system of task labor to negotiate less plantation work so they might spend more time tending their gardens. "Significantly," Carney observes, "subordinated peoples used their own knowledge systems of the environment they settled to reshape the terms of their domination."[11]

Corn became a food consumed in quantity by slaves, usually in the form of a cornmeal product. Corn originated in the Americas, and Native Americans used a wide variety of corn products. Although corn was nutritionally deficient in protein by itself, it was supplemented through the tradition of hunting small game—turkey, rabbits, raccoons, possum, and squirrels. European Americans and African Americans also quickly incorporated other Native American dietary practices, such as growing pumpkins, squash, and beans and gathering sassafras, other wild plants, berries, and nuts.[12]

Collection and Storage

The harvest season has traditionally provided a time of food abundance. The Thanksgiving holiday celebrated by European Americans, African Americans, and others in the United States (and derived from its English predecessor, the Harvest Home Festival) is now for most people solely a time for feasting, but in the past it was also linked to the many activities connected with the harvest and putting up food for the winter.

Grain could reasonably be stored for later use through drying and could then be ground and used as needed. Much southern cuisine is based on freshly ground and cooked grain. Spoon bread and hoecakes as well as other types of corn bread were usually eaten immediately out of the oven or ashes when they would taste best, but they could also be eaten hours or even days later.

In the absence of refrigeration, freezing, and canning technologies, there was less preservation of food than at present. Small animals such as rabbits and chickens were usually butchered and eaten soon thereafter. Large animals like pigs presented an abundance of meat, however, and both Africans and Europeans were familiar with the techniques of salting and drying. Europeans had used sugar for preserving fruit. Smoking (a technique possibly borrowed from Native Americans), salting, and pickling were additional preservation methods and applicable to meat (pig) and a variety of fish. In addition, one-pot meals lent themselves to ongoing heating next to an open fire, thus destroying whatever bacteria had grown during the cooling period.

Distribution

Saturday night was usually the time for distributing slave provisions. This made possible the tradition of a larger than normal Sunday dinner—a practice that has continued with minor modification in many African American households to the present.

Sam Bowers Hilliard indicates that a normal weekly slave ration of a peck of corn (a quarter of a bushel, often as cornmeal) and, in various forms, two to five pounds of pork per week was supplemented by fruit and vegetables in season—often from the slave's own garden—as well as fish and small game.[13] If slaves were fortunate, a chicken sometimes might be consumed on Sunday.

Since slavery, African Americans have participated in the food economy through a combination of commercial and personal family relationships that affect food distribution or redistribution. Although most contemporary African Americans use commercial sources of food, many low-income southern African Americans still participate in informal exchange networks in which food is used as a gift or exchanged informally for labor. In addition, a good number of northern urban and rural African American families continue to keep gardens—food that can be consumed by a family, shared by others, and often provide cultural autonomy.

Preparation

Food preparation is probably the area that demonstrates the widest range of cultural influences and creativity. Originally, one of the factors that separated human beings from animals was that humans, by cooking, transformed nature into nurture. The manner of cooking, the combination of ingredients, and the presentation all give evidence of cultural creativity. According to John Edgerton, "It was in the preparation of food that African Americans made the greatest contribution according to accounts of early southern foodways. . . . The kitchen was one of the few places where their (the slave cooks') imagination and skill could have free rein and full expression and there they often excelled."[14]

Furthermore, because people from widely different areas in West Africa came together only in America, there developed in the slave culinary experience a fusion cuisine, a creolization based on influences from a variety of tribal traditions in Africa. These, creatively adapted to the mixture of food staples and spices available from the traditions of Europeans, Native Americans, and

Africans, provided the originality and distinctiveness of the cultural creation we now term soul food.

A basic division (with some overlap) existed during slavery between food that the cook, usually an African American slave, prepared for the white master's family and that she or he prepared for the African American field worker. Whites, for example, kept for themselves what they considered the prime cuts from pigs, leaving the less desirable parts of the animal for slaves; creative cuisine was required for items like chitterlings and hocks. White masters frequently ate roasts, steaks, and chops, whereas slaves had to chop what meat they had into small pieces and use it in stews, soups, or other mixed dishes.

Slaves who worked in the master's "big house," as well as the mulatto offspring of the master and the slave women with whom he coupled (if they were favored by the master), usually ate more or less the same food as the whites, items such as "fried chicken, fried pies, potato salad, hot biscuits and yeast rolls."[15] Corn products such as hominy and grits were included in southern white cuisine as well as in the slaves' diet. In this context, Edgerton observes that "blacks invented new dishes, taught whites how to cook and even on occasion wrote cookbooks . . . but they seldom received credit for their accomplishments."[16]

One black cook who acquired some fame was the chef for Thomas Jefferson, the only gourmet American president. Jefferson took James Hemmings, brother of Sally Hemmings, said to be Jefferson's lover, to France to learn culinary skills. Hemmings subsequently favored certain foods and invented new uses for others, creating particular recipes that influenced American cuisine. Some of the items he helped make popular were ice cream, spaghetti, cornbread stuffing, waffles, and vanilla flavoring.[17]

Like Hemmings, other slave cooks were creative, regardless of their status. Generally, field slaves needed to make an adaptive response to the conditions that gave them less desirable (although not necessarily less nutritious) parts of a pig as well as a diet based on corn. Being that fieldwork limited available cooking time, it was necessary to find ingenious preparation techniques within demanding work schedules.

From those constraints come the continuing use of chitterlings (chitlins). Consisting of pig intestines, which southern whites would not eat, chitterlings involved (usually) slow cooking, all day while the slaves were at work. A wide variety of African spices, especially extremely hot peppers, made the nutritious dish palatable and sometimes a delicacy. Chitterlings also fulfilled the tradition of using an entire animal or plant.

Limited access to the full range of kitchen utensils also necessitated creative adaptations. Often slaves used a laundry tub for one-pot meals, and corn batter was sometimes cooked in the ashes (ash cake) or on the metal blade of the hoe (hoe cakes). Recent archaeological digs in slave quarters reveal the collective use of a common hearth, as in Africa.[18]

The other method of preparation that has continued as part of soul food is frying, the fastest manner of cooking that was available to slaves. Frying involved the use of African oils such as palm and coconut as well as lard.[19] After working all day, food that cooked quickly, contained plenty of calories, and was tasty was a necessity.

In the African cooking tradition, techniques of food preparation were passed on in a manner involving close sensory contact. Slaves used smell and taste, touch, sight, and sound in order to cook. Those techniques were rarely written down but were communicated within the oral tradition. The slave system's injunction against teaching slaves to read and write, of course, buttressed this oral tradition. Only recently has there been an emphasis on using cookbooks as a method of spreading the culture of soul food, and they are not a particularly reliable way of documenting what average families really eat or some of the fine points of preparation.

The slaves' synthesis of European, American, and African ingredients and preparation techniques resulted in certain traditional African American dishes that are now generally subsumed under the name *soul food*. Some of the most famous items are hopping John (boiled black-eyed peas and rice); smothered rabbit and squirrel (boiled and baked); venison (salt water–soaked, dried, and then cooked with vegetables); possum and 'taters (the animal parboiled, then boiled, seasoned, and simmered with sweet potatoes, brown sugar, and melted butter); pumpkin soup with chicken broth and light cream; fried catfish (salted, peppered, and covered in cornmeal before frying); hush puppies (a fried mixture of cornmeal, eggs, salt, buttermilk, and sometimes onions); barbecued ribs, either pork or beef (parboiled, marinated in a spicy sauce, then grilled or baked); chitterlings (pig intestines, cleaned and then simmered with garlic, hot peppers, other herbs and spices, onion, vinegar, and or/lemon as well as other ingredients, depending on local tradition); collard greens (boiled greens with pork pieces, usually served with corn bread to soak up the resulting liquid [pot likker]); and other greens (kale, mustard, spinach, poke but not the roots and lower stalks of pokeweed, cress, turnips, beet tops, dandelion, and chard).

A number of scholars assert that the cultural identity of West African food culture has been maintained as much in the preparation practices as in the particular ingredients of these dishes. Josephine Beoku-Betts, for example, notes that "one way in which Gullah women try to control their cultural boundaries is their way of cooking these foods as distinct from other southern practices . . . to assert that . . . their style of preparation and type of seasoning used are different."[20]

Consumption

The culture of consumption that has developed among African Americans is a synthesis of European, African, and American cultural influences in dialectical interaction with the exigencies of the slave experience. Sociologically, commensality (the act of eating together) defines the limits of a group's culture. In the American South, African Americans and whites usually did not eat together. It was therefore no accident that the civil rights movement of the 1960s began with lunch-counter sit-ins, where African Americans sought to eat as equals with whites.

Although there is now no official segregation of public facilities in the United States, the segregated nature of housing and the socioeconomic inequalities within American culture undergird significantly less than full-scale integration in eating. College cafeteria tables populated only by African Americans, for example, are a demonstration of de facto social segregation. Because a majority of African Americans are not affluent, their economic status perpetuates a generally segregated eating pattern. As a by-product, African Americans—north and south—have generally continued to consume as an ethnic racial group. As Kittler and Sucher write, "The sharing of food is considered an important factor in the cohesiveness of southern Black society."[21] In many parts of the North the same pattern is observed.

Just as the absence of cooking utensils favored one-pot meals such as soups and stews during the slavery period, a lack of eating utensils meant that hands were the favored method of eating communally. Ethiopian restaurants of today are famous for offering a communal eating experience, with diners using portions of spongy bread (*injera*) to scoop up food and the same bread being a kind of serving platter for that food.[22] Sharing utensils, or not using them at all, was a fairly common practice in the Colonies and Early Republic among blacks as well as whites but was especially prevalent in slave culture because slave masters preferred the efficiency of a common kitchen and feared that utensils could be used as weapons.

When it comes to actual meal patterns there is no uniformity in historical data concerning the African past. Most sources point to a tendency to have one big meal a day and snack at other times. Although the big meal did not come at breakfast, its timing depended on a variety of customs. It could occur at noon, at mid-afternoon, or in the evening.

The most economical slave pattern, making the most of sunlight hours, had the largest meal at the end of the day. With Emancipation, however, sharecropping former slaves often had the food preparer leave the fields at mid-morning and prepare a large midday meal. Leftovers were generally eaten at a smaller meal in the evening.[23] It was common for free agricultural laborers to partake of the general American pattern of having a large breakfast—ham or bacon, fried sweet potatoes, grits, biscuits, eggs, coffee, or tea.

Commensality took on a larger significance through the role of the African American church. Church feasts provided a mechanism to affirm traditional African American cuisine as a symbol of collective meaning. As Whitehead explains, "Feasts and their accompanying foodways also met communication needs by providing the opportunity to share information and to communicate to members the structure of their group realities. [They] provided an opportunity for group members to congregate and reaffirm their sense of corporateness and their bonds of rights and obligations."[24]

Regardless of the specific pattern of the meal, African Americans who eat together maintain ethnic and family solidarity. That is well illustrated in the film *Soul Food*, in which the performance of eating together re-cements familial bonds that had weakened in an African American family.

Disposal

Little conclusive research exists about exactly what was eaten and by whom. We do know, however, that the African American slave community ate (and thereby "disposed" of) many of the ingredients that white, planter-class families would not eat. Poorer whites ate many of the same foods as slaves, although that did not usually include cooked greens and chitterlings.

The eighteenth-, nineteenth-, and early-twentieth-century American family farm was traditionally sound ecologically (and, of course, some people still follow these conservation practices). Leftover food was either fed to the animals or composted. There was hardly anything near the enormous waste characteristic of the current industrial system, which makes massive attempts at advertising and marketing though elaborate packaging.

Conclusion

The peculiarly American phenomenon of soul food gives evidence of influence from Europe, the Americas, and Africa. In its production, collection, storage, distribution, preparation, consumption, and disposal, soul food is the synthesis of contributions from three continents.

As the cultural production of African Americans, soul food demonstrates the manner in which, in the face of unfavorable social conditions, slaves involved themselves collectively in creating a new cuisine that addressed problems of nutritional adequacy and ethnic and racial identity. As Mendes maintains, "Africans of different nations or tribes lived and worked side by side . . . they tasted each others' cooking and verbally exchanged recipes. This culinary exchange led to the development of an international cooking style in America. In spite of its many evils, segregation continued to provide Blacks with relative freedom from outside influences. Thus, they were able to preserve much of their own heritage and to evolve a culinary style of their own."[25]

In the sociology of the 1950s in the United States, African Americans were supposedly involved in assimilating into the modern melting pot of society. Yet the cooking pot was perhaps the only place in which that melting pot was in evidence in the succeeding half century.

Contemporary sociological theory has given increased emphasis to a postmodern perspective that relegitimizes the specific identity of various national, ethnic, and racial cuisines. There has also been increased pride in cultural background of whatever origin. Hence, soul food has reappeared as an emblem of ethnic and racial pride in developments such as the self-conscious creation of the African American celebration Kwanza.

The most serious creative nutritional work remaining for today's African Americans is decreasing the high fat content of traditional soul food. Whereas fat historically served the needs of the high physical activity that went with slave and agrarian society, that high fat content, along with high salt content, has become an impediment to a healthy and longer life span. Just as working-class consumers found McDonald's hamburgers a cultural substitute for emulating the 1950s' middle-class consumption of steak and roast beef, contemporary African Americans who can afford to do so may indulge in larger quantities of high-fat meat than their ancestors. In part as a result of dietary imbalances, African American life spans lag significantly behind those of Americans of lighter skin and generally higher income. Whitehead has noted that "a number of counties within . . . North and South Carolina, Georgia and North Florida have been dubbed the 'stroke belt' by cardiovascular disease researchers because of the higher prevalence of stroke and cardiovascular illnesses than in other parts of the country."[26]

There are now a number of attempts to create traditional soul food while making the recipes for it more healthful. One of the first such efforts came in 1994 with *In the Kitchen with Rosie* by Rosie Daley, a white woman who was then Oprah Winfrey's chef. Other health-conscious cookbooks include Barbara M. Dixon's *Good Health for African Americans*, the National Council of Negro Women's *Black Family Dinner Quilt Cookbook*, Howard Paige's *Aspects of African American Foods*, Wilbert Jones's *The New Soul Food Cookbook* and *The Healthy Soulfood Cookbook*, Jonell Nash's *Low Fat Soul Food*, Carolyn Quick Tillery's *The African-American Heritage Cookbook*, Lana Shabazz's *Cooking for the Champ: Muhammed Ali's Favorite Recipes*, George Forman and Cherrie Calbom's *George Foreman's Knock-Out-the-Fat Barbeque and Grilling Cookbook*, Ruby Banks-Payne's *Ruby's Low-Fat Soul Food Cookbook*, and Leah Chase and Johnny Rivers's *Down Home Healthy*.[27] Although not always an overwhelming culinary success, low-fat soul food must continue along its cultural and creative path in order to maintain ethnic and racial identity while helping African Americans find improved health in the twenty-first century.

Noting that African Americans benefit most from nutritional intervention, the American Dietetic Association has urged them to choose lower-fat pork options. One low-fat substitute for fatback when flavoring greens, for example, is Liquid Smoke. Furthermore, the ADA would like African Americans (as well as most Americans) to eat less sugar and salt, which both contribute to obesity and high blood pressure.[28]

There are those who bemoan changes to the traditions of soul food. Ultimately, however, one can view this process of recreating a cultural cuisine in new environments and under new influences as signs of the culture's durability and capacity for adaptive responses—dual mechanisms that have, for decades, constituted the essence of creating any successful cultural cuisine.

NOTES

My thanks to graduate student Amy Dobre-Cooper for her excellent technical assistance with this essay.

1. Tony L. Whitehead, "In Search of Soul Food and Meaning: Culture, Food and

Health," in *African Americans in the South: Issues of Race, Class, and Gender*, edited by H. A. Baier and Yvonne Jones (Athens: University of Georgia Press, 1982), 94–110, emphasis added.

2. Anne Murcott, "Sociological and Social Anthropological Approaches to Food and Eating," *World Review of Nutrition and Diet* 55 (1988): 13.

3. Helen Mendes, *The African Heritage Cookbook* (New York: Macmillan, 1971), 11.

4. For the stereotype of blacks lacking a culture see Winthrop D. Jordon, *White over Black: American Attitudes toward the Negro, 1550–1812* (Baltimore: Perican, 1969), 436–37; and Pamela Goyan Kitler and Kathryn P. Sucher, *Food and Culture in America: A Nutrition Handbook* (New York: Van Nostram, 1989), 182.

5. Thelma Barer-Stein, *You Eat What You Are: A Study of Ethnic Food Traditions* (Toronto: McClelland and Stewart, 1972), 14–15; Lynn Marie Houston, "African American Food," in *The Oxford Encyclopedia of Food and Drink in America*, edited by Andrew Smith (New York: Oxford University Press, 2004), 20.

6. Judith A. Carney, *Black Rice: The African Origins of Rice Cultivation in the Americas* (Cambridge: Harvard University Press, 2001), 156; Larry McKee, "Food Supply and Plantation Social Order: An Archaeological Perspective," in *"I, Too, Am America": Archaeological Studies of African-American Life*, edited by Theresa A. Singleton (Charlottesville: University Press of Virginia, 1999), 224–26.

7. Author interview with Veta Tucker, spring 2005, Grand Valley State University; Lucia Stanton, *Slavery at Monticello* (1993, repr. Charlottesville: University Press of Virginia, 1996), 38.

8. For a fuller discussion of slaves marketing produce and especially poultry see Philip D. Morgan, *Slave Counterpoint: Black Culture in the Eighteenth-Century Chesapeake and Lowcountry* (Chapel Hill: Published for the Omohundro Institute of Early American History and Culture, Williamsburg, Virginia, by the University of North Carolina Press, 1998), 359–72.

9. William C. Whit and Shatolnla Daniel, "It Ain't Soul Food—If It Ain't Got That Twang!!!" paper presented at the Association for the Study of Food and Society, Tuskegee University, June 1995.

10. Kittler and Sucher, *Food and Culture in America*, 187.

11. Carney, *Black Rice*, 97–106, 162.

12. Whitehead, "In Search of Soul Food and Meaning," 103

13. Sam Bowers Hilliard, *Hog Meat and Hoecake: Food Supply in the Old South, 1840–1860* (Carbonale: Southern Illinios University Press, 1972), 56–57.

14. Edgerton quoted in Whitehead, "In Search of Soul Food and Meaning," 104.

15. Sheila Ferguson, *Soul Food: Classic Cuisine from the Deep South* (New York: Grove Press, 1989), xxvi.

16. Edgerton in Whitehead, "In Search of Soul Food and Meaning," 34.

17. Ibid., 21

18. Ferguson, *Soul Food*, 100.

19. Mendes, *The African Heritage Cookbook*, 35.

20. Josephine Beoku-Betts, "'We Got Our Way of Cooking Things': Women, Food and the Preservation of Cultural Identity Among the Gullah," in *Food in the USA: A Reader*, edited by Carole Counihan (New York: Routledge, 2002), 287.

21. Kittler and Sucher, *Food Culture in America*, 191.

22. Very few slaves came from Ethiopia, but I use this example as a reminder that eating without utensils is still an accepted practice in various parts of the world.

23. Whitehead, "In Search of Soul Food and Meaning," 105.

24. Ibid., 107–8.

25. Mendes, *The African Heritage Cookbook*, 12.

26. Whitehead, "In Search of Soul Food and Meaning," 109.

27. Doris Witt and David Lupton, "Chronological Bibliography of Cookbooks by African Americans," in Doris Witt, *Black Hunger: Food and the Politics of U.S. Identity* (New York: Oxford University Press, 1999), 224–28.

28. Cathryn Boyd Burke and Susan P. Raia, *Soul and Traditional Southern Food Practices, Customs, and Holidays* (Chicago: American Dietetic Association, 1995), 13–15.

3

Excavating the South's African American Food History

Anne Yentsch

Nostalgia governs African Americans' recollections of family meals and the food that relatives cooked. Lively memories with accompanying recipes are a focus of cookbooks such as Maya Angelou's *Hallelujah! The Welcome Table: A Lifetime of Memories with Recipes* (2004). Other less nostalgic studies by such writers as Andrew Warnes, Caroline Rouse, and Janet Hoskins highlight connections between food and conflicts over race, class, religion, and ethnicity.[1] Each way of considering food's pivotal role speaks to who black people are, and each tells of social and cultural identities centered on special foods, dishes steeped today in black mythology. Yet the complex realities of African American food history are difficult to document.

Most African American cookbooks present themselves as drawing on long-standing southern traditions. They provide recipes for feather-light biscuits, chicken and dumplings, boiled crab or fried shrimp, pork-flavored beans, okra gumbo, rice in various guises, sweet potatoes, corn cooked in numerous ways, pecan and lemon meringue pies, coconut and caramel cakes, banana pudding, peach and blackberry cobblers, and, of course, divinity fudge.[2] Right away we find some incongruities. Few rural black nineteenth-century families ate luxurious deserts frequently. Pies such as Hattie Townsend's lemon meringue, one so good it "would make a rabbit hug a hound," were saved for special occasions.[3] Furthermore, many "traditional" recipes evolved well after the Civil War, including varieties of meringue pies—orange, peach, apple, and sugar—that are now dominated by lemon. In fact, much African American food history lies in twentieth-century realities.

Of course, whether cooks prepare dishes conforming precisely to archetypes doesn't matter within the realm of collective memory. What is critical is the connection between present and past, between ancestors and descendants. Complete and full replication is irrelevant. The tide turns on whether people *believe* the dishes are "authentic."[4] To understand African American food history requires separating myth and reality. One has to consider not simply what people ate but how they lived and how and where they obtained food. In addition, there is the issue of "outside foods" (commercial items or foods from other ethnic groups) and their companions, choice and change.[5]

As an archaeologist, my attention is drawn to two dimensions of the food system: first, the spaces in which people lived, worked, and ate and, second, the social relationships that guided behavior. There also are patterns of power, dominance, and resistance to consider as well as the varied paths of social change. My perspective on these is ingredient-oriented and gives attention to small, informative facts that speak to space, place, and social action.

Archaeologists look at changes in soil color to distinguish one stratum from another. They look at the presence and absence of specific objects or design motifs on pots. They consider how these were made to see how one change flowed into another, making something old into something new even as its maker tried to follow tradition. Archaeologists constantly confront individual imprints and ethnically driven derivations.

A similar approach can be taken toward foodstuffs and recipes, especially those in southern cookbooks. Two overlapping patterns are present. Conspicuous abundance, exotic ingredients, specialized utensils, and intensive labor mark meals among the wealthy. Here, culinary display is essential. Simple ingredients and cooking techniques, scarcity and want, few tools, and a focus on having enough food distinguish meals within poor southern families. Essentially, that is the difference between turtle soup and catfish stew, real coffee and peanut coffee. These differences created two food traditions that speak to social identity in much the way as would two artifact assemblages of similar age from two different cultures.[6]

Within historical archaeology, details emerge with greater clarity and inter-pretations grow richer as the past moves closer to the present, as material fact can be meshed with historical text. Detail fades when the material record is fragmentary or hard to see and historical narrative is unusually silent. Generic images appear. That is especially apparent whenever an archaeologist has to view the beliefs and behavior of an underclass through eyes of the elite.

There are similar phases to researching African American foodways. Pre–Civil War texts occasionally give first names of plantation cooks, but surnames are missing and most remain anonymous. Their social identities are vague. Yet as ghostly as those people are, they still appear more clearly than women who cooked in sharecroppers' homes. The latter are normally unknown, unsung, and occupy silent places in the historical record. Their muteness emphasizes the replacement of one form of white power by another, equally repressive system after the Civil War, one in which, according to Sidney Mintz, "the institutional fabric of slavery was lovingly preserved."[7] The years marked by social barriers and color lines that began after the Civil War and lasted into the twentieth century left scars on rural African American food customs that were as devastating as slavery. Their foodways show that black landowners, in contrast to tenant farmers and the urban poor, had more opportunity to break free of economic and social constraints. By the early twentieth century the historical record provides more information on African American cooks, chefs, and foodworkers and gives their names.

Because the war provides such a clear break, this essay is separated into two sections—foodways during slavery and those afterward and up to about 1935. Each section considers the domestic and commercial aspects of food. Through-out, the emphasis on tangible remains signals an archaeological perspective partnered with anthropology-based research in historical documents.

Foodways during Slavery

Within African towns and villages, eating was entwined with almost every as-pect of community life. Getting a meal was the day's daily work; everyone participated. In the New World, however, African traditions had to be incorpo-rated into other cultures, a slave's choice of what to eat was minimal, and food was highly regulated. In slave owners' eyes, only income-producing work was viable. Masters allocated food resources using a value system that cared not one whit for the rights, time constraints, or traditions of the black community.

Slaves adapted both European and Native American foods and cooking methods to African custom. Black cooks learned to prepare many new dishes. Corn and collards, deer and possum, pokeweed, persimmon, potatoes, and plantain were just some of the food that Africans began to eat. This adaptation surpassed simple food substitution or reworked recipes; the outcome was greater than anyone who just added its parts would see. Use of a specific ingredient, however, was often restricted by domineering masters. Countermaneuvers to circumvent white dictates and open alternate routes to foodstuffs prevailed.

The lineage of food preferences and cooking techniques was African. Slaves born in Africa and their descendants continued to create meals that had a vegetarian base, adding meat and flavoring to heighten taste. Whenever possible, they continued to hunt and gather. They applied such traditional cooking methods as boiling and frying, baking in ashes, fireside grilling, using earthen pits for roasting, and steaming food wrapped in leaves.[8] New vegetables—squash, peppers, green runner beans, and European greens—were easily prepared using familiar techniques. The use of hot oil to fry food crisp on the outside and keep it tender inside came into play. Cooks honed the technique to provide an array of deep-fried foods, from corn oysters to okra fritters and oyster puffs.

The slaves' phenomenal resourcefulness in overcoming hunger drew on fierce tenacity, but some obstacles were difficult to overcome. Plantation mistresses restricted access to certain foodstuffs. No slave could accumulate the ingredients needed for a meal if these included the wide range of staples used in plantation kitchens: salt, pepper, yeast, cheese, vinegar, pickles, and mackerel. Slaves had little access to luxury ingredients such as almonds, raisins, currants, citrons, cinnamon, cloves, nutmegs, ginger, gelatin, lemon and vanilla flavoring, coffee, tea, wine, brandy, cordials and champagne, pulverized sugar, sugar ornaments, and candy kisses.[9] Just a few of the assorted foods offered at breakfast on Louisiana plantations were ever provided in the quarters: prawns, grilled fowl, New Orleans fish, eggs and ham, potted English salmon, preserved meat from Europe, big hominy, little hominy and cornmeal mush, African-prepared vegetables, coffee, tea, and claret. And, obviously, no slave could serve early-morning juleps: glassfuls of "brandy, sugar, and peppermint beneath an island of ice."[10]

In the quarters, lack of time demanded that weekday meals be easily prepared, contain readily available ingredients, and be easy to serve and eat. Foods that could be eaten by hand (e.g., bread, biscuits, and roast potatoes) had an advantage. People could cart peas, beans, and bacon to the fields in buckets or pots and cook them over fires where they worked.[11] On Saturday nights and Sundays, cooks paired ingenuity with "cooking ahead"; the aroma of food rose with smoke from outdoor fires, awakening hungry tummies. On some plantations people worked collectively to get a meal, at some it was an individual task, and at others one or more slaves were designated to cook for all. It is noteworthy that within the slave community men and women shared food preparation in ways not customary in white households.

There were male domains within food procurement and preparation: butchering, distilling hard liquor, and hunting. For holidays, political events, and seasonal celebrations men also dug shallow, narrow (i.e., animal-length) trenches, gathered wood, butchered, tended the fire, and basted slowly roasting shoats, goats, rabbits, and chickens through the night. The gender divisions and the prerogatives of rank in plantation life carved out different social niches, each of which occupied its own physical space (i.e., distinct activity areas offering separate food options). Access to these and the food therein varied, as shown in a diagram designed by Larry McKee.

McKee's model is focused on two aspects of the slaves' food procurement: the locus of control (planter or slave) and whether the food activities were sanctioned. Archaeologists can fairly easily analyze a set of faunal remains and determine quantity, quality, and nutritional components, but it is harder to see the links between slave, planter, and the larger society. McKee's model shows a straightforward pattern of provision when foods were supplied by the planter; the pattern that emerges when slaves obtained food for themselves is more complex.

Sometimes it is useful to set aside nutritional value or flavor and look at food in terms of space. Consider the places where food might be found on a plantation and the paths leading to them. There is a continuum from the interior domestic space (the white woman's domain) shown in McKee's model as the plantation kitchen. There food was centrally processed. Within the big house (not shown by McKee) and its kitchen the household staff garnered a few amenities, more molasses, extra cornmeal, snippets of meat, or even a handful of sweets, but most obtained food in the form of carefully distributed rations distributed on the basis of worker productivity.[12] Planters and their families gave apples, oranges, tea, coffee, stick candy, molasses, brown sugar, and liquor as favors.[13] Beef was normally allotted at Christmas, when a whole animal was slaughtered and given to families in the quarters. (Some planters also butchered in summer.)[14] It was not an ethical system of food distribution. Access to liquor, coffee, and tea, sweets, flour, and domestic meat was highly regulated.

Near the mansion, formal gardens sometimes contained decorative ponds stocked with edible carp. Outbuildings usually included, besides the kitchen,

SOURCES OF FOOD IN THE DIET OF PLANTATION SLAVES

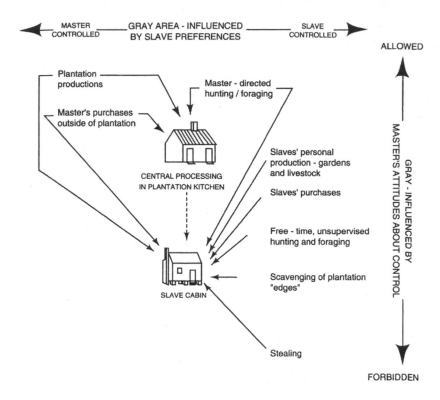

From Larry McKee, "Food Supply and Plantation Social Order: An Archaeological Perspective," in "*I, Too, Am America*": *Archaeological Studies of African American Life*, edited by Theresa A. Singleton (Charlottesville: University Press of Virginia, 1999).

a storehouse, smokehouse, and well. Some planters also built a mill, a spring-house, a dairy, a granary, even an ice house or greenhouse. Specific outbuildings were often locked; all were closely watched. The kitchen gardens, usually supervised by the planter's wife and tended by slaves, also lay near the mansion house. These were tempting places offering opportunities to grab fresh vegetables. The overall space immediately surrounding the big house was one of heightened awareness. Here the master of a well-run plantation fully governed what was allowed and what was not. Some planters could stand on their back porches, look out over the quarter's dwellings, and watch families eating or socializing on their own porches.

The barnyard domain, with its stable, cow barn, corn crib, hen house, pigpens, and dog kennels, lay slightly further away but was tightly connected to the big house. Planters controlled, or tried to control, these back areas, tension remained high, and slaves took foodstuffs at their peril. Set somewhat apart lay the planter's orchard, where children stole eggs from bird nests and almost everyone took fresh fruit according to its season: apples, pears, peaches, figs, cherries, quince, plums, apricots, and nectarines.[15] After Emancipation the orchard's food resources disappeared because sharecroppers had neither space nor time to spend raising fruit trees.

Beyond the orchard were planted fields, fenced pastures, and rice paddies where slaves worked and gathered to eat lunch. As a special privilege meant to reward conformity, some masters allowed them to raise livestock in this area. Slave narratives include some accounts of those few masters who were humane, but most were not. Planters also placed slave housing within this zone, outside the immediate vicinity of their own homes but still close by. They usually laid out these dwellings in regular fashion, using European architectural forms. People had little privacy in their work yards and adjacent garden plots.[16] Activities could be observed by any and all. Wary men made themselves well acquainted with their neighbors' habits and let that knowledge guide their own food search. The slave-quarter homes and yards were thus situated in a border area between the mansion's carefully ordered cultural space and its less orderly fringes. In coastal areas the latter contained piers, landing places, rivers, and creeks that served as roads. Here, slaves used whatever they could find and took chances on whether or not to obey rules.

On all plantations the built landscape merged with natural land, unimproved and under no one's control. Such spots offered freer access to food although masters never let slaves forget that they themselves, the land, and its game were white man's property.[17] Still, among the woodlands, meadows, swamps, forests, marshes, creeks, and open bays, black folk possessed a modicum of independence. There networks forged with Native Americans provided additional knowledge of the terrain and its resources. Families came into being that included both black and Indian; children had parents and relatives among both groups with vested interests in making sure the youngsters were enculturated to Native American norms. The techniques they were taught and the training they received infused food collection and preparation within slave and maroon communities.[18] One former Carolina slave pointed out that a smart man "et a heap o' possums an' coons der bein' plenty o' dem an' rabbits and squirrels."[19] Foraging in these freer zones remained an important part of daily life within rural black communities long after slavery ended.[20]

Basically, slaves had few foodstuffs with which to work. Skeletal analysis reveals malnutrition, especially in young children.[21] Planters often doled out the coarsest flour—dredgings and shorts. Many were stingy, supplying but a monthly peck of rice or cornmeal for adolescents and adults and five to eight quarts for children. Some planters fed children like animals: a little bit of bread in the morning and nothing at noon. Dinner arrived in a huge wooden trough and consisted of greens or bones or corn bread in buttermilk.[22] Children ate by hand or scooped up food with oyster or mussel shells. Annie Burton of Clayton, Alabama, remembered it vividly: "This bowl served for about fifteen children, and often the dogs and the ducks and the peafowl [guinea hen] had a dip in it."[23]

Archaeology at slave-quarter sites yields evidence of substandard rations supporting the documentary record and its accounts of the slaves' dismal situation. Take the Georgia and South Carolina rice coast as an example. Once a week, Sea Island planters supplied either a peck of corn or a bushel of sweet potatoes; once a month, they handed out a quart of salt. As one observer wrote, "On this they lived." He continued, "When the hardest work was required, [slaves] received a little molasses and salt meat."[24]

It took tenacity to survive. It was also imperative to look out for one's interests. As McKee observes, throughout slavery, anyone who built a workable food procurement strategy, who rarely went hungry and had a choice of food, "had achieved a kind of independence."[25] A planter's power reached into the heart of his slaves' homes and lives and attended to the smallest details. (Poor whites across the South might not have had much to eat either, but they freely expanded and contracted their food intake and controlled their private life.)

When it came to parsing out butchered meat on plantations, just as with other foodstuffs, planters gave slaves the meat they thought least desirable.[26] Blacks received the head, innards such as intestines, fatback, necks, tripe, and sometimes the heart, kidney, liver, or ribs. Lamb went into the plantation ovens; goat was grilled in the quarters. Even poultry could be divided so slaves got only innards, gizzards, or feet.[27]

Slaves improvised the use of fat and meat from different parts of swine or cattle, turning less-desirable pieces into notable dishes. There were special recipes for each part of various animals; families gradually developed distinctive ways of cooking each piece of the anatomy and taught their children how to do so as well. Cookbook writers offer evidence of this in separate recipes for pig's tails, fried brains and eggs, tripe stew, gizzards and gravy, neck bones and rice, livers and lights, simmered chitterlings, and maw salad as well as baked, fried, or pickled pig's feet and ears.[28]

The lack of food was egregious; the inhumanity staggering. Surely planters knew that hungry men would steal and that men, women, and children would ease hunger any way they could. Inadequate rations were a tacit license for theft.[29] Singly or in groups, slaves stole hogs and sheep, chickens, turkeys, and geese. They milked cows at night and surreptitiously roasted oxen and fattening swine. They took corn, cabbage, potatoes, pumpkins, turnips, sugar cane, and virtually anything that grew, usually from the ends of rows and other unobtrusive places. Small children snatched chicken feet and biscuits away from dogs. Slaves quickly mastered scrounging, scavenging for food, and hiding the evidence.[30] Archaeological assemblages indicate that adults stole preserved foods such as hams and sometimes took the platter, too. Adults also took rice saved for seed and feed (i.e., corn) from horse and mule troughs. Theft, an essential, adaptive maneuver, often brought pleasure.[31] A northern observer concluded, "Corn, chickens, flour, meal, in fact, everything edible, became legitimate plunder for the Negroes when the rations furnished them were scanty."[32]

Families ate many wild foods. Children gathered greens and berries, picked fruit and nuts, searched for quail eggs, and brought home stray turtles. Men hunted, and women learned to fish. Both men and women planted vegetable gardens for family use and for market. The responsibility to acquire food crossed all age and gender lines.[33] Some families began to raise a few animals because, like poor whites, they, too, could sell goods at market, on street corners, or door to door and keep the cash. Other canny slaves gifted planters with fresh fish, eggs, oysters, or shrimp. There was an unspoken assumption behind this: You let me hunt and fish for my family, and I will keep bringing to your door that which you can't get by yourself. Even though hunting was a mechanism of white male competition, a means of male bonding, and a way to demonstrate superiority over peers and slaves, both planter and slave honored this silent agreement.

Slaves ate from hunger, for nourishment, and with little opportunity to select their own food. They used whatever was available. The animal bones archaeologists recover at slave cabins do not say much about decision making, risk avoidance, gendered behavior, patronage, or food preference. Plant remains decompose quickly in the soil. Roasted sweet potatoes vanish without trace below ground, as do greens. Neither butter beans nor field peas survive, although sturdy fruit pits and hard nutshells may endure.[34] Occasionally archaeologists recover corn cobs, but these speak to the development of better varieties (as denoted by the number of rows and size of cobs) and not to corn's role in a recipe. So the archaeological record is more informative about meat than about herbs, fruit, and vegetables.[35] The archaeological record for meals among any group of individuals who depend primarily on vegetable protein is lean; beverages go by the board. The remains decompose, leaving no trace although written records tell us that slaves drank, among other beverages, real coffee (rarely), peanut coffee, parched-corn coffee, cottonseed tea, apple cider, corn whiskey, grape wine, dandelion wine, elderberry wine, dewberry wine, persimmon wine, and buttermilk.[36]

Animal bones, however, tell us what was eaten (horse, sheep, or cow), whether it was nourishing, and if the cut was choice (a chop or t-bone steak) and taken from a young or old animal, but they don't say much about how the meat was cooked. Yes, one can tell that a wide range of foods was eaten, from pork ribs to pig's feet, from quail to wild duck.[37] But when were they cooked—and how? Outside or inside? Which were liked best? Was the meat provided by the master, raised by the slave, hunted, or stolen? As Larry McKee points out, "A rib from a stolen pig looks no different from one from an animal distributed as rations."[38]

By and large, documents are also silent on precisely how slaves cooked. The truth is that slave *cooking*, with some exceptions, exists only in imagination unless it was observed and recorded by someone able to read and write and who had time to do so—whites.[39] There are snippets of information in legal documents and fragments in a few autobiographies (e.g., Louis Hughes's description of peach cobbler).[40] One discovers more by mining slave narratives, but overall the coverage is scanty. Works Progess Administration (WPA) records are invaluable and insightful, but their content is based on recollections where the focus is the pleasure of eating and not the specifics of food preparation.

One fact stands out in both black and white accounts: the best black cooks and superior chefs worked in slave owners' own kitchens (i.e., in a relatively private space). Many white families believed their own cook's skills topped all others, but confidence in, and praise of, a cook's skill did not ensure that she received credit for her recipes. Occasionally, plantation mistresses and urban white women acknowledged their cooks' creations and contributions (e.g., okra à la Maulie).[41] More often they did not. White mistresses claimed ownership of not only their cooks but also their cooks' everyday creations. Fancier dishes, however, were normally a cooperative venture between the slave cook and mistress. Because few slaves read, a plantation wife or daughter had to read aloud a recipe until her cooks mastered it.[42] She also had to release the more expensive ingredients from under lock and key.

Barbecue as a celebratory food, part of a highly public performance, *is* discussed in detail in a number of narratives. Louis Hughes's description is well rounded and even includes the ingredients for sauce, but people don't dine on barbecue alone.[43] What accompanied it? How was it apportioned? What special favors did a black barbecue master receive? Were barbecues, a masculine food provenance, supervised differently than making beaten biscuits in the kitchen? Such questions are rarely answered in historical narratives. Cookbooks, as working texts, are amplified in letters, diaries, and descriptive accounts. Ingredients, as individual foodstuffs, appear most clearly in legal documents and business records, but during the period in question the information is not well rounded.

Documents give the most information for foods that were (a) served to guests with conspicuous abundance; (b) prepared for slave owners under white supervision; (c) chosen or ordered by a planter and his wife; (d) celebratory in type and form (e.g., wedding cakes); or (e) exchanged in reciprocal transactions (jams, jellies, and fresh fruit). A culinary tension exists between extraordinary dishes and the everyday food on which slaves depended; we know significantly less about the latter. That tension can be seen in Booker T. Washington's childhood memories of ginger cakes, so tempting and delicious that his thought of eating one was the "height of ambition."[44] With the continued rise in sugar consumption (8.4 pounds per person in 1801, 70.06 in 1905, and perhaps as much 150 pounds in 1999), one needs to know how rare it was for a black child to have sweets to understand the depth of feeling in Washington's words.[45]

Slaves had to do a day's work before they could cook for themselves. Where the task system prevailed they might have time after work. Where they toiled day long and into the night that was not possible. There was very little with which to work, and people often used any extras to swap, barter, or sell.[46]

Black men and women, both slave and free, joined the market chain as suppliers, resellers, and buyers. They worked face to face, built personal networks, drew on favors, haggled, and traded. They bought and sold small barnyard birds—chickens, fowl, turkeys, and geese—and a few animals in addition to freshwater and saltwater fish, clams, oysters, shrimp, crabs, turtles, eggs, honey, Spanish moss, rice, corn, wheat, figs, peaches, berries, melons, sweet potatoes, Irish potatoes, peanuts, and perishable green vegetables. When slaves sold market commodities to their masters at below-market prices that custom made good sense to slave owners. When it created scarcity it did not.

When slaves' (and free blacks') commercial practices interfered with urban merchants' profits white men retaliated by rewriting laws to regulate how and when black families could sell foodstuffs. Such laws can be found throughout the South. In South Carolina, legislators wrote new laws for commerce in 1737 restricting black participation.[47] White merchants believed that placing city markets out of bounds to slaves would stop forestalling (buying produce before it reached the market and jacking up its price) and lower the rising cost of fresh food. The laws satisfied no one. Shopping for food was highly personal, based on social relationships between buyer and seller. Hence, the legislation outraged white women accustomed to sending their household staff to market. Charleston women fought the law. They saw no reason they should have to shop for food when they owned other women who could more easily do so by forging market alliances that brought fresher foodstuffs into their kitchens. Food purveyors were many, but greengrocers were few; grocery stores as we know them were nonexistent.[48]

City leaders continually and unsuccessfully tried to control the food trade among blacks. The legal wrangle reveals many aspects of southern life, especially the role slave women held in food procurement and distribution. They raised greens, herbs, and other vegetables and either sold the produce themselves or to market women who then resold it. Their city sisters bought it at the instruction of their white owners to use in the town's mansions. The produce also made its way into plantation kitchens and middle-class homes. This is one reason, among others, that favored African foods slipped into culturally conservative homes.

The heritage of slavery includes barbecue and malnutrition; gardening skills with New World and Old World plants; experience raising domestic livestock; learning how to trade with white folks; and learning how to steal, hunt, fish, and gather. Slaves came to highly value ingenuity, creativity, independence, and self-reliance. These remain part of black ideology.

The heritage also includes detailed knowledge of country terrain and its natural resources, something that stood African Americans in good stead for some three hundred years. Yes, the New World's ecological systems were unfamiliar to African immigrants, but Africans began, almost instantaneously, a sustained social interaction with Native Americans. They quickly learned to take advantage of this hemisphere's resources. They compiled a repertoire of recipes for finger-friendly, quick-cooking food and for items that cooked slowly without much supervision. They learned how to bake fruit cobblers over open fires and make meals from crop pests such as raccoons, rabbits, possums, and tree squirrels.

Black families acquired an intimate acquaintance with all phases of butchering and meat preparation, honed marketing and bargaining techniques, and became well aware that sugar exemplified power and prestige. Slaves knew as well as planters that in the southern oligarchy food made the man. They knew it wasn't just the food a planter ate that set him apart but the skill with which it was made and displayed, how it was shared among family and friends, its hospitable distribution, the value of generosity, and the privilege of abundance. They took these values into freedom.

Free blacks encountered situations quite different than those of slaves, and many were deeply embedded in the commercial food domain. Peddlers sold street food. Poor women found "hawking and carrying" to be one of the few avenues they had to support themselves and their families. Peter Earle, describing London in the 1850s, might have been writing of the American South: "The biggest group [of market women] were those who sold fruit and vegetables, followed by fishwives and old clothes dealers, while other products sold in the streets included bread, pies, baked puddings, butter and eggs, sausages, tea."[49] It was a New World reincarnation of ancient and informal trade networks built on personal ties between rural providers and city suppliers. Its heart lay in open markets and a growing number of free, urban blacks.

City life offered many ways to make money within the food world and gave opportunities to increasingly more free black folk to earn enough to buy homes or freedom for relatives.[50] Energetic women took to cooking at the market and peddling door to door. By 1823 Savannah's free women kept shops, baked pastries, and prepared and sold sausage. Others served in bars and hotels. One kept an oyster house, and almost a dozen peddled small wares. Men fished for a living, raised sheep and cattle, opened butcher shops, sold fruit or vegetables from pushcarts, baked bread, and sold delicacies. In all southern cities slaves, slaves for hire, and free blacks, especially the women, found ways to get and use local food, which they either sold or, going one step further, baked and fried in portable form. They supplied food to private households and in more public venues.[51]

Most families ate at home, and the public clientele such as soldiers, sailors, unmarried lodgers, transients, and single travelers contained few who stood high on the social ladder. Tourism and working life, as known today, did not exist. Both men and women cooked, catered, and served food on street corners and in the market or in public dining places: taverns, lodging houses, and inns. Both men and women ran cafes, restaurants, and oyster houses. Initially, the food, entertainment, and lodging business did not generate large profits for very many families.

A small number gained prestige by participating in food-related lines of work.[52] A few grew wealthy as elite travelers fought to stay at their inns and hotels. In Charleston, Jehu Johnson ran the Jones Hotel from 1815 to 1833; Eliza Lee, known as an excellent black cook, ran the Carolina Coffee House and the Carolina Hotel; and Susan Wilkie was in charge of the Farmers Hotel.[53] Black hoteliers were present in Newport, New Orleans, and later in Savannah. Black women also ran boardinghouses, serving daily meals cooked by their own workers. Rachel Brownfield, for example, by hiring her own time and that of her daughters, first rented and then bought a sixteen-room boardinghouse in Savannah.[54]

The food trades taken up by Savannah's free black community, like those elsewhere, went from street vendor to shop owner and included two confectionery shops. The one at the center of town was owned by an Afro-Haitian, Aphasia Merault.[55] Her name provides one clue, as do the names of other confectioners in places like Baltimore (Honore Jaffe), that knowledge of candy making and ice cream production entered the black community in the 1790s and early 1800s with the flow of Dominican (i.e., Afro-Haitian) refugees from sugar plantations. The intricacies of cooking with chocolate and vanilla also flowed into the South and then up the Mississippi from the Caribbean islands, South and Central American countries, and Mexico. A major entryway was via the city streets of the South.

Street food was an art unto itself. At least sixty-four women were hawking "cakes, nuts, and so forth" by 1778 in Charleston.[56] By 1820, more than two dozen female hucksters cried their wares on Savannah's streets. Their goods ranged from fruit and produce to cooked rice, cakes, candies, and sweetmeats. The street calls that Harriette Leiding recorded in Charleston would have been familiar in Savannah. Walt Whitman's memories of New Orleans include "a large cup of delicious coffee with a biscuit . . . from the immense shining copper kettle of a great Creole mulatto woman. . . . [I] never have had such coffee since."[57] Women also made and sold delightful candies on New Orleans streets and squares—*la colie, mais tic-tac,* and *candie tiré à la melasse* (based on molasses)—plus white, creamy pink, almond, peanut, molasses, and pecan pralines. Emily Burke, in 1840, saw street vendors in Savannah working the crowds wherever and whenever people congregated and noted that "many are seen with large trays on their heads, loaded with fruit, sweetmeats and various kinds of drinks." They arrived at Savannah's market just before dawn. The market opened at 5 A.M. and normally closed at 10 A.M. but remained open on Saturday evenings.

In the market, an open shed with a brick floor, women worked in individual stalls. Anything not sold had to be carted away or the market-keeper took it, sold it cheap, and kept the profit. Burke described the range of edibles: fresh vegetables, shell fish and fin fish, birds both wild and tame, fruit from cold climates, and tropical fruit from the Caribbean. "Here," she concluded, " almost every eatable thing can be found."[58] The Charleston and New Orleans markets were equally, if not more, well supplied.

Many more black women than appear in city records were food vendors, some on a casual basis and some full time. Their vigorous sales of cakes and apples on Savannah streets prompted the city council to require badges by the 1790s. The council claimed it was afraid the opportunity to hawk food would decrease the number of black women willing to nurse the ill during the yearly "sickly season."[59] One has to doubt their benevolence because a similar move was made against black males at a later time. The women, apparently, ignored the legislation.

In 1823 six black Savannah women made and sold pastry. Four of them, Phillis Hill, Frances Carly, Nancy Golding, and Susan Jackson, were so successful that they were able to purchase slaves and buy real estate. "Pastry" had a more inclusive meaning then, subsuming pies, tarts, cakes, tea cakes, puddings, and candy. It also included the mouth-watering fruitcakes that one of these women made and shipped overseas to fill English orders.[60] There were fifteen professional female pastry cooks in Savannah by 1860, and black men also joined their ranks. The energetic William Claghorn hired black and white workers alike, giving jobs to immigrant German bakers who stocked his store with European-style baked goods.[61] The numbers of small confectioneries continued to grow after the slavery era; in 1937, 370 black candy makers lived inside or near the city (i.e., in Chatham County, Georgia).[62]

From the Revolution onward, women led the commercial food trade, joined by a growing number of men, including fishermen and butchers, as the nineteenth century progressed. In 1810 Savannah had one black butcher, and in 1823 there were five. About that time, the city council forbade any black man from apprenticing himself to a white butcher.[63] Prudent men such as Joshua Bourke and Adam Whitfield decided to interpret the law literally, stayed away from city market, and took their trade to the streets. Later, black butchers returned in force. Nine were forced to work under a white butcher to provision the Confederate Army in the 1860s. Savannah's Jackson B. Sheftall, a mulatto, opened his own shop in 1849 and began to sell choice cuts of meat: "steaks, chops, and cutlets." An 1894 article in the *Savannah Tribune* noted its continuous operation, addition of western beef, and the fact that Sheftall had grown rich. Concurrently, Capt. F. F. Jones had one of the largest butcher stalls in the city market, and Josephine Stiles Jennings ran a combined meat and grocery store in Yamacraw, one of Savannah's oldest black neighborhoods.[64] Whether from street vendors, food peddlers, or greengrocers selling produce in small, informal, open-air markets, members of black communities in Chatham County, as elsewhere, prospered in the broad domain of commercial food.

Foodways after Emancipation, 1865–1935

African descendants, their food, and their cooking techniques made such an indelible impression on white southern families, generation after generation, that whites pulled cooks and cooking techniques from the black world both before and after Emancipation. African-derived cooking techniques proved so irresistibly tempting that (as only one example) by 1878 most cooks in Mobile, Alabama, were making fritters from the supper's vegetables.[65] Eventually, as happens in mythic history, people forgot the origins of this technique. African fruit and vegetables became commonplace, although knowledge of their origin was not. Along with this trend, specific African, African American, and African Native American cooking styles took precedence in preparing comfort foods, and all evoked the essence of white southern country cooking.

Both Emancipation and technological advances increased the divide between country cooking and urban foods. The postwar years from 1865 onward also left their mark on cooking in rural black communities, but the effect was not beneficent. The white community twisted and crushed freedom at every opportunity. As Grace Hale expressed the leitmotif of liberation, "Freedom may not be an easy place or time to be, but it [was] the only place and time to be."[66] That held true whether on city streets, in country fields, or inside black kitchens.

In practice, the war tore apart the style of cooking epitomized by the plantation kitchen, yet it endured, rock-solid, romanticized, and aggrandized, in mythic history. Annabelle Hill wrote a cookery book designed for the thousands of young, inexperienced, southern (white) housekeepers who "in this particular crisis" could no longer depend on "Mother's [black] Cook."[67] One can see in various other books a similar intent, drawn from nostalgia, but none of this had any influence on newly freed cooks, especially in rural areas.

With Emancipation, black people began new lives. Men started small businesses, marketing fruit, wood, and produce; women were less mobile and stayed closer to home.[68] Those who had cooked in the big house took their skill for fancy cooking with them; some were able to find work cooking as domestics or in commercial establishments. Freedmen filled southern cities to overflowing and then moved into Chicago and its suburbs and to Detroit, Kansas City, and Cleveland. A smaller number went west during this first wave of northern migration, among them the African Americans who influenced the ways in which other Americans ate on trains, in large cities, and in Montana homes (e.g., Rufus Estes, Abby Fisher, Mammy Pleasant, and numerous cateresses and railroad chefs).[69] Most, however, remained in the South as sharecroppers or tenant farmers.

Like plantation slaves, sharecroppers lived in restricted spaces over which they had only a pinch of control. As was true in slavery, much of the food they ate was substandard and minimally nourishing.[70] Unless they worked for their former owners, most black families were not welcome on a planter's land. Thus, although plantations contained a wide range of food sources, sharecroppers obtained food from a narrower one. They had few cooking utensils and sometimes used lard or soup cans to bake cakes of assorted sizes.[71] The kitchen in a sharecropper's home was never an "easy place to be."

Women who carried the knowledge of plantation cookery into freedom had simultaneously lost access to the resources it required. There were barriers such as time, utensils, and appliances. There was also the lack of special ingredients and no money to buy them where they were available. Such restrictions forced women, black and white alike, to adapt plantation cooking to what they had available. In both cases their new lives made its reproduction next to impossible. In rural black homes where overworked women sometimes didn't have time to wash dishes, women must have hungered for culinary continuity and ingredients such as sugar, butter, ginger, and other baking spices.[72] For many, bringing food home from the plantation kitchen had been a perquisite of their work, part and parcel of their lives; clearly, that source of foodstuffs was gone.[73]

Storekeepers shattered culinary aspirations further because they had their own ideas about who should buy what and how much they should pay. They catered to wealthier white farmers whose wives enjoyed the privilege of serving things, especially fancy cakes, not seen in black homes. Black women found buying groceries a particular hassle because men lounged around the stores, whittling, gossiping, and watching who came and went, what they brought to trade, and what they took with them.[74] Black customers had to wait until all the white customers were served and usually saw their orders set aside if one appeared. Some women found it easier to send their children or men to the market whenever they could. Being poor and black made it impossible to buy the ingredients to bake a cake at some stores. Then, too, the cost of baking powder, baker's chocolate, vanilla extract, figs, dates, nuts, oranges, bananas, and, in some places, apples put many ingredients out of reach. Cooks without the newer utensils were at a further disadvantage.

It was a double blow when large landowners also owned local stores outside black neighborhoods. Make no bones about it. These white men used intimidation to construct a racial divide, placing fancy baking on their side. Needing cheap labor to prosper, they circumvented the law and used any means at hand to keep black folk down, in debt, dependent, and subservient. Both diet and nutrition showed the effect of limited access to limited goods. According to Howard Odum, "Those least able to buy their food [bought] the largest proportion."[75]

Because sharecroppers had little money in the bank or cash on hand, storekeepers could keep families in debt by deducting from their earnings whatever the sharecroppers spent for seeds, tools, mules, shelter, clothing, food, coffee, and tobacco; they also charged outrageous prices.[76] People paid off debts by doing odd chores and trading with storekeepers such items as homemade candy, peanuts, eggs, hens, small fryers, turkeys, rabbits, corn, peas, and cabbage.[77]

Deep-seated, unimaginable rural poverty affected black and white alike and fueled resentment among embittered former slave owners. The tight hold that landowners maintained on land use enabled them to force tenant families to plant field crops right up to their cabin doors.[78] This fact, combined with the demands of labor-intensive agriculture, made it almost impossible to keep substantial kitchen gardens. Photographs document the lack of growing space. Some tenant contracts further limited food options by banning livestock (excluding poultry), thus forcing sharecroppers to purchase pork or other meat at high cost.[79]

Meanwhile, some who were free still felt enslaved. In Annette Coleman's memories of her Georgia childhood, she wasn't free. Forget that she was born around 1910. A white landowner handed out a food allowance each week—molasses, meat, cornmeal, and flour. Much of the food was scraps from his table, and those scraps had to be shared with his dogs. He whipped her for disobedience, insolence, and laziness and whenever she didn't do what he wanted as quickly as he wanted it done. Annette was, in essence, his kitchen slave. Together with her family, she learned to help herself to the corn, sugarcane, and sweet potatoes that grew in the outermost field rows. Survival took precedence.[80] All women in similar situations dreamed about was "a little home, a pretty yard of flowers, and a garden, even some chickens."[81]

Many families lived in drafty, unheated, small wooden cabins that were sparsely furnished and without kitchen cupboards or shelf space, screened doors, or screened, glass windows. These were homes that had no gas or electric stoves, iceboxes, or refrigerators and no running water or sanitary facilities.[82] According to Peter Daniel, "Farmers joked that they could see the stars at night and watch the dogs and chickens run . . . through cracks in the floor."[83]

Think what it would be like to cook in the South Carolina home that Julia Peterkin described: "The chimney's wide, black, sooty mouth . . . was filled with logs of wood. A great fire licked at them." It contained pot hooks holding "iron pots in the blaze. The sandy hearth held three-legged pots. Pots with handles. Iron kettles. Iron spiders. All had tight fitting lids." Sweet potatoes roasted in a corner beneath mounded ash, and corn husks peered through another where ash cake cooked. "A frying pan sat on live coals pulled out from the fire. Slices of fat bacon sputtered and spit and curled around the edges."[84]

Women rose at dawn to prepare the fire while men gauged its heat by the steam rising from pots. Cooks used whatever they could find to prepare a meal. Recorded recollections show that sharecroppers managed on very little. WPA oral histories tell of a bare-bones existence: "We usually eats butts meat an' rice for supper," Effie Burns said, "an' if I'm lucky, we has some sort o' vegetubbles, an' maybe a little stewed peaches or such for sweetin' . . . [there is] butt meat an' grits for the chilluns' breakfast, . . . we don' worry bout no midday meal." The titles of some recipes encoded the need to watch pennies. For example, the recipe for "nickel beans" instructed, "Take a nickel worth of bean, half beans, half rice; a side of meat, 5 cents worth; add half onion and half garlic, 5 cents worth; cook until done."[85] Scratch cooking was the norm. Recipes worked by approximation as portions expanded and contracted as needed. Women used what was available in the local store, what was sold from the wagons of Jewish peddlers, and what was on hand. Southerners consumed, on average, five hundred pounds of cornmeal a year. One study of black tenant farms in Mississippi indicated that a third of them had no cow, and "one seventh [of the farmers] went a whole year without eating chicken or eggs."[86]

Women baked food on stone hearths in winter and outdoors in summer, regulating heat by shifting pots closer to or farther from the fire. Cooks flavored dishes with bits of salt pork. Mothers fed infants bits of their own food—cornmeal mush or catfish stew. Life was tough, as Mason Crum's details of Sea Island life reveal. Flies were everywhere, and there was no lawn, no bath, and no toilet. It was a hand-to-mouth existence that included a diet of grits, fatback, collards, cabbage, sweet potatoes, molasses, butt meat, and, rarely (except when winter began), fresh pork, sausage, and spareribs. Families also took whatever nature provided.[87]

Good food storage was merely a wish in cabins where chickens ate crumbs from the floor. Home canning was not an option.[88] Beans could be dried for use year-round, and from fall to spring, families lived off root crops—turnips, rutabagas, and potatoes—that had been "banked" in back yards and root cellars. Perishable fruit appeared seasonally for short bursts of time; gardeners reaped vegetables from spring to early fall but grew only a limited number.

Southern cookbooks offer recipes whose relevance to tenant family cooking is questionable. Marcellus, a black cook in a white Kentucky home around 1900, had several recipes for breakfast breads.[89] The ingredients now seem ordinary—cornmeal, soda, salt, eggs, grits, and lard—but even some of those ingredients would often have been unavailable to poorer families. Simpler recipes found in accounts of Sea Island cooks include batters made from nothing more than meal and water. Sea Island women also mixed meal with cold water and then added hot water to make mush.[90]

In truth, sharecropping had no food-enhancing qualities and posed a number of cooking dilemmas. To move past this form of peonage with enough money to buy land demanded ferocious saving, a hoarding of nickels, dimes, and pennies, that in turn required eating sparingly and depending solely on what one could gather, grow, trap, or hunt. People were clear about how they felt: "We was raised up just like cattle is, and we experienced hard times . . . [but] I rather get on with eating once a week on bread and water than be a slave with plenty."[91]

Tenant farmers became landowners by surviving on bare necessities and using the most basic clothes, tools, and cooking utensils. Successful families eyed the popular Dixie Pink salmon but didn't buy it. Shoppers who splurged on canned goods, who bought fresh fruit (bananas, oranges, lemons) or liquor, had little left to buy land. Prudent families prided themselves on the ability to feed their households while spending as little as possible. An archaeologist looking for commercially produced material culture might conclude such families barely lived at all.

Gradually, from about 1890 to 1910, more black farmers became landowners.[92] Once a family owned its land, it created a series of discreet spaces whose organization, as with Native American yards, appeared disorderly to many white observers.[93] People raised a larger variety of foodstuffs. Families became more self-sufficient and autonomous, and, as one consequence, they also had higher self-esteem. They showed their thankfulness in church donations, at church suppers and summer revivals, and by sharing with less-fortunate kin.

Black landowners still had to deal with racist storekeepers, but because their yard space was not in white hands their vegetable gardens could be any size a family chose.[94] They could plant fruit trees. They could raise more than chickens and add a hog, a mule, or a cow, or they could plant a flowering crape myrtle. Soon farms boasted pecan trees, fig trees, cane fields, and sweet potato patches. Gardeners grew collards, okra, tomatoes, and watermelons and irrigated tiny rice fields. Fruit and vegetables composed a larger percentage of farm products.[95] Farm agents taught canning and encouraged decorative planting. Food limitation was voluntary and more limited in scope, although cost stayed a concern.

When one elderly white woman described her pre–World War II childhood home she spoke for countless families, black and white, in surrounding states. "The house was very small. The outside looked like an old farmhouse. The boards were unpainted. The yard was mostly dirt with scattered flowers. . . . The kitchen included a dishpan with water from the well, iron skillets to cook with, cabinets containing food, and a wood stove. To cook, you would have to go outside to get the wood for the stove. We also had to chop it. There was no electricity; we managed other ways."[96] The culture of rural poverty gradually yielded to technological advance during the 1940s as the federal government installed rural electric lines, families put in indoor plumbing, and both agricultural and home economics extension agents touted new tools and techniques.

Susan Holt compared two African American North Carolina families, one that owned land and one that did not. Everyone in the tenant family worked, whether farming, selling produce door to door, or cooking for a white family. Their diet was little more than fatback and bread. Nothing else was affordable. In contrast, the landowner ran a drayage, and his wife and children raised fruit, vegetables, and livestock. The children sold berries, and their mother took in laundry. This family, Holt notes, had "money in the bank."[97] Their kitchen would have held equipment well above and beyond that the tenant family used. A wood stove, cupboards, and closets filled with jars of home-canned products meant the family could have pickles for dinner and jam on breakfast bread in summer and in winter. The complement of utensils would have grown to include an egg beater, more bowls, and some baking pans. Baking soda, baking powder, and flour might reside on cupboard shelves beside the cornmeal. The differences—hoe cakes rather than biscuits, or fruit cobbler rather than red velvet cake—seem insubstantial cast against today's food domain but were immense for their time.

Edna Lewis draws readers into such a black landowner's world in *Taste of Country Cooking*. Her family's concerns mirror those in other rural black communities: literacy, expressive performance (poetry, plays, and music), education, swapping seeds and ideas, sharing farm labor, and exchanging setting hens. She describes the care of chickens and guinea hens and writes of planting when the sun, moon, and stars are auspicious. She recounts seasonal celebrations and a longer cycle of major events—births, weddings, and burials. Lewis remembers various family members "preparing delicious foods" to honor each season, drawing on sources from the farm, the store, and nature. Her spring and early summer desert list—junket, custard, blanc mange, and bread pudding—show the rhythms of the seasons and the presence of fertile cows who abundantly supplied the dairy. A pressed-glass butter dish that sat on the family table symbolized the above-average material wealth of a landowner.[98] Cake stands and desert cups were also part of the household inventory.

Because family income was tied to farming and food production, differing degrees of prosperity created culinary variation. Some vegetables, however, were universally grown. Farm wives had good access to local fruit and vegetables but saved for expensive ingredients for special events. Gradually, the availability and lowering cost of commercial foods enabled women to try more exotic dishes using marshmallow fluff, Karo Syrup, California almonds, dates and apricots, canned pineapple, tuna, canned ham and Spam, and Hellmann's Blue Ribbon Mayonnaise.

Across the South it was common to see men with hunting dogs. Even possum deadfall was skinned and tossed in a pot. Families enjoyed roast possum served with sweet potatoes, corn bread, and gravy; men saw it as a special breakfast treat. Alert hunters also brought home muskrat, beaver, and other game. Families bought large wood stoves on time. Some had iceboxes stocked with blocks of ice shipped from northern states or upland areas of the South, where winter brought freezing temperatures and frozen lakes. Well water became the norm.[99]

Throughout the spring, summer, and fall, rural families (whether sharecroppers or landowners) also gathered wild plants, fruit, and nuts. Forests and fields provided a variety of greens—lamb's quarter, dandelion, pokeweed, sorrel, wild mustard, watercress, and winter cress—as well as numerous summer berries (blueberries, whortleberries, raspberries, and blackberries) and other fruit such as peaches, persimmons, ground cherries, papaws, and even maypops (*Passiflora incarnata*) for cobblers, pies, and preserves. Sassafras leaves—dried, pulverized, sifted, and bottled—provided one flavoring, and peppergrass, chives, garlic, and young onions produced others. Scuppernong grapes were ready to pick in autumn, when haws, hickory nuts, pecans, walnuts, butternuts, and chinquapins also dropped.

No matter where one went, landowners usually had an abundance of bacon fat, lard, butter, eggs, and cream. Preserved food—bread and butter pickles, pickled fruit, or peach leather—was also common. Local food in the upland Carolinas, Kentucky, and Tennessee, however, differed somewhat from that in the lowlands. Apples flourished; wheat flour was readily available, whereas rice flour was not; and pasturage was richer than along the Georgia coast.[100] More recipes called for beef, lamb, or mutton. North Carolinians found abundant blueberries but could not grow bananas, whereas bananas and oranges overflowed New Orleans fruit shops. Women in Louisiana could bake with home-grown sugar cane, and men had a greater choice of fruit trees for their backyard orchards and arbors.

Variations in flora and fauna, in climate and weather created regional garden nuances. Individual emphases also varied. Rice, corn, or wheat might dominate; pork might take precedence over beef; and hot breads might be favored over cold. In Louisiana, Effie Burns's grandpa raised yellow and red plums, figs, dates, sweet oranges, sour oranges, grapes, and pecans.[101] Citrus farmers raised ten varieties of orange trees near New Orleans, and bananas grew wild on Pecan Island. Along the Gulf Coast and in the Deep South, families could grow two crops a year, filling winter gardens with white cabbage, rutabaga, turnips, onions, shallots, garlic, endive, mustard, roquette, radish, cauliflower, beets, cress, lettuce, parsley, leeks, English peas, and celery. Gardeners put in a second planting that additionally held ginger, okra, tomatoes, peppers, cucumbers, cashews, bene plants [sesame], pinders [peanuts], potatoes, arrowroot, strawberries, and melons.[102] The accessibility of a wide range of fresh fruit and vegetables spurred a variety of different recipes, visible in cookbooks, and gave more complex flavors to regional dishes. People in the uplands had a single, and shorter, growing season. Yet as railways grew quicker and added more efficient refrigeration, grocers began to offer more fruit out of season from outside the region.

Changes in traditional African American foodways occurred first within cities and towns. The unequal partnership between white housewives and black housekeepers was one nexus. The daily journeys of black domestic workers between black and white communities opened a path through which food habits and preferences flowed from one group to the other and back again. Dori Sanders describes how this worked in her family. Aunt Vestula, a housekeeper near Charleston, always boarded the train for home bearing bags of fancy food and enticing ingredients. Dori's mother and aunt would then shut themselves in the kitchen to experiment while the children played and wondered what new dish the two women were cooking.[103] Multiply this a thousand fold, give it bit of folk wisdom and a dollop of individualism, and one can see how new foodways spread like ripples on a pond.

As historians point out, however, the kitchen in white, middle-class homes was contested terrain where white women had racial superiority yet needed dishes to serve in undeniably rivalrous table contests. The rivalry appeared at church dinners and quilting parties in black communities, too. Craig Claiborne remembers his childhood in Sunflower, Mississippi, where Mrs. Diggs and Mrs. Lancaster "competed to set the best table in town."[104] Maya Angelou gives a recipe for her grandmother's caramel cake and explains, "Momma would labor carefully over her selection, because she knew but would never admit that she and all the women were in hot competition . . . none of the other cooks would even dare the Caramel Cake."[105]

Resourceful domestics used employers to their own advantage.[106] Food that was easy to pack came home on a regular basis in baskets and tin cans. Employers viewed the unspoken benefit in varied ways. It made some very unhappy. Others took it in stride, believing, as one man said, "If the cook don't take care of herself before she puts the food on the table, it's her own fault."[107]

A common assumption is that black cooks were in charge of the kitchens of their employers, but often cooks did not control the menu or purchase the food. In small-town Georgia, grocers sent black workers with order books to white homes, where women wrote out their lists; grocers then saw that the orders were delivered.[108] There were some cooks, like Rosa, who sometimes bought food and later were reimbursed. On such occasions Rosa cooked "turnip greens and cornbread, black eyed peas, or sweet potatoes."[109] Marcie Cohen Ferris provides many examples of black cooks introducing similar foods into southern Jewish homes.[110] Recipes attributed to black cooks became more varied in urban texts by the turn of the century.

Throughout much of the nineteenth century, the food system was restricted in some ways, broad and expansive in others, and pieced together with simplicity, abundance, and local flavor. A changing set of favorite dishes evolved. Plantation kitchens introduced African American families to cakes, pies, puddings and tarts and to jams, jellies, preserves, fruit-based wines, brandies, and vinegars. White households demanded these from each and every cook they hired. African American country cooking gained new depth as black women blended traditional European recipes into their home cooking and family rituals and as they acquired more foodstuffs and new appliances. Ice-cream makers appeared at church picnics, and Sunday meals were embellished beyond necessity.

Across the South, black foodways were a product of change, assimilation, and acculturation. The puny food rations during slavery led to an expansive use of edible wild food in the daily diet. That, along with what they produced on their own, grew the base of foods upon which black families drew. Food choices gradually and steadily increased among landowning families and brought more "outside" foods into their homes. Young women who entered historically black institutions such as Spelman College in Atlanta took classes in home economics, although domestic service was not their goal. Others took similar lessons at Hampton Institute and Tuskegee. In local schools cooking was taught by means of simple textbooks published in northern cities and containing northern recipes. That, too, expanded and "whitened" the range of food selection. Progressive reformers reached out to families outside schools, especially in the countryside. Farm Bureau and home demonstration agents from the U.S. Department of Agriculture taught hygiene, sanitation, food preservation, and home gardening using venues such as girls clubs. Some, like Amelia Boynton Robinson, a Georgia native who became a home demonstration agent, had immense influence in their counties.[111] Seaman Knapp captured the philosophy in a 1911 letter to Susie V. Powell: "Through the tomato plant you will get into the home garden and by means of the canning you will get into the farm kitchen."[112]

The goal of such efforts was not to revitalize southern cuisine (although it certainly had an impact on it) but rather to improve health among rural families, raise their incomes, and create more independence for farm women. Without doubt, one result was greater variety at the dinner table. Women in Beaufort County, North Carolina, who learned how to build hotbeds and cold frames and then grow crops in them further modified their home gardens so produce could appear in kitchens early or out of season.[113] Home demonstration agents encouraged women to improve horticultural techniques as they tried new and unfamiliar vegetables. Expanding the range of food available in each season brought change to the dining table. Last but not least, women baked and brought their very best creations to summer revivals and church suppers, thereby raising expectations throughout communities.

Other forces acted upon black families. Northern publishers of African American newspapers smuggled papers south using a network of Pullman porters. The newspapers included columns on food and health that offered ideas on new dishes, ingredients, and methods. They also warned against unsightly street wagons and "unsanitary" eating places where "southern" food was served (probably barbecue or fry shacks). Such cautions may have had more effect in the South than the North.[114]

People who moved out of the South during the Great Migration wanted familiar homegrown cuisine once they arrived in the North or the West. Migrant black women in California mourned the loss of familiar ingredients, and families that had grown their own food or bought it in rural markets became shoppers. Enterprising men and women turned this to advantage by opening sidewalk barbecue stands and "chicken shacks." Cafes, restaurants, grocery stores, and butcher shops in segregated neighborhoods catered to the newcomers.[115] The food domain in selected areas of cities such as Chicago, Philadelphia, Newark, New York, and Los Angeles reverberated to a new rhythm.

Black people in northern cities kept culinary memories alive by shopping for food on each return trip home. Relatives baked, preserved, canned, and saved favorite food—so dearly missed—and sent it north packed in paper bags and suitcases. The southern touch was especially vibrant in the Harlem market; sweet 'tater pone sold by peddlers was particularly popular. It didn't take long for men and women to start selling produce in Chicago and New York markets, where, just as in the South, vendors sang to attract buyers. They sang to tout fish and greens: "Ah got string beans! Ah got cabbage! Ah got collard greens! Ah got um! Ah got um! . . . Ah got anythin' you' need." Canny men varied their cries, emphasizing the tune and adding more swing, drawing on the rhythm of old spirituals: "I caught shad, I caught 'em in the sun; I got shad, I caught just for fun." Another might claim, "Ah come fum down in New Orleans, Whar dey cook good vittles, Speshly greens." Clyde "Kingfisher" Smith told a WPA interviewer, "Yes, I sing them different. I put the words to the tune, to fit the occasion."[116] Cries changed with each product, depending on whether clams, catfish, oysters, fish, raw shrimp, blackberries, blueberries, or watermelons were for sale.

Out in the hinterland, especially in the South, other men and women opened juke joints where bluesmen played while meat roasted over smoky fires (in the North, some speakeasies functioned in similar ways). Lowcountry artist Jonathan Green has re-created these in a series of paintings that draw on memories of his grandmother's joint—a place to talk, gossip, listen and learn, eat and drink, and dance or romance. Kathy Starr recounts the food her grandmother prepared, the daily meals for local laborers, and the location and role of her grandmother's joint in a Delta town.[117] Starr's grandmother served one clientele during the day and another at night or on weekends. The mask of a juke joint, its curtain of ordinariness, vanished when the sun went down, and local people knew it. They spoke of the "Devil Children" to be found there. Liquor, sometimes illegal, sometimes legal, sometimes just clear moonshine in a plain glass jar, graced the night. In an odd reversal of southern apartheid, throughout the first half of the twentieth century white men sneaked in quietly and cautiously to pick up food and liquor in plain paper bags.

The grilled chicken, spare ribs, spicy pork, and whole range of smoky barbe-cued meat cooked so well in these places—which still exist—are a continuum of the cooking that males did, beginning with those on plantations. Steamboat cooks brought these foods up the rivers, and railroad cooks and chefs took them across the prairies. Juke joints had urban alter egos, and whether sited on an alley or by a cotton field their down-home food was but one focus. Music was another. The cooks had southern roots, and the food was simple yet complexly layered. Orich LaMoneda promoted his place in West Side Savannah as one where food was "strictly home cooked."[118]

Conclusion

Both prejudice and poverty forced pre– and post–Civil War African Americans to create a cohesive cooking tradition built with limited resources and mak-ing do. Before the Civil War, as we have seen, slaves learned how to combine food and cooking methods from their own African heritage with European and Native American traditions. Plain versus fancy cooking marked the divide be-tween slaves (and some free blacks) and the plantation elite and wealthy, white urban households. With Emancipation the boundaries that dictated what slaves should, could, and did eat were breached, yet the meals that black sharecrop-pers ate mirrored the slave diet. In contrast, black landowners enjoyed a steadily growing repertoire of foods while still making use of those familiar to both slaves and sharecroppers. Families sold and shared foodstuffs, added better stoves, and learned to can and preserve. When they had little cash to spare, rural families drew on plants, birds, and animals from sea and shore. Many southerners also made game and wildfowl, fish, and shellfish part of their regular diets.

Local fauna was a significant source of food for rural families until World War II, and southern cookbooks, black and white alike, reiterate this fact. But changing technologies and economic conditions permitted a new, wider range of choices. For example, as railway networks spread, small exotic luxuries like canned sardines entered the black community. Yet racial prejudice still shaped eating patterns, dictating when and where one could eat. In the cities, families became consumers. Women bought from curb markets or neighborhood stores and patronized Jewish grocers who stocked shelves with African Americans in mind.[119] Black cooks worked in white homes, where they taught immigrant women how to cook southern-style vegetables and took home for themselves knowledge of different cuisines. Many became formidable cooks with a talent for food fusion.

Women carried their culinary skills into wider arenas through church suppers, restaurant work, and catering. They cooked in boardinghouses and in commercial establishments. They became well acquainted with "outside" foods that added sophistication to their own creations. They were both resourceful and experimental. Their food exchanges built communal strength, and when they exchanged a recipe for pecan pie or pound cake with a Jewish store owner they made a crack in the barrier of segregation.

This review of the black side of southern food history illustrates how a rich culinary tradition was born out of necessity and innovation. By including information from archeological deposits, court and business records, cookbooks, slave narratives, memoirs, and other sources I have tried to provide a sense of the forces that acted on Africans and their descendants, and, in turn, on the way they fought against limiting conditions—through steadfastness, stealth, commerce, and inventiveness—to eat food of much greater variety than is often acknowledged.[120]

NOTES

This essay has benefited greatly from the advice and encouragement of Anne Bower; comments by an anonymous reviewer; Psyche Williams-Forson's *Building Houses Out of Chicken Legs: Black Women, Food, and Power* (Chapel Hill: University of North Carolina Press, 2006); and Marcie Cohen Ferris's dissertation, "Matzoh Ball Gumbo, Goober Goo, Gefilte Fish, and Big Momma's Kreplach: Exploring Southern Jewish Foodways," George Washington University, 2003. I also thank Mary C. Beaudry for providing some of the reference materials.

1. Andrew Warnes, *Hunger Overcome: Food and Resistance in Twentieth-Century African American Literature* (Athens: University of Georgia Press, 2004); Caroline Rouse and Janet Hoskins, "Purity, Soul Food, and Sunni Islam: Explorations at the Intersection of Consumption and Resistance," *Cultural Anthropology* 19 (May 2004): 226–50. According to Rouse and Hoskins, Elijah Muhammad "argued that southern cuisine was a tool used by whites to physically, morally, and intellectually weaken blacks" because of its role in racial identity. They cite statements such as "peas, collard greens, turnip greens, sweet potatoes and white potatoes are very cheaply raised foods. The Southern slave masters used them to feed the slaves, and still advise the consumption of them" (234–36).

2. This partial list was inspired by Sheila Ferguson, *Soul Food: Classic Cuisine from the*

Deep South (1989, repr. New York: Grove Press, 1993); Rebecca Sharpless, "Traditional Summer Cooking: Not Gone with the Wind," *Phi Kapa Phi Forum* (Baton Rouge) no. 3 (2002): 10–15; and Williams-Forson, *Building Houses Out of Chicken Legs.*

3. Maya Angelou, *Hallelujah! The Welcome Table: A Lifetime of Memories with Recipes* (New York: Random House, 2004), 4.

4. Sidney Mintz, *Tasting Food, Tasting Freedom: Excursions into Eating, Power, and the Past* (Boston: Beacon Press, 1997).

5. In "Eating 'Out': Food and the Boundaries of Jewish Community and Home in Germany and the United States," *Nashim* 5 (2002): 53, Ruth Abusch-Magder defines outside food as that prepared either outside the home (commercially prepared) or not historically included in an ethnic cuisine. In the context of this essay that would be food not eaten at ordinary meals or only on special occasions by African or African American slaves, sharecroppers, and landowners. Note that outside foods, over time, can be incorporated into a cuisine and lose their outside status.

6. An excellent example of archeological work on food is Maria C. Franklin's "The Archaeological Dimensions of Soul Food: Interpreting Race, Culture, and Afro-Virginian Identity," in *Race and Archaeology of Inequality*, edited by Charles Orser Jr. (Salt Lake City: University of Utah Press, 2002), 88–107.

7. Sidney Mintz, "Enduring Substances, Trying Theories: The Caribbean Region as Oikoumene," *Journal of the Royal Anthropological Institute* 2 (1996): 298.

8. Jessica Harris, *Iron Pots and Wooden Spoons: Africa's Gifts to New World Cooking* (New York: Atheneum, 1989); Anne Yentsch, *A Chesapeake Family and Their Slaves: A Study in Historical Archaeology* (New York: Cambridge University Press, 1994), 196–208. Zainabu Kpaka Kallon provides contemporary recipes for a wide variety of African foods, some of which seem to be prototypes for African American dishes made in the South (e.g., *gombondoh*). Okra is called *bondoh* by the Mende. Zainabu Kpaka Kallon, *Zainabu's African Cookbook with Food and Stories* (New York: Citadel Press, 2004).

9. These items were needed for a mid-summer event on a Georgia plantation in 1855. E. Merton Coulter, "A Century of a Georgia Plantation," *Mississippi Valley Historical Review* 16, no. 3 (1929): 337.

10. William Howard Russell, *My Diary North and South* (Boston: T. O. H. P. Burnham, 1863), 276.

11. Genia Woodberry account in *The American Slave: A Composite Autobiography*, edited by George P. Rawick (Westport: Greenwood Press, 1972–79), pt. 4, 221.

12. Plowden C. J. Weston drew up an overseer's contract for use on his South Carolina lowcountry plantations in which he identified three cooks: one on the island, one on the mainland, and one for the children. They were to "cook cleanly and well." The child's cook was to be particularly careful to ensure that no child ate anything considered unwholesome. Rations for the children were half that provided to adults. Children received two quarts of potatoes in potato time; one pint of grits and one pint of salt during grits time (October to April); and a half pint of small rice from April first to October first on Tuesdays and Fridays together with meat. Each Thursday the children got molasses, but no adults received molasses unless they had behaved well and remained healthy. The Christmas allowance for the children was one and a half pounds of fresh meat, one and a half pounds of salt meat, one pint of molasses, and two quarts of rice. Mason Crum, *Gullah: Negro Life in the Carolina Sea Islands* (1940, repr. New

York: Negro Universities Press, 1968), 246–49. On the nearby Sea Islands, corn used for rations had to be husked, shelled, and then, using large log mortars and hand mills, ground into meal. Reported in *Letters from Port Royal*, edited by Elizabeth W. Pearson (Boston: W. B. Clarke, 1906), 52.

13. Virginia store accounts also show purchases of rum, brandy, molasses, and sugar by slaves, while freedmen's claims for lost property after the Civil War in the lowcountry indicate that a number had been able to purchase store goods. Barbara Heath, "Slavery and Consumerism: A Case Study from Central Virginia," *African American Archaeology Newsletter*, no. 3 (Early Winter 1997): 1–2.

14. James Mellon, ed., *Bullwhip Days: The Slaves Remember: An Oral History* (New York: Grove Press, 1988), 310, 323.

15. In plantation records Eli J. Capell listed the fruit trees in his Mississippi orchard: forty varieties of apples — northern and southern — thirty of peaches, twelve of pears, six of plums, four of cherries, and two each of apricots, nectarines, and grapes. Each variety had a slightly different taste and time of ripening. Slaves would have eaten these as fresh fruit. Wendell Holmes Stephenson, "A Quarter-Century of a Mississippi Plantation: Eli J. Capell of Pleasant Hill," *Mississippi Valley Historical Review* 23, no. 3 (1936): 364. See also Daniel Dennett, *Louisiana as It Is* (New Orleans: Eureka Press, 1876), 41.

16. Take, for example, the family at Oakley Plantation whose porch faced the back of the Great House. Laurie A. Wilkie, *Creating Freedom: Material Culture and African American Identity at Oakley Plantation, Louisiana, 1840–1950* (Baton Rouge: Louisiana State University Press, 2000). In more recent years archaeologists have paid close attention to these spaces. Wilkie, *Creating Freedom*; Barbara J. Heath and S. Amber Bennett, "The Little Spots Allow'd Them: The Archaeological Study of African American Yards," *Historical Archaeology* 34, no. 2 (2000): 38–55; see also P. A. Gibbs, "'Little Spots Allow'd Them': Slave Garden Plots and Poultry Yards," *Colonial Williamsburg Interpreter* 20, no. 4 (1999): 9–13.

17. The suggestion that a plantation's lands belonged to both planter and, in a surreptitious fashion, to its slaves can be seen in an account of a slave who was hunting with his master's son at Lebanon Plantation. Stuart A. Marks, *Southern Hunting in Black and White: Nature, History, and Ritual in a Carolina Community* (Princeton: Princeton University Press, 1991), 2

18. Native Americans, for example, used buds, nuts, seeds, and tubers from the live oak, chinquapin, hickory, walnut, wild artichoke, persimmon, prickly pear, redbud, red mulberry, mesquite, yaupon, mandrake, and thistle, among others. Bartram writes that the women gathered a wide range of wild (i.e., native) vegetables, cultivated others, and quickly adopted peaches and watermelons as edibles. William Bartram, *William Bartram on the Southeastern Indians*, edited by Gregory A. Waselkov and Kathryn E. Holland Braund (Lincoln: University of Nebraska Press, 1995). They gathered greens from spring into fall, concentrating on nuts as fall progressed. The strength of the alliance between Indian and black gave rise to a Louisiana term, *grif*, identifying the mixed ethnicity. Gwendolyn Midlo Hall, *Africans in Colonial Louisiana: The Development of Afro-Creole Culture in the Eighteenth Century* (Baton Rouge: Lousiana State University Press, 1992), 118; see also Daniel H. Usner Jr., *Indians, Settlers, and Slaves in a Frontier Exchange Economy: The Lower Mississippi Valley* (Chapel Hill: University of North Carolina Press, 1992).

19. Julius Nelson in *The American Slave*, ed. Rawick, pt. 4, 144–46.

20. On Georgia's Sea Islands, different niches supplied different foods. August's rice birds, picked off the shrubbery that lined the fields, were made into pies. Partridges lived in the pinelands, and doves hovered over pea fields. Deer from swamps provided venison. Some wild ducks preferred open water, others fed in the marsh, as did coons and muskrats, whereas nocturnal possum took to the woods. Shell banks of oysters lined the shores of bays whose waters were seined for fish, crab, and shrimp. Bass, drum, catfish, rockfish, sheepshead, flounder, croaker, and shad were caught in creeks and rivers. Crum, *Gullah*.

21. Joyce Hansen and Gary McGowan, *Breaking Ground, Breaking Silence: The Story of New York's African Burial Ground* (New York: Henry Holt, 1998).

22. Ralph B. Flanders, *Plantation Slavery in Georgia* (1933, repr. Cos Cob, Conn.: J. E. Edwards, 1967); Mellon, ed., *Bullwhip Days*, 38.

23. Annie Burton, *Memories of Childhood's Slavery Days* (Boston: Ross Publishing, 1909). Concerning food in troughs, Russell provides the following from a set of printed directions for overseers, "Troughs of animal swill were prepared in a similar fashion: sound cotton seed, a gallon of corn meal to the bushel, a quart of ash, a handful of salt, and a good proportion of turnips or green food of any kind, even clover of peas . . . thoroughly cooked" (*My Diary North and South*, 361).

24. Whitelaw Reid, *After the War: A Southern Tour, May 1, 1865 to May 1, 1866* (1866, repr. New York: Harper Torchbacks, 1965), 94–95.

25. McKee, "Food Supply," 233.

26. Before the nineteenth century and a sea change in the way in which animals were butchered, planters provided whole animals as provisions. Joanne Bowen, "Foodways in the Eighteenth Century Chesapeake," in *The Archaeology of Eighteenth-Century Virginia*, edited by T. R. Rheinhart (Richmond, Va.: Spectrum Press), 87–130; Franklin, "The Archaeological Dimensions of Soul Food."

27. This practice is described by Booker T. Washington and recounted in Carolyn Tillery, *The African American Heritage Cookbook: Traditional Recipes and Remembrances from Alabama's Renowned Tuskegee Institute* (Secaucus: Carol Publishing, 1998), 93–94. See also Kathy Starr, *The Soul of Southern Cooking* (Jackson: University of Mississippi Press, 1989).

28. After the civil rights movement, black food writers began to reach back to their roots and describe the hardscrabble foods of the nineteenth and early twentieth centuries. One good example is Ruth L. Gaskin's *A Good Heart and a Light Hand* (New York: Simon and Schuster, 1968). Poor white families ate many of the same dishes. For centuries, European farm families were noted for the penurious use of every possible piece of a slaughtered animal, from head to toe. Lettice Bryant, *The Kentucky Housewife* (1841, repr. Bedford, Mass.: Applewood Books, 2002). It is notable, however, that cookbooks written by black authors before the civil rights movement contain far fewer dishes using poor cuts of meat. See, for example, Rufus Estes, *Good Things to Eat, as Suggested by Rufus: A Collection of Practical Recipes for Preparing Meats, Game, Fowl, Fish, Puddings, Pastries, Etc.* (1911, repr. Jenks, Okla.: Howling at the Moon Press, 1999); Lena Richard, *New Orleans Cookbook* (Boston: Houghton Mifflin, 1940); and Freda de Knight, *Date with a Dish: A Cook Book of American Negro Recipes* (New York: Hermitage Press, 1948). Williams-Forson provides a detailed discussion in "'Building Houses Out of Chicken

Legs,'" 124–72, as does Tracy N. Poe in "The Origins of Soul Food in Black Urban Identity: Chicago, 1915–1947," *American Studies International* 37, no. 1 (1999): 4–33.

29. Alex Lichtenstein, "That Disposition to Theft with which They Have Been Branded: Moral Economy, Slave Management, and the Law," *Journal of Social History* (1989): 413–40.

30. Mellon, ed., *Bullwhip Days*, 43. They burned chicken feathers and dumped the bones and guts of shad far out in rivers to escape detection. Charles Ball, *Slavery in the United States: A Narrative of the Life and Adventures of Charles Ball, a Black Man, Who Lived Forty Years in Maryland, South Carolina and Georgia, as a Slave* (1837, repr. New York: Dover Publications, 2003).

31. An ethnographic parallel exists. American POWs interned in Japanese concentration camps applied the term *quan* to food not included in rations. It meant any dish prepared solely from unrationed (appropriated) ingredients or from a blend of rations (rice) and nonrationed foodstuffs. The POWs described quanning as pleasurable and thrilling. As Jan Thompson interpreted it, the experience of joyful anticipation when mixing, and if need be cooking, quan was inexpressible. Thompson, "Prisoners of the Rising Sun: Food Memories of American POWs in the Far East during World War II," in *Food and the Memory: Proceedings of the Oxford Symposium on Food and Cooking 2000*, edited by Harlan Walker (Blackston, Totnes, Devon: Prospect Books, 2001).

32. Russell, *My Diary North and South*, 351.

33. Parents and Gullah elders customarily teach children, regardless of gender, to be self-sufficient and know how to hunt, fish, and gather. Josephine Beoku-Betts, "'We Got Our Way of Cooking Things': Women, Food and the Preservation of Cultural Identity among the Gullah," in *Food in the USA: A Reader*, edited by Carole Counihan (New York: Routledge, 2002).

34. Anna Wright gives cursory information about the food slaves ate, including chicken, catfish, ham gravy, cornmeal, flour, "taters," onions, turnip greens, snap beans, collard, cabbage, pot likker, blackberry pie, and cake with jelly filling. She notes two utensils, an iron griddle and an iron pot (Mellon, ed., *Bullwhip Days*, 42). An archaeologist might see fish bones and could recover chicken bones. If the iron utensils were deposited in the archaeological record they would be the most visible. It is a different case with Lucinda Williams's succinct directions: "bile de greens—all kinds of greens from out in de woods—and chip up de pork and deer meat, or de wild turkey meat; maybe all of dem, in de big pot at de same time! Fish too, and de big turtle dat lay out on de bank!" T. Lindsay Baker and Julie P. Baker, eds., *The WPA Oklahoma Slave Narratives* (Norman: University of Oklahoma Press, 1996), 107–17. Archaeologists would be able to identify the bones from each animal. If they were smashed or broken open, that is a clue that they had been used in soup or stew but there would be no reliable evidence they were cooked together.

35. Because it is difficult to tell whether a seed has worked into the soil by itself or whether earlier occupants of a site were responsible, archaeologists place most weight on charred seeds, believing that only those can be irrefutably associated with human activity. One of the few African American sites where charred seeds were found is the Rich Neck slave quarter. The seeds include corn, grains (wheat, rye, pearl barley), squash, a variety of peas and beans (bean, lima bean, common bean, cow pea, and peanut), cultivated fruit (melon and cherry), and native plants such as blackberry, acorn,

black walnut, honey locust, bedstraw, and sedge. Stephen Mrozowski and L. Driscoll, "Seeds of Learning: An Archaeobotanical Analysis of the Rich Neck Slave Quarter, Williamsburg, Virginia," manuscript on file, Department of Archaeological Research, Colonial Williamsburg Foundation.

36. Mellon, ed., *Bullwhip Days,* 310–11, 351.

37. Extensive lists of faunal remains from southern plantations can be found in three studies: William H. Adams, ed., *Historical Archaeology of Plantations at Kings Bay, Camden County, Georgia,* Report of Investigation no. 5, submitted to Naval Submarine Base, U.S. Dept. of the Navy, Kings Bay, Ga., by the Department of Anthropology, University of Florida, Gainesville (Gainesville: University of Florida, 1987); Elizabeth Reitz and Nicholas Honnerkamp, "British Colonial Subsistence Strategies on the Southeastern Coastal Plain," *Historical Archaeology* 17 (1983): 4–26; and Elizabeth Reitz, Tyson Gibbs, and Ted A. Rathbun, "Archaeological Evidence for Subsistence on Coastal Plantations," in *The Archaeology of Slavery and Plantation Life,* edited by Theresa Singleton (Orlando: Academic Press, 1985).

38. McKee, "Food Supply," 232. A broader overview is Theresa Singleton, "The Archaeology of Slavery in North America," *Annual Review of Anthropology* 24 (1995): 119–40. More focused studies based on single sites include Brian W. Thomas, "Power and Community: The Archaeology of Slavery at the Hermitage Plantation," *American Antiquity* 63, no. 4 (1998): 531–51; and Garrett Randall Fesler, "From Houses to Homes: An Archaeological Case Study of Household Formation at the Utopia Slave Quarter, ca. 1675 to 1775 (Virginia)," Ph.D. diss., University of Virginia, 2004.

39. In the early nineteenth century it became illegal to teach a slave to read and write. The few who could do so were not apt to waste this talent by risking detection on topics as frivolous as how to bake a pie. Oral tradition substituted for literacy, but it easily collapses time and makes change invisible. When spices were expensive and ovens unavailable, mothers taught daughters to cook one way, but the daughters, as spices dropped in price and more homes had ovens (albeit without good temperature gauges), modified the recipes. As temperature gauges became more reliable and oven heat more regulated, granddaughters again modified the recipes, as did great-granddaughters. Recipes are fluid entities, but their attributions are not (e.g., Nonnie's cinnamon cake), and thus they have auras of authenticity. The nuances in flavor and cooking techniques were not codified as they were in cookbooks. Modifications to recipes in the *Fannie Farmer Cookbook* (Boston: Little Brown, 1896) over its thirteen editions and hundred-year history can be tracked, but changes via the oral tradition cannot be unless recorded on tape or via another medium.

40. Louis Hughes described a July 4 barbecue where peach cobbler and apple dumplings were baked on a rotating basis in iron (Dutch) ovens over open fires. These large apple dumplings were plainly made and without spices or extra fruit flavoring (e.g., lemon or cranberry). The warm, brown-sugared fruit became a delicious, pielike concoction that remained in Hughes's memory. For peach cobbler, he continued, "the crust or pastry was prepared in large earthen bowls, rolled out like any pie crust, only it was almost twice as thick. A layer of this crust was laid in the oven, then a half peck of peaches poured in, followed by a layer of sugar; then a covering of pastry was laid over all and smoothed around with a knife." Hughes, *Thirty Years a Slave: From Bondage to Freedom,* edited by William Adams (Milwaukee: South Side Printing, 1897), 49.

41. Anne Sinkler Whaley Leclercq, *An Antebellum Household: Including the South Carolina Low Country Receipts and Remedies of Emily Wharton Sinkler* (Columbia: University of South Carolina Press, 1996). A more typical example appears in an 1897 letter from Ida Matthews about fig pudding: "My cook says it is one of the easiest puddings to make and she often in winter gives it for Sunday as she prepares it on Saturday . . . [cooks it] only a hour on Sunday, for my cook goes to church and only gets back a little before 1 o'clock and I dine at 3." Archaeologists have tentatively identified Silvia Freeman as the cook and her monthly salary as $4. Wilkie, *Creating Freedom*, 100.

42. Many saw literate slaves as subversive agents rebelling against white domination. Legislators throughout the South tried stringent enforcement of the rule against teaching a slave to read or write as the century progressed. Charleston, Columbia, and Savannah city councils paid particular attention to black literacy because it provided a lifeline to the broader world. Kenneth M. Stamp, *The Peculiar Institution: Slavery in the Antebellum South* (New York: Vintage Books, 1956), 177. Still, some did learn to read and write. In a letter to Mary Campbell, dated May 2, 1838, Hannah Valentine, a house slave wrote, "The strawberry vines are in full bloom, and promise a good crop of fruit. I should like to know what you would wish done with them. If you wish any preserved, and how many. If you do I will endeavor to do them as nicely as possible. If you have no objection I will sell the balance, and see how profitable I can make them. . . . The currants and gooseberries look well, and are tolerably full of fruit. Please let me know if you would wish me to make any currant jelly, and if you would like me to bottle the gooseberries." Campbell Family Papers, Special Collections Library, Duke University. In cities such as Savannah, free blacks ran covert schools, so urban cooks were more apt to be able to read a recipe than were those on plantations.

A comparison of illiteracy rates for whites and blacks in the South, compiled using 1900 U.S. Census data available on line from the Fisher Library at the University of Virginia, provides the following information: in Alabama, there were 2,100 literate blacks and 338,000 literate whites; in Georgia, 1,300 and 379,000; in Louisiana, 18,000 and 284,000; in Mississippi, 1,400 and 314,000; in North Carolina, 600 and 210,000; in South Carolina, 600 and 284,000; and in Virginia, 7,000 and 214,000. Robert Higgs, however, asserts that black literacy quickly rose from 10 percent in 1880 to 50 percent in 1900. Higgs, *Competition and Coercion: Blacks in the American Economy, 1865 to 1940* (Chicago: University of Chicago Press, 1977), 177. A local historian, Sunny Nash, has pointed out that many blacks were quiet about their abilities, to the point that some would not reveal to census takers that they could read or write. Nash, "From Excavation to Oral History," *Ancestry Magazine* 20, no. 6 (2002), accessed online at http://www.ancestry.com/learn/library/article.aspx?article=6919. Even so, there remained a staggering number who, like many poor white women, could not read a cookbook much less write one. For a bibliography of African American cookbooks see Doris Witt, *Black Hunger: Food and the Politics of U.S. Identity* (New York: Oxford University Press, 1999), 221–28.

43. Hughes, *Thirty Years a Slave*, 48–49.

44. Mellon, ed., *Bullwhip Days*, 358, 360; Booker T. Washington, *Up from Slavery: An Autobiography* (New York: Barnes and Noble, 2003), 1: 11.

45. U.S. Department of Agriculture, Economic Research Service, *Sugar and Sweetener Situation and Outlook Yearbook 2001*, Report SSS-231 (May 2001), accessible at

http://www.ers.usda.gov/publications/so/view.asp?f=specialty/sss-bb/; Wendy Woloson, *Refined Tastes: Sugar, Confectionary, and Consumers in Nineteenth-century America* (Baltimore: Johns Hopkins University Press, 2002), 194.

46. Williams-Forson writes of Bella Winston, who, following in her mother's steps, sold fried chicken across from a train station. Her children, she remembered, didn't know "there were other parts of the chicken besides wings, backs, and feet" until they were teenagers and old enough to leave home. "When Gordonsville was the Chicken Capital of the World," *Orange County Review*, July 9, 1970, quoted in Williams-Forson, "'Building Houses Out of Chicken Legs,'" 50.

47. Thomas Cooper and David J. McCord, eds., *The Statutes at Large of South Carolina*, 10 vols. (Columbia: A. S. Johnston, 1836–73), 3: 487–88; see also Yentsch, *A Chesapeake Family*, 245–46.

48. Grocery stores of the past bore little resemblance to commercial establishments of today. Chain stores appeared gradually. S. S. Pierce and Company opened its first food store in Brookline, Massachusetts, in 1831, and the Great Atlantic and Pacific Tea Company (A&P) opened in 1859, just before the Civil War. Both began as "counter-service" stores with home delivery. Buying groceries for cash became an option early in the 1900s but was not initially popular. Safeway and Piggly Wiggly opened their doors around World War I, with the latter the first major chain to offer self-service, in 1916. See "Did You Bring Bottles?" at www.groceteria.net.

49. Peter Earle, "London Female Labour Market," *Economic History Review* 42, no. 3 (1989): 341.

50. Whittington B. Johnson, *Black Savannah, 1788–1864* (Fayetteville: University of Arkansas Press, 1996), 188, discusses the purchase of slaves by Savannah's free black community. A similar practice existed in the Caribbean and across the South, but it differed from white slave ownership. Sometimes free blacks bought relatives, who although technically not free were at liberty to behave as if they were. Women often purchased other women and taught them a trade. Nancy M. Socolow discusses this practice in the French Caribbean, and there is no reason to think it did not operate in Savannah, too. Socolow, *The Women of Colonial Latin America* (New York: Cambridge University Press, 2000), 130–46.

51. Johnson, *Black Savannah*, 157, 186, 188.

52. Ibid., 188.

53. Jane H. Pease, *Ladies, Women, and Wenches: Choice and Constraint in Antebellum Charleston and Boston* (Charlotte: University of North Carolina Press, 1990), 54. The hotel was well situated, widely known, and served excellent food that included luxuries unavailable at most commercial establishments. Also see Marina Wikramanayake, *A World of Shadow: The Free Black in Antebellum Charleston* (New York: Free Press, 1973), and Mrs. St. Julian Ravenel, *Charleston: The Place and the People* (New York: Macmillan, 1927).

54. Timothy J. Lockley, "Spheres of Influence: Working White and Black Women in Savannah," in *Neither Lady nor Slave: Working Women of the Old South*, edited by Susanna Delfino and Michele Gillespie (Chapel Hill: University of North Carolina Press, 2002), 106.

55. Johnson, *Black Savannah*, 71.

56. *South Carolina and American General Gazette*, Feb. 19, 1778, quoted in Robert

Olwell, *Masters, Slaves, and Subjects: The Culture of Power in the South Carolina Low Country, 1740–1790* (Ithaca: Cornell University Press, 1998), 98.

57. Harriette Kershaw Leiding, *Street Cries of an Old Southern City* (with music and illustrations) (Charleston: Daggett Printing, 1927); Walt Whitman in the *New Orleans Picayune*, Jan. 25, 1887.

58. Emily Burke, *Reminiscences of Georgia* (1850, repr. as *Pleasure and Pain, Reminiscences of Georgia in the 1840s* [Savannah: Beehive Press, 1978]), 27, 9–10.

59. Johnson, *Black Savannah*, 70–71; Georgia Bryan Conrad, *Reminiscences of a Southern Woman* (Hampton, Va.: Hampton Institute, n.d.), 16.

60. Conrad, *Reminiscences of a Southern Woman*, 16.

61. Charles L. Hoskins, *Out of Yamacraw and Beyond: Discovering Black Savannah* (Savannah: Gullah Press, 2002), 13–14. In the 1850s, approximately 50 percent of Savannah's white population was foreign-born, primarily immigrants from Ireland and also Germans and a number of East European Jews. These numbers come from Hoskins, quoted in Ferris, "Matzah Ball Gumbo, Goober Goo"; see also Johnson, *Black Savannah*, 156–58.

62. Johnson, *Black Savannah*, 156–58.

63. Betty Wood, *Women's Work, Men's Work: The Informal Slave Economies of Lowcountry Georgia* (Athens: University of Georgia Press, 1995), 212–13; Johnson, *Black Savannah*, 69, 66.

64. Johnson, *Black Savannah*, 57, 99–100; Hoskins, *Out of Yamacraw*, 40, 46, 121.

65. In Mobile, vegetables underwent more than their share of frying. Cauliflower, corn, eggplant, figs, grits, okra, onions, parsnips, plantain, potatoes, sweet potatoes, rice, salsify, squash, and tomatoes were either fried or frittered in at least 25 percent of recipes. *The Gulf City Cookbook*, compiled by the Ladies of the St. Francis Street Methodist Episcopal Church, South, Mobile, Ala. (Dayton: United Brethern Publishing House, 1886).

66. Grace Hale, *Making Whiteness: The Culture of Segregation in the South, 1890–1940* (New York: Vintage Books, 1999).

67. Annabelle P. Hill, *Mrs. Hill's Practical Cookery and Receipt Book* (1867, repr. Columbia: University of South Carolina, 1995), 12.

68. Leslie A. Schwalm, *"A Hard Fight for We": Women's Transition from Slavery to Freedom in South Carolina* (Urbana: University of Illinois Press, 1997), 176.

69. Rufus Estes, *Good Things to Eat as Suggested by Rufus* (1911, repr. Jenks, Okla.: Howling at the Moon Press, 1999); Abby Fisher, *What Mrs. Fisher Knows about Old Southern Cooking, Soups, Pickles, Preserves, etc.* (1881, repr. [edited by Karen L. Hess] Bedford, Mass.: Applewood Books, 1995); Emma Harris, *Choice Recipes of Cateresses and Best Cooks of the State* (Billings: Montana Federation, Negro Women's Clubs; Ways and Means Committee, 1927).

70. Sam B. Hilliard, "Hog Meat and Cornpone: Food Habits in the Antebellum South," *Proceedings of the American Philosophical Society* 113, no. 1 (1969): 1–13; see also Hilliard, *Hog Meat and Hoecake: Food Supply in the Old South, 1840–1860* (Carbondale: Southern Illinois Press, 1972), 56–69.

71. The description of Maun Hanna's baking is in Julia Peterkin, *Scarlet Sister Mary* (1928, repr. Athens: University of Georgia Press, 1998), 28–29.

72. Noralee Frankel, *Freedom's Women: Black Women and Families in Civil War Era Mississippi* (Bloomington: Indiana University Press, 1999), 88–89.

73. Jacqueline Jones, *Labor of Love, Labor of Sorrow: Black Women, Work and the Family from Slavery to the Present* (1985, repr. New York: Basic Books, 1995), 80.

74. Picture lowcountry stores as weather-worn structures with stout shutters, barred windows, and a bench where men gathered, gossiped, and whittled. Crum, *Gullah*, 26–27.

75. Country stores stocked less food than one might think. The focus was on goods that had a long shelf life. Joseph W. Reddoch ("As It Was: A Family Portrait," 1978, typescript on file in the Louisiana State Archives) listed the contents of an Alabama store around 1915, a list similar to one compiled from the 1897 invoice book for W. L. Tillery and Company of Greensburg, Louisiana (Louisiana State Archives). The Alabama country store, according to Howard Odum, "held groceries, canned goods, coffee, crackers, sugar in barrels, molasses, salt, sacks of flour, corn meal, hominy grits, rice, sweet and sour pickles, salt meat, kits of salt mackerel, large tins of link sausage packed in cottonseed oil . . . canned salmon, sardines, Vienna sausage, potted meat, oysters, a wheel of American cheese." Reddoch noted the storekeeper took eggs in exchange for store goods. A boy could also buy cookies such as gingersnaps, and "stick candy in many flavors." The Louisiana store was a reliable source for whiskey, and store invoices also reveal a few spices. Only limited provisions were normally available in rural areas, but there were regional variations. A Tennessee store, for example, also offered cinnamon bark, chestnuts, maple sugar (a local product), dried peaches, vinegar, Irish potatoes, mustard, nutmeg, coffee, tea, sorghum, lard oil, baking powder, cayenne pepper, and other spices. J. C. Williams Daybook, 1879–81, in Jacqueline P. Bull, "The General Merchant in the Economic History of the South," *Journal of Southern History* 18, no. 1 (1952): 56 (quotation by Odum).

76. An example from Eli Capell's store accounts shows how this worked. On January 1, 1867, he owed a freed slave, Willie Dotson, $97.87. After deducting for Dotson's 1866 expenses ($94.62.5), Dotson had exactly $3.25.5 in profit—money he immediately spent buying additional goods from Capell. Stephenson, "A Quarter-Century of a Mississippi Plantation," 373; see also Bull, "The General Merchant," 40.

77. Sharon Ann Holt, *Making Freedom Pay: North Carolina Freedpeople Working for Themselves, 1865–1900* (Athens: University of Georgia Press, 2000), 33; Julia Peterkin, *Green Thursday: Stories* (1924, repr. Athens: University of Georgia Press, 1998), 12.

78. Pete Daniel, *Standing at the Crossroads: Southern Life in the Twentieth Century* (New York: Hill and Wang, 1986), 84.

79. Prejudice, along with greed, is readily apparent in explanations of why freedmen could not keep livestock. Asked why a black tenant farmer wanted to raise livestock and how he would feed them, a Sea Island agent replied, "Feed them? Out of your corn-crib, of course . . . he would steal the corn you fed your mules . . . out of the very trough from which the mules were eating it." Reid, *After the War*, 463; see also Jones, *Labor of Love*, 82–83.

80. Oral interview with Caroline Davis, Nov. 2002, in possession of the author.

81. Interview with Emma McCloud in Daniel, *Standing at the Crossroads*, 223.

82. Jones, *Labor of Love*, 86.

83. Daniel, *Standing at the Crossroads*, 87.

84. Peterkin, *Green Thursday*, 119–20.

85. Typescript of oral interview with Effie Burns, born in 1900, Friends of the Cabildo transcripts, Special Collections, Tulane University Library.

86. Bull, "The General Merchant," 51, 55.

87. Crum, *Gullah*, 15–17.

88. Much later this fact prompted a massive campaign throughout the South to promote canning of tomatoes. It began with white families and gradually incorporated black families. The first Tomato Club for young black girls and women was organized in 1917. Extension service work among fully grown black women in South Carolina started earlier, however, in 1914, and was based on the premise that "no race of people can rise above the level of their women. . . . Teach girls to raise tomatoes, and the next generation will understand the arts of farming better than we do." Ransom W. Westberry quoted in Carmen Harris, "Grace under Pressure," in *Rethinking Home Economics: Women and the History of a Profession*, edited by Sarah Stage and Virginia B. Vincenti (Ithaca: Cornell University Press, 1997), 206–7.

89. Minnie C. Fox, *The Blue Grass Cook Book* (New York: Duffield, 1911).

90. Peterkin, *Scarlet Sister Mary*, 61. Another account notes how a Sea Island woman made cornbread: "mix meal and water together with a little salt. This was done by eye and her proportions always varied, much to the author's dismay." Charles Stearns, *The Black Man of the South and the Rebels* (Boston: N. E. News Co., 1872), 86.

91. A woman from Vicksburg, Mississippi, quoted by Clifton Johnson, *Highways and Byways of the Mississippi Valley* (New York: Macmillan, 1906), 61.

92. Charlene Gilbert and Quinn Eli, *Homecoming: The Story of African-American Farmers* (Boston: Beacon Press, 2000), 40–41.

93. Dianne D. Glave, "Gardening, Progressive Reform, and the Foundation of an African American Environmental Perspective," *Environmental History* 8, no. 3 (2003): 395–411.

94. Crum, *Gullah*, 15.

95. Holt, *Making Freedom Pay*, 33.

96. Oral interview, November 2002, typescript in possession of the author. Although this white woman grew up in poverty, even middle-class or wealthy country families used wood stoves well into the 1930s. Emily Whaley, *Mrs. Whaley Entertains: Advice, Opinions, and a Hundred Recipes from a Charleston Kitchen* (Chapel Hill: Algonquin Books, 1998), 8; Crum, *Gullah*, 15–17.

97. Holt, *Making Freedom Pay*, 20–21. Dietary differences between sharecropper and landowner were dramatic across the South. Williams-Forson, "'Building Houses Out of Chicken Legs,'" particularly 125–28.

98. Edna Lewis, *Taste of Country Cooking* (New York: Knopf, 1976), xiv–v, 2–7, 13–14.

99. For information on some of the newer processed items see the Borden Company's *Nutrition and Health* (1924): 25–29. Borden's Eagle Brand Condensed Milk is pure cow's milk combined with unadulterated cane sugar. According to the company history at www.karosyrup.com, until Karo Syrup's introduction "the American housewife carried her syrup jug to the grocery store to be refilled from the grocer's barrels of syrup." For information on hunting, see Crum, *Gullah*, 55; Irving E. Lowery, *Life on the Old Plantation* (Columbia: University of South Carolina Press, 1911), 53; and Mellon, ed., *Bullwhip Days*, 44. Concerning use of recipes, see Edna Lewis and Scott Peacock, *The Gift of Southern Cooking: Recipes and Revelations from Two Great American Cooks* (New York: Knopf, 2003), 12.

100. Planters supplied flour as part of rations (Mellon, ed., *Bullwhip Days*, 43), where-

as in Sarah Rutledge's 1847 cookbook, wheat flour is used sparingly although recipes using rice flour appear throughout. Rutledge, *The Carolina Housewife; or, House and Home. By a Lady of Charleston, S.C.* (Charleston: W. R. Babcock, 1847).

101. Typescript of oral interview with Effie Burns.

102. Dennett, *Louisiana as It Is*, 20, 41, 123, 149–50.

103. Dori Sanders, *Dori Sanders' Country Cooking: Recipes and Stories from the Family Farm Stand* (Chapel Hill: Algonquin Books, 1995). Throughout "Matzah Ball Gumbo, Goober Goo" Ferris documents the process among Jewish families in Savannah, Charleston, New Orleans, Montgomery, and Memphis.

104. Craig Claiborne, *A Feast Made for Laughter* (Garden City: Doubleday, 1982), 11–12.

105. Angelou, *Hallelujah!* 13.

106. Jones, *Labor of Love*, 132

107. Leigh Campbell in Susan Tucker, *Telling Memories among Southern Women: Domestic Workers and Their Employers in the Segregated South* (New York: Schocken Books, 1988), 49.

108. LuAnn Landon, *Dinner at Miss Lady's: Memories and Recipes from a Southern Childhood* (Chapel Hill: Algonquin Books, 1999), 99.

109. Campbell in Tucker, *Telling Memories*, 51.

110. Ferris, "Matzah Ball Gumbo, Goober Goo," passim.

111. Amelia Boynton Robinson, *Bridge across Jordan* (Washington: Schiller Institute, 1991), passim.

112. Danny Moore, "To Make the Best Better": The Establishment of Girls' Tomato Clubs in Mississippi, 1911–1915," *Journal of Mississippi History* 63 (Summer 2001): 101–18.

113. Dianne D. Glave, "Gardening, Progressive Reform, and the Foundation of an African American Environmental Perspective," *Environmental History* 8, no. 3 (2003): 395–411.

114. *The Defender*, Jan. 10, 1920, editorial page. Whether in advertisements, weekly health or home economics columns, or restaurant reviews, *The Defender's* middle-class prejudices were often demonstrated in discussions of food (9). Feature articles such as one entitled "Pig Ankle Joints" warned against the "unsightly, unsanitary eating places and wagons" that catered to the migrant class's desire for familiar, down-home foods (10). In the South, people found excuses to visit neighbors who received the paper so they could read it for themselves and fantasize about (and sometimes experiment with) the recipes.

115. Poe, "The Origins of Soul Food," 9–10.

116. The first is from a cry of Clyde "Kingfisher" Smith, the second was recorded by Terry Roth in 1938, and the third is from an interview with Smith. All in *Street Cries and Criers of New York* in American Life Histories: Manuscripts from the Federal Writers' Project, 1936–1940, Manuscript Division, Library of Congress.

117. Starr, *The Soul of Southern Cooking*, xvii–xx.

118. Hoskins, *Out of Yamacraw*, 39.

119. Ferris, "Matzah Ball Gumbo, Goober Goo," 160.

120. Among the cookbooks that form the basis for this essay are Martha McCullough Williams, *Dishes and Beverages of the Old South*, facsimile (Knoxville: University of Ten-

nessee Press, 1988), which imitates plantation cooking, as does Mrs. Porter's *New Southern Cookery Book* (Philadelphia: J. E. Potter, ca. 1871). The WPA slave narratives contain many examples of plantation cooking from a black perspective. Starr's *Soul of Southern Cooking* is a good illustration of hardscrabble cooking, and Sanders's *Country Cooking* and Lewis's *Taste of Country Cooking* convey evocative accounts of country cooking. Gaskin's *A Good Heart and a Light Hand* is an earlier example. Any number of charity cookbooks present imitative or nostalgic plantation cooking, a style also codified in *Mrs. Dull's Southern Cooking* (New York: Grossett and Dunlap, 1928). At least two cookbooks distill the sophistication of food among the black elite before 1950: Estes's *Good Things to Eat as Suggested by Rufus* and de Knight's *Date with a Dish*. *The Picayune Creole Cookbook* (1901, repr. New York: Random House, 1995) splendidly represents the urban milieu, contrasting nicely with earlier texts like Mrs. E. J. Verstille's *Mrs. Verstille's Southern Cookery: Comprising a Fine Collection of Cookery and Other Receipts Valuable to Mothers and House-Keepers* (New York: Owens and Agar, 1866, 1867), which details Louisiana country cooking (with Germanic nuances), and Mary Land's *Louisiana Cooking* (Baton Rouge: Louisiana State University Press, 1954). Few early texts exemplify commercial cooking in the South, but see S. Thomas Bivens, *The Southern Cookbook: A Manual of Cooking and Lists of Menus, Including Recipes Used by Noted Colored Cooks and Prominent Caterers* (Hampton, Va.: Press of Hampton Institute, 1912); and Lena Richard, *New Orleans Cook Book* (1940, repr. Mineola, N.Y.: Dover Publications, 1985). Two examples of published cookbooks with ethnic variations of southern cooking for Jewish and German cuisines include Mrs. Charles Moritz and Adele Kahn, *Every Woman's Cookbook* (New York: Cupples and Leon, 1926), and the Georgia Salzburger Society, *Ye Olde Time Salzburger Cookbook* (Ebenezer, Ga.: n.d., n.p.).

PART 2

Representations of
African American Food

4

From Fiction to Foodways: Working at the Intersections of African American Literary and Culinary Studies

Doris Witt

Around 1989, while a graduate student in English at the University of Virginia, I conceived the idea of writing a dissertation about food thematics in the work of several contemporary African American women writers. My idea had originated largely in response to what I perceived as the tendency of then-prevailing theories about African American literature to use male-centered paradigms. In particular, I refer to Houston Baker's work on blues music and Henry Louis Gates's work on signifying.[1] I had a workable outline for the dissertation—cooking in Toni Morrison's work, eating in Gloria Naylor's, vegetarianism in Alice Walker's, and recipes in Ntozake Shange's. Along the way, however, I was sidetracked. Initially, in response to the experience of reading Shange's novel *Sassafrass, Cypress and Indigo* (1982), which embeds recipes in the text of the narrative as gifts handed down from mother to daughter, I became fascinated by African American cookbooks.[2] I started compiling bibliographies of them, prowling used bookstores and interlibrary loaning en masse.

As the work progressed and I realized how little traditional scholarship was available about African American foodways, I felt increasingly less inclined to focus solely on either literature or cookbooks. Nevertheless, my main interest continued to be not so much the material history of specific foods or what people actually ate but how they *represented* what they ate and why. These are not distinct concerns, obviously; it is more a matter of relative emphasis.

Eventually, I found my niche when I started exploring the emergence and evolution of popular discourses about "soul food." While growing up in rural south central Kentucky in the 1960s and 1970s, I ate many of the foods that have been associated with soul in both hardscrabble and upscale versions, depending on whether the cook was my maternal grandfather, a twice-widowed coal miner, or my paternal grandmother, a farm wife.[3] Only later did I hear the phrase *soul food*, and then I began to assume that this was the way black people had historically referred to their versions of the food my white relatives and I had called "country," to the extent we called them anything at all.

When I arranged my African American cookbook bibliography in chronological order, however, I realized that the actual rubric of soul food, if not the concept itself, was of relatively recent vintage.[4] Before the late 1960s, cookbooks by African Americans did not use the label. My curiosity piqued, I redirected my research toward this topic and eventually focussed almost the whole of my first book on debates over soul food during the black power era. Why did the concept emerge when it did, for example, and what about this particular cultural moment made soul food catch on and become so controversial?

As an outgrowth of my interest in food and cultural studies, in this essay I explore some of the provocative intersections between African American literary and culinary history, using cookbooks as a bridge between the two domains. My main focus will be on the twentieth century, but for purposes of periodization I will use as a template the organizational schema of *The Norton Anthology of African American Literature*, which has emerged as the standard literary survey of the field.[5] (The section headings that follow quote titles used for sections of *The Norton Anthology*.) I have two fundamental aims in this essay: to explore what sorts of contributions people trained to analyze ideology and aesthetics rather than material culture might make to the study of African American foodways and, conversely, to explain why increased attention to food can benefit African American literary and cultural studies.

The Vernacular Tradition

Providing evidence for my perception that the Baker and Gates models have continued to dominate the field, the subheadings in this segment of *The Norton Anthology* are heavily weighted toward music and oral traditions, including "Spirituals," "Gospel," "The Blues," "Secular Rhymes and Songs, Ballads, and Worksongs," "Jazz," "Rap," "Sermons," and "Folktales." There are no cookbook excerpts or recipes to discuss specifically under this ahistorical rubric—an absence to which I will return—but the vernacular tradition is an excellent source of information for people who work on black culinary history. One of the work songs included in *The Norton Anthology*, for example, is "We Raise the Wheat": "We raise de wheat, / Dey gib us de corn; / We bake de bread, / Dey gib us de crust; / We sif de meal, / Dey gib us de huss; / We peel de meat, / Dey gib us de skin; / And dat's de way / Dey take us in; / We skim de pot, / Dey gib us de liquor, / And say dat's good enough for nigger."[6]

Consider in greater detail the import of the first two lines: "We raise de wheat, / Dey gib us de corn." In *¡Que Vivan Los Tamales! Food and the Making of Mexican Identity*, Jeffrey Pilcher explores debates in Mexico over the value of wheat versus corn as a staple food grain.[7] His goal is to understand the broader significance of these culinary debates for ideologies of race, gender, class, and Mexican national identity. At the turn of the twentieth century, for example, the Mexican ruling classes attributed the poverty of indigenous people to their continuing preference for corn instead of wheat-based diets rather than to their lack of access to arable land. The failure of peasants to eat wheat, they argued, undermined Mexico's pursuit of modernization. Corn thus became a scapegoat for the legacy of colonialism. Although conflicts between wheat and corn have had a different history in the United States, Pilcher's study demonstrates why a work song such as "We Raise the Wheat" would be relevant to an exploration of the historical connections among food, race, slavery, and nationality.

Drawing on the same types of materials, a textually rather than historically oriented scholar might instead undertake a study of food thematics in African American vernacular traditions. When I lived in Charlottesville, Virginia, a local disk jockey periodically put on a program called *Songs about Food*. Inasmuch as he was particularly knowledgeable about blues and jazz, that meant listeners could look forward to hours of pleasure from titles such as "Struttin' with Some Barbecue," one of Louis Armstrong's releases of the 1920s.[8] The disk jockey eventually coauthored a book on African American music, but I have never heard of anyone trying to formulate a systematic analysis of black music and food. Such a study could consider how and why the food references have changed over time, whether there are noticeable differences among genres, and how the food references function as discourses of sexuality, class, and political ideology.

One of the more intriguing artists who could be included in such a survey is the rapper Kool Keith, whose work includes such funk-inspired albums as *Black Elvis/Lost in Space*.[9] During one live concert performance in fall 1999, Kool Keith threw plastic bags filled with fried chicken into the audience.[10] Because African American science fiction writers such as Octavia Butler often use the genre of fantasy fiction to imagine wildly alternative foodways — in Butler's novel *Dawn* (1987), for example, the alien spaceships and living quarters are made of organic material that automatically regenerates food supplies as needed — Kool Keith's decision as a techno-artist to deploy one of the foods most stereotypically associated with the African American diet would be worth scrutinizing.[11]

Finally, in addition to suggesting that literary scholars interested in food-ways might do well to follow the lead of the compilers of *The Norton Anthology of African American Literature* by incorporating vernacular and musical traditions into their analyses, I also maintain that excerpts from cookbooks, including recipes, should be included in texts such as *The Norton Anthology*. Sermons make the cut, yet it is not hard to find evidence that in many black churches the post-sermon meal is no less an art form than the sermon itself.[12]

Granted, for the editors of *The Norton Anthology* to include recipes as part of the vernacular tradition would raise several fascinating but vexed questions regarding the relationship of African American performative culture to written texts, questions that have long been asked of efforts to transcribe oral traditions such as song lyrics. As feminist scholars have demonstrated, however, cookbooks and recipes are not just transcriptions of performative culture — far from it. They are complex rhetorical structures that can be decoded using the sorts of tools literary critics typically bring to, say, a novel. Hence, the title of one pathbreaking essay collection in food studies is *Recipes for Reading*, and many of the essays therein explore the interpretive challenges that cookbooks and other types of recipe exchange pose.[13]

The Literature of Slavery and Freedom: 1746–1865

During this period one can begin discussing the precursors to African American cookbooks, although very few such books have been uncovered thus far.

The majority of African Americans in this country during the antebellum period were slaves, and it was illegal for slaves to read and write. Much African American cultural transmission was oral. The earliest of the books currently known is Robert Roberts's *The House Servant's Directory* (1827). Twenty-one years later, Tunis Campbell followed suit with *Hotel Keepers, Head Waiters, and Housekeepers' Guide* (1848).[14] Roberts, a member of black Boston's antebellum elite, was a delegate to the Second National Convention of Free People of Color; Campbell was an early activist against slavery, who, after leading a group of free Sea Island farmers working to support the Union Army during the Civil War, was eventually elected to the Georgia State Senate.[15]

As do the editors of *The Norton Anthology*, scholars who study African American literature of this era have traditionally focused on such issues as the conditions under which a given text was produced, the constraints on an author's ability to speak freely, and the use of "legitimating" prefaces by white people. Similar concerns are relevant to any study of advice books such as these. As Rafia Zafar explains elsewhere in this volume, Roberts and Campbell, in the process of offering up recipes and remedies for everything from sauces and beer to cures for alcohol breath and lusterless furniture, were also busy making veiled comments on codes for interracial behavior, techniques for African American men to survive in a white-dominated business world, and class relations within African American society.

One aspect of Zafar's approach that I especially value and would wish to advocate in the field of African American food studies—not just in this early period but in more recent ones as well—is her decision not to treat black culinary writing in isolation from the broader range of multiethnic culinary writing in the United States. Zafar considers the literature of African American foodways in relation to that of Native American, Chicana/o, Italian American, and other cultural traditions.[16]

Yet even as I would want to encourage scholars to move away from an often-reductive black/white analytic binary and develop multiethnic or multicultural models of inquiry, the emergence in recent years of the interrelated domains of postcolonial, diasporic, border, hemispheric, and globalization studies would suggest that there is also no reason to stop at the boundaries of the nation-state in developing frameworks for culinary research and critique.[17] That would seem particularly true given the criticisms against discourses of U.S. multiculturalism leveled by such scholars as Robyn Wiegman and David Palumbo-Liu. In particular, they assert that multiculturalism in the humanities has too often fixated on equality of representation rather than equality of access to material services and goods.[18] Those interested in cultural representations of food, whether in literature, film, or the visual arts, need to understand how such portrayals have been shaped by, and in turn help shape, various material histories, including agricultural labor, land distribution policies, industrial production techniques, and international trade agreements.

One important domain of inquiry for this and even earlier eras would be the impact of the transatlantic slave trade on African diasporic culinary traditions in the Americas and around the world. Sidney Mintz's classic *Sweetness and Power*, which explores the role of Caribbean sugar cultivation in the development of British capitalism, remains the touchstone in the field.[19] In addition, however, those trained in the humanities who wish to work on African American foodways should perhaps not always automatically invoke the historical and spatial imaginary most commonly deployed to analyze African American literature or even African diasporic history. The editors of *The Norton Anthology*, for example, understandably use 1865 as the termination date for the segment on "Slavery and Freedom," but one might also ask how the domains of African American literature and foodways would appear if, say, the Mexican American War were commonly invoked as a nodal point. After all, Tunis Campbell's book was published in that war's terminal year. Given recent work in the area of hemispheric studies, attention to the impact of the Mexican American War might help alter the spatial imaginary of African American culinary history in ways that would foreground cross-border culinary exchange between, for example, African Americans and members of the African diaspora in Latin America. My aim is not to suggest that more traditional historiographical models lack value or should be discontinued but rather to acknowledge that other paradigms might offer different, and potentially very useful, insights.

Literature of the Reconstruction to the New Negro Renaissance: 1865–1919

In the standard version of African American historiography, this period includes the Reconstruction Era, from about 1865 to 1876, when African Americans in the South made some sociopolitical gains under the pressure of Republican occupation from the North. It also includes the years after the demise of Reconstruction, when southern state governments began instituting the repressive system of Jim Crow laws and condoning the racial terrorism that contributed to the mass migration of African Americans to the North and the West. In traditional African American literary terms the era is often understood to have given rise to the literature of racial uplift and passing. That literature frequently features middle-class, light-skinned, and virtuous African American characters. A paradigmatic plot line—as, for example, in Frances Harper's novel *Iola Leroy* (1892)—finds the unsuspecting "white" protagonist learning that she possesses the requisite drops of black blood to render her existence as a freewoman precarious.[20]

Among white southern writers, by contrast, the era gave rise to discourses about the "servant problem" and thus also a proliferation of plantation-school literature celebrating the virtues of old-time "happy darkies" such as the mammy cook. A good many white southern cookbooks were written to preserve recipes it was feared would be lost in the wake of the demise of slavery.[21]

In this respect, Abby Fisher's *What Mrs. Fisher Knows about Old Southern Cooking* (1881) is particularly significant because its existence undermines one of the key mythologies that white plantation-school writers and southern cookbook authors propagated about black women cooks—that they cooked "by instinct" and knew not what they did. In all likelihood born a slave, Fisher eventually relocated from the South to San Francisco, perhaps by serving as a cook on a wagon train.[22] The culinary historian Karen Hess points out that while in California, Fisher received numerous awards and medals for her cooking. Presumably, she would have had some exposure to West Coast recipes and foods, including those of an Asian American population that had been growing until the exclusion laws were enacted beginning in the 1880s. That exposure would, in theory, make Fisher's text an intriguing place to look for multiethnic interactions of the sort I have described. Hess, however, notes that although Fisher "used what we call the Chinese method of cooking rice rather than the Carolina method, . . . this was already being done in some parts of the rice lands and had nothing to do with being in San Francisco."[23] Fisher's recipes for cakes, breads, meat, jellies, and other foods are consistently those associated with "old Southern cooking." In that respect she might be understood to have distanced herself from the mammy stereotype in stressing the transcribability of what she "knows" while, paradoxically, recuperating aspects of the mammy's emerging culinary aura to further her own celebrity.

Meanwhile, another African American cookbook from this era and geographical region, *The Federation Cookbook: A Collection of Tested Recipes, Contributed by the Colored Women of the State of California* (1910), went even farther toward rebutting the plantation mammy stereotype.[24] Like much contemporaneous African American literature, it foregrounds a middle-class model of black female identity. For example, an opening poem, "Cookery

Jingles" by the novelist and activist Katherine Tillman, participates in the classic Victorian "marriage plot" by making clear that the recipes are intended to enable women readers to attract husbands, not employers:

> She could draw a little, paint a little,
>   Talk about a book.
> She could row a boat, ride a horse,
>   But alas she couldn't cook.
>   She could gown, she could go,
>   She could very pretty look
>   But her best beau he was poor
>   And he couldn't hire a cook.
> When he learned the fatal truth
>   His flight he quickly took
> And his girl is single still,
>   Because she couldn't cook!

This private, familial orientation contrasts to the cookbooks of the era by black men, which largely reflect the authors' experiences as cooks in the public domain: H. Franklyn Hall's *Three Hundred Ways to Cook and Serve Shell Fish, Terrapin, Green Turtle, Snapper, Oysters, Oyster Crabs, Lobsters, Clams, Crabs, and Shrimps* (1901), Rufus Estes's *Good Things to Eat, as Suggested by Rufus* (1911), and S. Thomas Bivins's *The Southern Cookbook* (1912).[25] All these books are reticent about personal information; the focal point is the recipes, not the cook. As I continue working through the historical periodizations provided by *The Norton Anthology* one of the developments I trace is the movement of African American cookbooks away from the textually spare, domestic-science ideal that predominated at the turn of the twentieth century toward increasingly more discursive—often memoiristic—modes that lend themselves to the techniques of literary explication.

The recipes in books such as *The Federation Cookbook* and Mrs. W. T. Hayes's *Kentucky Cookbook* (1912) share substantial commonalities with those popularized at this same time by white domestic scientists, both in terms of the type of recipes offered and their clinical mode of presentation.[26] As the culinary historians Laura Shapiro and Harvey Levenstein have explained, domestic science was an important corollary to the turn-of-the-century growth of consumer capitalism and the high rates of immigration from southern and eastern Europe that helped make that growth possible.[27]

For domestic scientists, food was a domain not of individuality and pleasure but of assimilation and progress. Accordingly, one suspects that many of the

African American authors I have mentioned would have been taken aback at the claim, which seems first to have emerged in print in African American cookbooks during the black power era, that the defining quality of African American culinary practice is improvisation.[28] The scientific mode of recipe presentation was significant precisely because the ethos of that era for many upwardly striving blacks was less about preserving one's heritage or proving one's racial authenticity than achieving the rights and benefits of American citizenship. Raising the stature of domestic labor—legitimating it through science—was one means to that end.

Harlem Renaissance: 1919–1940

Of course, African American cookbook authors working within the domestic-science paradigm could also have been encouraged by programs at historically black colleges in the South, such as the Hampton and Tuskegee Institutes, because home economists and other proponents of Americanization through dietary standardization had made inroads there early in the twentieth century. One way literary scholars have discussed the artistic efflorescence of the Harlem Renaissance, in fact, is in terms of the widely known (if often reductively portrayed) debate between Booker T. Washington and W. E. B. Du Bois over the best strategies for assuring African American progress toward equality. Tuskegee Institute founder Washington famously encouraged African Americans to "cast down your bucket where you are," in the South.[29] By that, he meant gain an economic foothold via agricultural and other manual labor and avoid challenging the emerging Jim Crow status quo. Du Bois, by contrast, urged African Americans to pursue higher education and the white-collar professions and demand social equality. Despite efforts to recuperate the much-maligned Washington as a precursor to the Harlem Renaissance, by and large scholars tend to view the era as a symbolic victory for Du Bois.[30]

The Harlem Renaissance had left a complicated legacy for representations of black foodways in literature and the production of African American cookbooks. Particularly in the early years, priority was often given to creating still more imagery of genteel blacks as a way of countering the *Emperor Jones*–oriented primitivism of contemporaneous white bohemian fascination with black culture. Moreover, had the authors committed to portraying what Du Bois termed the Talented Tenth (such as *Crisis* literary editor Jessie Fauset) depicted characters engaged in the act of eating, the food would probably not have been the down-home "chicken and chitlins" typically associated with the migrating black masses. As it turned out, these authors only rarely portrayed characters eating anything at all because to do so would have been to call attention to their physical embodiment and desires. Characters in the fiction of the black bourgeoisie of the period tend to be passionate about art and ideas, especially racial uplift, rather than about satisfying gastronomic desire. Witness, for example, Joanna Marshall, the protagonist of Fauset's novel *There Is Confusion* (1924). Singularly ambitious, Joanna dreams about achieving success as a theatrical performer. "You'll see!" she tells her boyfriend Peter, himself far less of a striver than Joanna. "They'll have on the billboard, 'Joanna Marshall, the famous artist.'"[31]

Once again, vernacular traditions tend to be a more promising site, as evidenced by Bessie Smith's famous anthem "Gimme a Pigfoot and a Bottle of Beer."[32] But by later in the decade a younger generation of writers such as Langston Hughes and Zora Neale Hurston had rebelled against the perceived dictates of their mentors by incorporating vernacular traditions into their own work. In his controversial *Home to Harlem* (1928), for example, Claude McKay was attuned to the desire of displaced southerners for the foodways of their homes. Of one character in particular McKay writes, "Susy could cook. . . . [S]he belonged to the ancient aristocracy of black cooks, and knew that she was always sure of a good place, so long as the palates of rich Southerners retained their discriminating taste. Cream tomato soup. Ragout of chicken giblets. Southern fried chicken. Candied sweet potatoes. Stewed corn. Rum-flavored fruit salad waiting in the ice-box. . . . The stars rolling in Susy's shining face showed how pleased she was with her art."[33] Whereas passages such as this pay homage to black women's culinary expertise, the entire middle section of the novel is set among black male cooks and dishwashers on a railroad car. *Home to Harlem* might thus be said to continue the "public sector" orientation of cookbooks published by African American men earlier in the century.

In terms of the cookbooks of the era, there were at least two notable developments related to the Washington–Du Bois debate. The first is that cookbooks associated with historically black colleges began to proliferate, including Carrie Alberta Lyford's *A Book of Recipes for the Cooking School*, published at the Hampton Institute in 1921. George Washington Carver's "105 Different Ways to Prepare the Peanut for the Table," a collection of the famous Tuskegee Institute scientist's bulletins, appeared as an appendix to a 1929 biography of Carver by Raleigh H. Merritt.[34]

Of course, both texts could just as properly be associated with the preceding Progressive Era as much as with the 1920s. Thus, what I instead take to be the most significant food text of the Harlem Renaissance (and this reflects the second notable development) was Harlem-based bibliophile Arthur (Arturo) Schomburg's unpublished typescript proposal for a history of African American foodways.[35] Part of what makes Schomburg's proposal so stunning for a contemporary reader is his perception that African American foodways need to be treated as part of a broader diasporic tradition. Far from just focusing on the northern migration of southern blacks, Schomburg's proposal moves from West Africa to the Sea Islands to New Orleans to New York City and elsewhere in a fashion geared toward showing connections among all these varied dietary traditions. In so doing, moreover, he insinuates food into the pan-Africanist politics then associated with Du Bois.

Yet even as Schomburg's proposal anticipates many of the directions taken in more recent years by historians of Africana foodways, George Washington Carver still warrants further study, including by students of American popular culture, because of his international celebrity. I have contemplated pursuing this topic since encountering a poem about Carver by June Jordan. Written in the late 1970s—perhaps not coincidentally during the reign of the peanut-farming southern president Jimmy Carter—"Notes on the Peanut" begins:

> Hi there. My name is George
> Washington
> Carver.
> If you will bear with me
> for a few minutes I
> will share with you
> a few
> of the 30,117 uses to which
> the lowly peanut has been put
> by me
> since yesterday afternoon.
> If you will look at my feet you will notice
> my sensible shoelaces made from unadulterated
> peanut leaf composition that is biodegradable
> in the extreme.
> To your left you can observe the lovely Renoir
> masterpiece reproduction that I have cleverly
> pieced together from several million peanut
> shell chips painted painstakingly so as to
> accurately represent the colors of the original![36]

Notwithstanding the tongue-in-cheek tone that probably reflects a post–black power era willingness to poke fun at Carver's historical status as a "credit to the race," Jordan provides an astute commentary on the ingenuity with which African Americans have survived under oppressive conditions and the absurdity of a society that gave Carver so little choice but to focus on peanuts in the first place. Perhaps not accidentally, Schomburg never mentions Carver's work, but given contemporary debates over the genetic modification of food, Carver's research and celebrity as a food scientist warrant renewed attention.

Realism, Naturalism, Modernism: 1940–1960

This period has more commonly been known among African American literary historians as the "protest era," and until feminist critics intervened discussions had focused mainly on three towering figures: Richard Wright, Ralph Ellison, and James Baldwin. The work of these writers has been thus labeled because it tended to function (in vastly divergent ways) as a corollary to the prevailing sociopolitical development of these decades: the civil rights movement. The period is especially intriguing with respect to the topic of this essay. The types of cookbooks published continued to diversify, and black writers continued delving into issues such as the impact of black migration and class-stratification on black foodways—in part because writers such as Hurston and Hughes helped legitimate the idea that black art should explore all aspects of black life rather than function first and foremost as propaganda against white racism.

At the outset of this period Wright explored the practice of interracial culinary slumming in his novel *Native Son* (1940).[37] Set in Chicago, the narrative includes a scene in which the protagonist, Bigger Thomas, serves as chauffeur for the evening for Mary Dalton, the rebellious daughter of his wealthy white employers, and Jan, her boyfriend, a card-carrying communist. The following notorious exchange takes place while all three are in the car:

> "Say, Bigger," asked Jan, "where can we get a good meal on the South Side?"
> "Well," Bigger said, reflectively.
> "We want to go to a real place," Mary said, turning to him gaily.
> "You want to go to a night club?" Bigger asked in a tone that indicated that he was simply mentioning names and not recommending places to go.
> "No, we want to eat."
> "Look, Bigger. We want one of those places where colored people eat, not one of those show places."[38]

Against Bigger's wishes they eventually end up at Ernie's Chicken Shack. Jan and Mary consider themselves to be demonstrating nonracist credentials through their choice of this eatery, but Wright damns them precisely because of their inability or refusal to understand the situation from Bigger's perspective. He is far more interested in his friends seeing him with the Daltons' expensive car than with Mary Dalton and her boyfriend. Indeed, his experience in the restaurant with them is humiliating.

Even as novelists such as Wright and Ellison were incorporating scenes in their fiction that explored the ways in which race, gender, class, and other boundaries were negotiated through food, African American cookbook writers were beginning to map out some new directions as well. There were continuations of preexisting types of cookbooks. Harry H. Hart's *Favorite Recipes of Williams College, with Training Table Records, Notes, and Menus* (1951), for example, furthers the tradition of black male "public sphere" cookbooks, albeit with the innovation of including height and weight charts for members of various Williams College football teams.[39] As had previous generations of whites, writers such as Edith Ballard Watts published books that exploited the recipes of their cooks. Watts's contribution to this tradition is *Jesse's Book of Creole and Deep South Recipes* (1954).[40] In turn, a private servant published a book featuring her work as a cook for a white family. Rebecca West's persona in *Rebecca's Cookbook* (1942) would strike many contemporary readers as evocative of contemporaneous Hollywood portrayals of black women as mammy cooks. She uses, for example, phonetic spellings and repeatedly refers to her obviously wealthy employer as "my lady." Yet she also mentions the period of life when she "use to go round a lot" (i.e., travel widely) and the resulting columns she wrote for what I take to be a black-owned newspaper, thus undermining efforts on the part of readers to locate her text as a straightforward contribution to the plantation cookbook tradition.[41]

The cookbook from this era that I consider most important, however, is Freda de Knight's *Date with a Dish: A Cook Book of American Negro Recipes* (1948). De Knight was the food columnist for *Ebony* magazine, which had only recently begun publication after World War II. *Date with a Dish* is likely the first nationally advertised and distributed cookbook that attempted to present a synthetic picture of African American foodways. In keeping with *Ebony's* middle-class focus and integrationist outlook, its recipes include a substantial number of dishes that would have been at home in cookbooks directed toward white women of the era (spaghetti with rolled flank steak, for example). De Knight also includes some that many readers would have associated with the legacy of slavery. There are, for instance, two versions of cracklin' bread. A decade later, in 1958, the National Council of Negro Women published its own rendition of such a text, *The Historical Cookbook of the American Negro* (which is also discussed in the final essay of the present volume).[42] In addition to recipes, the book includes sketches of such notable figures from black history as Frederick Douglass.

During the 1990s the NCNW resumed publishing cookbooks, some of which I think are problematic in their deployment of the historically conservative rhetoric of racial uplift.[43] My heart remains with de Knight, in part because in 1962 and 1973 *Ebony* published a revised version of her book under the title *The Ebony Cookbook: A Date with a Dish*. In the process, the editors removed much of the personal narrative that makes the first book such a pleasure to read—including an intriguing narrative persona de Knight called the Little Brown Chef—in a fashion parallel to what Susan Leonardi has demonstrated happened to *The Joy of Cooking* over the years.[44]

The Black Arts Movement: 1960–1970

This is the era on which I focus in *Black Hunger*, although I extend my terminal date to around 1975. By the mid-1960s a younger generation of African American students and activists had grown disillusioned with the southern, largely church-based, civil rights movement. Around 1966, as the rhetoric of "Black and White Together" was left behind and demands for black power intensified, many writers, notably Amiri Baraka, began conceiving of themselves as the cultural vanguard of the emerging black power political movement. It was by no means a homogeneous group, but by the late 1960s the prevailing rhetoric was oriented toward the need to create revolutionary art. In popular culture, meanwhile, "soul" became one of the most celebrated concepts of the era, particularly as immortalized in music. Around 1968—appropriately enough the year when everything else seemed to explode—soul food cookbooks were born.

No one has been able to offer a definitive narrative of origins for the rubric "soul food," although its link to "soul music" has been often stated. It began being popularized in the early 1960s among northern-based writer-activists such as Baraka, who wanted to challenge the notion that black people had developed no viable cultural traditions under slavery. In a 1962 essay, "Soul Food," he waxed euphoric about food he associated with the diet of southern blacks—everything from fried chicken and porgies to grits and greens—and recommended places where readers could go "for a good grease" when away from home.[45]

As the decade evolved, however, debates over soul food quickly emerged. Writing from prison in 1965, future Black Panther Eldridge Cleaver dismissed soul food as "counterrevolutionary black bourgeois ideology." He insisted that "eating chitterlings is like going slumming," thus focusing attention on what soon became, at least for the popular press, the most fetishized of soul foods.[46] Nation of Islam leader Elijah Muhammad, who had influenced Cleaver, was simultaneously expanding his efforts to condemn the consumption of pork and other food associated with soul and did so through two *How to Eat to Live* dietary manuals published in 1967 and 1972.[47]

Muhammad's belief in the health dangers of pork seems sincere—and his critique of the mass-food industry is largely admirable—but his obsession with black dietary practices was also connected to his efforts to proselytize against the black Christian church. Oriented toward nationalism rather than integration, Muhammad found black Christianity's role in the civil rights movement objectionable. Oriented toward patriarchy, he feared that "church sisters" were using their culinary expertise to turn unsuspecting black men into biscuit-craving mamas' boys who were rendered too complacent by a belly full of soul food to fight for their rights as men.[48]

By the early 1970s the comedian and activist Dick Gregory had also joined the ranks of dissenters. Although his political views varied considerably from Muhammad's, he, too, began to view the rise of soul food as an unhealthful practice of racial genocide. Slaves, he insisted, had eaten not soul food but "soil food," which included fresh, organic garden fruit and vegetables and mostly dairy-free grains. Eventually, Gregory began promoting a fruitarian diet, particularly by means of a book subtitled *Cookin' with Mother Nature* (1973).[49] Meanwhile, Vertamae Grosvenor, a native of South Carolina who has become well known because of her work on National Public Radio and the Public Broadcasting Service, also advanced a critique. Although she was more willing to use the label *soul food* than she has since wanted to admit, Grosvenor called her 1970 cookbook-travelog-memoir *Vibration Cooking; or, The Travel Notes of a Geechee Girl,* in part as a way of distancing herself from what she believed was the popular understanding of soul food as "massa's leftovers." It was an understanding that not coincidentally tended to reify black women in the stereotypical role of the mammy cook.[50]

Whereas "soul" was thought to refer to the black past, Grosvenor presented "vibration" as being avant-garde. The term itself likely resulted from her experience as a "space chantress" with the iconoclastic jazz musician Sun Ra. Grosvenor worked in the tradition of Schomburg by foregrounding connections between black American dietary practices and the foodways of people of the African diaspora around the world. *Vibration Cooking* is also significant as the first African American cookbook I know of that transgresses generic boundaries by situating its recipes in a full-fledged narrative. At the same time, Grosvenor was still only one among many black women of the era who used cookbooks to create a counterdiscourse to black power's notorious masculinism by celebrating black mother-daughter traditions, demonstrating the historical resilience of black communal life, and insisting that black women's cooking is itself an art.

Before turning to the final period I should mention chef Edna Lewis, who also distanced herself from the concept of soul food by referring to it in a *Southern Living* interview as "hard-times food in Harlem—not true southern food."[51] A worthy subject of culinary inquiry would be the ramifications of Lewis's decision in the bicentennial year of 1976 to publish a cookbook that adopted the term *country* rather than *soul: The Taste of Country Cooking*.[52] Two years earlier the Pulitzer Prize–winning writer James Alan McPherson had published a now-famous short story entitled "Why I Like Country Music."[53] The joke of the story was that its narrator was black. It was a joke that would have been abundantly clear at the time to anyone who knew the difficulty faced by a black country singer such as Charlie Pride in gaining acceptance for his music. Using these parallels with the music industry as a framework, one might explore the ways in which "country" has functioned since the 1960s as a discourse of "white soul," thus posing challenges for writers such as Lewis who have attempted to reappropriate the label for black culinary history.

Literature since 1970

Inasmuch as the editors of *The Norton Anthology* were unwilling to commit themselves to a specific rubric for the contemporary past, I am hesitant to do so myself. Had I to make a choice, though, I would probably opt for something like "Blackness in a Post-Ethnic Era" or "Blackness and the Global Marketplace." By the mid-1970s the black power movement had largely eroded, being undermined by internal shortcomings as well as outside forces such as the F.B.I. The 1980s witnessed increasing bifurcation between the black middle and working classes; by the late 1980s and early 1990s the mass market was rediscovering black inner-city youth culture. Films ranging from Spike Lee's *Do the Right Thing* (1989) to John Singleton's *Boyz N the Hood* (1991) reflected urban discontent yet lured affluent viewers eager for a safe, virtual-reality version of slumming. By the late 1990s, though, as the effects of a booming economy somewhat blunted the continuing reality of the vast racialized disparities in wealth distribution in the United States and around the world, Hollywood began to pay more attention to the black middle classes, as evidenced by the movie *Soul Food*. Similarly, the inauguration in 1999 of a new magazine, *The Black Issues Book Review*, was surely a function of the growing upscale market niche occupied by black writers and readers.

Not surprisingly, the numbers of cookbooks published by African Americans each year since 1970 also increased, particularly in the 1990s. The decades since the 1970s have given rise to a wide range of cookbooks, whether smaller community cookbooks or the mass-marketed ones on which I focus because of my interest in popular culture. There are soul food cookbooks, raw foods and vegetarian cookbooks, barbecue cookbooks, hog cookbooks, how-not-to-eat-hog cookbooks, Kwanzaa cookbooks, family reunion cookbooks, Afro-Atlantic cookbooks, Muslim cookbooks, dessert cookbooks, entertaining cookbooks, uptown cookbooks, down-home cookbooks, Sea Island cookbooks, Creole cookbooks, jazz cookbooks, and zydeco cookbooks.[54] There are cookbooks by famous individuals—from Pearl Bailey and Mahalia Jackson to Bobby Seale and George Foreman.[55] There are cookbooks to accompany many well-known black-owned restaurants, including Dooky Chase in New Orleans, Sylvia's in Harlem, and Mama Dip's in Chapel Hill.[56] Nearly all the cookbooks include some sort of information in addition to recipes, the twenty-seven-page autobiographical essay at the outset of *Mama Dip's Kitchen* (1999) being typical. The novelist Dori Sanders has offered *Dori Sanders' Country Cooking* (1995), and Ntozake Shange is the author of a full-fledged version of a cookbook-memoir, *If I Can Cook, You Know God Can* (1998).[57]

As has been the case with my discussions of earlier historical periods, it is impossible here to delineate in adequate detail the complex social circumstances from which these books have arisen. I can, however, note that their heterogeneity reflects the challenges inherent in efforts to articulate the meaning of blackness in the so-called global era. One of the most noticeable trends that these cookbooks document—the recuperation of southern foodways among African Americans—might be seen as an outgrowth of the widely discussed reverse migration of blacks to the South since the 1990s. At the same time, the related revival of interest in regional and subethnic foods stemming from Gullah and Creole traditions critiques homogenizing conceptions of blackness and responds to concerns about the loss of unique cultural traditions under the pervasive pressure of the mass culture industries.

Another trend evident in the cookbooks, interest in the food of diverse cultures, as exemplified in the work of Vertamae Grosvenor and Ntozake Shange, has been fueled at least in part by the rise of culinary tourism, whether in virtual form via the Food Channel or as a result of the black middle class's increasing ability to travel widely. Such cookbooks are, paradoxically, both complicit with and resistant to the global traffic in the iconography of ethnic multiplicity that Paul Gilroy, among others, has identified as a distinguishing and problematic feature of the late-capitalist marketplace.[58]

Similar tensions or contradictions in the construction of African American identity via culinary practices can be found in the simultaneous "McDonaldization" of African American youth (as fast-food employees and consumers) and the proliferation of ethnic-themed restaurants geared toward the public performance of blackness.[59] On the one hand, the fast-food industry, like the fashion and film industries, has worked hard to associate its products with the trappings of black urban youth culture. On the other hand, many black urban professionals have, by contrast, been able to affirm that economic success is compatible with continued identification with African, African diasporic, and African American culture by patronizing black restaurants ranging from, say, the upscale Georgia Brown's in Washington, D.C., to the more casual Africa Hut in Milwaukee.

In her best-selling novel *Brothers and Sisters*, Bebe Moore Campbell takes notice of the latter trend by going out of her way to portray the importance of down-home comfort food for her protagonist Esther Jackson, who is a successful Los Angeles banker. Memorably, when visiting Washington, D.C., Esther instructs her former college girlfriends, "'I must go to the Grille and have my fried chicken and greens and world famous biscuits. And following that, I must go over to Georgia Avenue and have a drink or two at Traces.'"[60]

At the same time, Campbell's portrayal of Esther's careful attention to diet and exercise elsewhere in the novel registers what is perhaps the most significant trend in African American cookbooks published since 1970: concern with healthful eating and weight loss. Many of these cookbooks specifically target black audiences, for instance, by promoting low-fat versions of soul food. Presumably, low-carbohydrate versions will not be far behind. But fixation on health and body image is by no means unique to African American culture. Discussion of the rapidly rising rates of obesity around the world is widespread, as is the concomitant growth of the weight-loss industry.

One of the more intriguing developments for those who follow black culinary practices has been the advent of lawsuits against the fast-food industry by consumers who claim to have been misled by false advertising. Plaintiffs argue, in other words, that when consumption of fast food results in obesity the fast-food industry can be held legally culpable. Appropriately enough given the long-standing efforts of chains such as McDonalds and KFC to target minority consumers, a black man was the lead plaintiff in one of the most high-profile of the suits.[61] Although the lawsuits probably have little chance of surviving the wave of legislation intended to insulate the fast-food industry from the sort of court battles that have battered the tobacco industry, one cannot help but wonder about the impact that a plaintiff's race might have on a lawsuit's chance of success.

The range of African American cookbooks now published reflects the multiplicity of African American culture, including the inadequacy of a still-common tendency to equate black culinary traditions with soul food, however broadly that term is construed. Accordingly, in keeping with my roots as a literary critic I conclude by looking briefly at a passage from a contemporary novel by an African American writer that has much to say about the continuing importance of food stereotypes that many ethnic cookbook writers have been working hard to banish. The passage is taken from Gayl Jones's vast, sprawling, and brilliant *Mosquito*.

The narrator of *Mosquito* is Sojourner Nadine Jane "Mosquito" Johnson, an African American truck driver in the Southwest who finds herself involved, accidentally, in "the new underground railroad"—the sanctuary movement for Mexican immigrants. Cross-cultural food exchange is a recurring theme in the narrative. Jones attempts to understand how ethnic boundaries among people of color in the Americas are being renegotiated through culinary border crossings. Early in the novel, Mosquito shares a meal with her Chicana friend Delgadina, which leads her to meditate on the power of culinary stereotypes: "We nibbles on them omelet sandwiches. Mexican omelets with onions, green peppers, pimentos and jalapenos. Them jalapenos little too hot for me, though, but I figure she likes them jalapenos being Mexican. I ain't mean to stereotype her, though. Delgadina she be telling me they's some agringado Mexicans likes jalapenos but don't eat them because they thinks they be stereotyping themselves, like African Americans that don't eat watermelon, and they don't eat them tacos neither. They likes tacos but don't eat them."[62]

Delgadina encourages Mosquito to distinguish, however, between stereotypes that "vulgariz[e]" another culture and those derived from "reality." Mosquito agrees, noting that "when people be running from them stereotypes based on some kinda reality a lot of times they be running from they own culture, they be running from theyselves."[63] For example, she thinks, black women in America have been called "Aunt Jemima" for wearing headscarves despite the fact that headscarves have been commonly worn by black women in Africa. Rather than dismissing out of hand the culinary stereotypes associated with African American culture—here Aunt Jemima, watermelon, and "chit'lins"—Jones thus encourages readers to try to understand why these stereotypes emerged in the first place and what makes them so charged.

As the conversation continues, Delgadina and Mosquito consider how practices of cross-cultural culinary patronage have structured the relationship between African Americans and Mexican Americans:

> Delgadina says she knows this Mexican American who likes African-American culture, or what he considers African-American culture—jazz and soul food and calls himself a Chitlins con Carne Mexican. And what about a African American that likes Mexican food? That truckstop restaurant specializes in them omelet sandwiches and got one of them salad-type bars with different omelet ingredients. You can even put them chickpeas in your omelets and they even got them fruit omelets. So I guess whatever your culture, you can make you one of them omelets. Ain't got no watermelon omelet, though. Delgadina she allergic to them jalapenos, but she eat them anyway. Cause they's her culture, I guess.[64]

As the nonexistent watermelon omelet might be taken to suggest, *Mosquito* is by no means a novel that offers a simplistic fantasy of multiculturalism as the solution to structural forms of inequality. Jones views food as a domain through which cultural differences can be explored, but she does not pretend that adventurous taste buds alone are the route to social justice. Food can, however, play a role—as a source of pleasure and a site of struggle—and that is why students of African American literature and culture should pay as much attention to food as to music. If I ever *do* write that book on food thematics in contemporary African American women's writing, the title of one chapter will have to be not "Chitlins con Carne" but rather "Omelets con Watermelon."

NOTES

I am grateful to an anonymous reader for pointing out errors of fact in an earlier version of this essay and also for making valuable suggestions about issues that I needed to address, particularly in the final segment on the contemporary era.

1. Houston Baker, *Blues, Ideology, and Afro-American Literature: A Vernacular Theory* (Chicago: University of Chicago Press, 1984); Henry Louis Gates, *The Signifying Monkey: A Theory of African-American Literary Criticism* (New York: Oxford University Press, 1988). I discuss my reasons for viewing these paradigms as male-centered in *Black Hunger: Soul Food and America* (Minneapolis: University of Minnesota Press, 2004), 9–10.

2. Ntozake Shange, *Sassafrass, Cypress and Indigo* (New York: St. Martin's Press, 1982).

3. In my immediate family, by contrast, we ate mostly the standard white, middlebrow food fare of the era such as Hamburger Helper, spaghetti, tuna casserole, meatloaf, and grilled cheese sandwiches.

4. In *Black Hunger*, I include an appendix on African American cookbooks that contains a brief introductory essay and a chronological listing of almost three hundred books.

5. Henry Louis Gates Jr. and Nellie Y. McKay, eds., *The Norton Anthology of African American Literature* (New York: W. W. Norton, 1997).

6. Gates and McKay, eds., *The Norton Anthology*, 38.

7. Jeffrey Pilcher, *¡Que Vivan Los Tamales! Food and the Making of Mexican Identity* (Albuquerque: University of New Mexico Press, 1999).

8. The Armstrong song is collected in Thomas L. Morgan and William Barlow, *From Cakewalks to Concert Halls: An Illustrated History of African American Popular Music from 1895–1930* (Washington: Elliott and Clark, 1992), 109. Morgan is the disk jockey to whom I refer.

9. Kool Keith, *Black Elvis/Lost in Space*, Columbia-Ruffhouse, 1999, BOOOOOJWG7.

10. Jon Pareles, "An Obsession with Space, Sex and Fried Chicken," *New York Times*, Sept. 4, 1999, A20.

11. Octavia Butler, *Dawn* (New York: Warner Books, 1987). Psyche Williams-Forson's *Building Houses Out of Chicken Legs: Black Women, Food and Power* (Chapel Hill: University of North Carolina Press, 2006) provides rich insight into the material and symbolic functions of chicken among African Americans.

12. For valuable work on the role of food within the black Christian church see Williams-Forson, *Building Houses Out of Chicken Legs* and Jualynne E. Dodson and Cheryl Townsend Gilkes, "There's Nothing Like Church Food: Food and the U.S. Afro-Christian Tradition: Re-Membering Community and Feeding the Embodied S/spirit(s)," *Journal of the American Academy of Religion* 63, no. 3 (1995): 519–39.

13. Anne Bower, ed., *Recipes for Reading: Community Cookbooks, Stories, Histories* (Amherst: University of Massachusetts Press, 1997). This collection takes its title from Susan J. Leonardi's essay "Recipes for Reading: Summer Pasta, Lobster à La Riseholme, and Key Lime Pie," *PMLA* 104, no. 3 (1989): 340–47.

14. Robert Roberts, *The House Servant's Directory; or, A Monitor for Private Families: Comprising Hints on the Arrangement and Performance of Servants' Work . . . and Upwards of One Hundred Various and Useful Receipts, Chiefly Compiled for the Use of House Servants* (1827, repr. Bedford, Mass.: Applewood Books, 1995); Tunis G. Campbell, *Hotel Keepers, Head Waiters, and Housekeepers' Guide* (1848, repr. as *Never Let People Be Kept Waiting: A Textbook on Hotel Management* [Raleigh, N.C.: Graphic, 1973]). The reprinted version of Roberts's book includes an introduction by Charles A. Hammond.

15. Those who wish to learn more about Campbell's political career should consult Robert Duncan, *Freedom's Shore: Tunis Campbell and the Georgia Freedmen* (Athens: University of Georgia Press, 1986). Robert Roberts seems to have passed his leadership skills along to his children. His son became a printer for the abolitionist movement in the 1840s and 1850s, and his daughter was the plaintiff in a desegregation case in Boston in the 1850s.

16. Rafia Zafar, "And Called It Macaroni," manuscript in progress. Similarly, in *We Are What We Eat: Ethnic Food and the Making of Americans* (Cambridge: Harvard University Press, 1998), Donna Gabbacia approaches African American foodways as one component of a more encompassing U.S. culinary history shaped by the dynamics of colonialism, immigration, urbanization, and consumer capitalism.

17. I have written about the impact of globalization on scholarship about transnational feminism and food studies in "Globalization and Food: A Review Essay," *Meridians* 1, no. 2 (2001): 73–93.

18. Robyn Wiegman, *American Anatomies: Theorizing Race and Gender* (Durham: Duke University Press, 1995); David Palumbo-Liu, *The Ethnic Canon: Histories, Institutions, and Interventions* (Minneapolis: University of Minnesota Press, 1995).

19. Sidney Mintz, *Sweetness and Power: The Place of Sugar in Modern History* (New York: Penguin, 1985).

20. In order to highlight large trends I am, of necessity, offering broad generalizations that do not do justice to the complexity of literary output during this period. A more nuanced approach is found in such classics as Hazel Carby, *Reconstructing Womanhood: The Emergence of the Afro-American Woman Novelist* (New York: Oxford University Press, 1987), and Claudia Tate, *Domestic Allegories of Political Desire: The Black Heroine's Text at the Turn of the Century* (New York: Oxford University Press, 1992).

21. I discuss plantation-school cookbooks in chapter 1 of *Black Hunger*.

22. Abby Fisher, *What Mrs. Fisher Knows about Old Southern Cooking, Soups, Pickles, Preserves, etc.* (1881, repr. [edited by Karen L. Hess] Bedford, Mass.: Applewood Books, 1995), 81. The book is marketed as the "first" African American cookbook, although more recent scholarship by Jan Longone has shown that Malinda Russell's *A Domestic Cook Book: Containing a Careful Selection of Useful Receipts for the Kitchen* (Paw Paw, Mich.: Published for the author by T. G. Ward, 1866) was published earlier than Fisher's book. Hess, in an editorial afterword, speculates about Fisher's means of reaching California (77–78).

23. Fisher, *What Mrs. Fisher Knows*, 81.

24. Bertha Turner, comp., *The Federation Cookbook: A Collection of Tested Recipes, Contributed by the Colored Women of the State of California* (Pasadena: n.p., 1910).

25. H. Franklyn Hall, *Three Hundred Ways to Cook and Serve Shell Fish: Terrapin, Green Turtle, Snapper, Oysters, Oyster Crabs, Lobsters, Clams, Crabs and Shrimps* (Philadelphia: Christian Banner, 1901); Rufus Estes, *Good Things to Eat, as Suggested by Rufus: A Collection of Practical Recipes for Preparing Meats, Game, Fowl, Fish, Puddings, Pastries, Etc.* (1911, repr. Mineola, N.Y.: Dover Publications, 2004); S. Thomas Bivins, *The Southern Cookbook: A Manual of Cooking and List of Menus, Including Recipes Used by Noted Colored Cooks and Prominent Caterers* (Hampton, Va.: Press of the Hampton Institute, 1912).

26. Mrs. W. T. Hayes, *Kentucky Cook Book: Easy and Simple for Any Cook, by a Colored Woman* (St. Louis: Tompkins, 1912).

27. Laura Shapiro, *Perfection Salad: Women and Cooking at the Turn of the Century* (New York: Farrar, 1986); Harvey Levenstein, *Revolution at the Table: The Transformation of the American Diet* (New York: Oxford University Press, 1988).

28. I discuss this issue at length in chapter 3 of *Black Hunger*.

29. Washington made this comment during a speech at the Atlanta Exposition in 1895. He quotes from the speech in his 1901 autobiography *Up from Slavery*, reprinted in *Three Negro Classics* (New York: Avon, 1965), 146–50.

30. See, most notably, Houston Baker, *Modernism and the Harlem Renaissance* for an effort to situate Washington as a forefather of black modernism (Chicago: University of Chicago Press, 1987). In *When Harlem Was in Vogue* (New York: Oxford University Press, 1981) David Levering Lewis offers the more common interpretation of how the Du Bois–Washington debate played out in Harlem Renaissance cultural politics.

31. Jessie Fauset, *There Is Confusion* (Boston: Northeastern University Press, 1989), 45. Furthermore, Joanna's father Joel is proudly described by his mother as "a great caterer, feedin' bank presidents and everything" (9), but Joel is said to be disappointed in his profession because his idea of greatness "had been that which gets one before the public eye, which makes one a leader of causes, a 'man among men'" (10).

32. Bessie Smith, "Gimme a Pigfoot," *Bessie Smith: The Collection*, New York: CBS/Columbia, 1989.

33. Claude McKay, *Home to Harlem* (Boston: Northeastern University Press, 1987), 77–78.

34. Carrie Alberta Lyford, *A Book of Recipes for the Cooking School* (Hampton, Va.: Hampton Normal and Agricultural Institute, 1921); George Washington Carver, "105 Different Ways to Prepare the Peanut for the Table," rpr. as appendix to Raleigh H. Merritt, *From Captivity to Fame; or, The Life of George Washington Carver*, 2d ed. (Boston: Meador, 1938), 133–230.

35. Arthur A. Schomburg, untitled typescript (proposal for a history of African American cooking), ca. 1920s, Arthur A. Schomburg Papers, Activities, and Writings, folder 7, box 12, SC micro 2798, reel 7, New York Public Library Schomburg Center for Research in Black Culture.

36. June Jordan, "Notes on the Peanut," in *Passion: New Poems, 1977–1980* (Boston: Beacon Press, 1980), 44.

37. Richard Wright, *Native Son* (New York: HarperPerennial, 1993). It is, admittedly, counterintuitive to cite *Native Son* in this context because in some other ways the novel lacks a nuanced representation of black communal life. For a fascinating study of food thematics in the work of Wright, Zora Neale Hurston, and Toni Morrison, see Andrew Warnes, *Hunger Overcome: Food and Resistance in Twentieth-Century African American Literature* (Athens: University of Georgia Press, 2004).

38. Wright, *Native Son*, 78.

39. Harry H. Hart Sr., *Favorite Recipes of Williams College, with Training Table Records, Notes and Menus* (Williamstown, Mass.: Author, 1951).

40. Edith Ballard Watts, with John Watts, *Jesse's Book of Creole and Deep South Recipes* (New York: Weathervane, 1954).

41. Rebecca West, *Rebecca's Cookbook* (Washington, D.C.: n.p., 1942), 5, 3.

42. Freda de Knight, *Date with a Dish: A Cook Book of American Negro Recipes* (New York: Hermitage Press, 1948); National Council of Negro Women, *The Historical Cookbook of the American Negro*, edited by Sue Bailey Thurman (1958, repr. edited by Anne Bower [Boston: Beacon Press, 2000]).

43. Kevin K. Gaines, *Uplifting the Race: Black Leadership, Politics, and Culture in*

the Twentieth Century (Chapel Hill: University of North Carolina Press, 1996) contains an extended discussion of the problems associated with African American ideologies of racial uplift.

44. Leonardi, "Recipes for Reading."

45. Amiri Baraka (LeRoi Jones), "Soul Food," in *Home: Social Essays* (New York: Morrow, 1966), 101–4.

46. Eldridge Cleaver, *Soul on Ice* (New York: Laurel-Dell, 1992), 40.

47. Elijah Muhammad, *How to Eat to Live* (Chicago: Muhammad Mosque of Islam No. 2, 1967); Elijah Muhammad, *How to Eat to Live, Book No. 2* (Chicago: Muhammad's Temple of Islam No. 2, 1972).

48. Witt, *Black Hunger*, ch. 4, contains an extended discussion of Elijah Muhammad, including his attitude toward black Christian women. My thanks to an anonymous reader for pointing out that Muhammad's dietary prescriptions have much in common with those promoted by the famed dietary reformer Sylvester Graham.

49. Dick Gregory, *Dick Gregory's Natural Diet for Folks Who Eat: Cookin' with Mother Nature*, edited by James R. McGraw, with Alvenia M. Fulton (New York: Perennial-Harper, 1974); see also Witt, *Black Hunger*, ch. 5.

50. Vertamae [Grosvenor], *Vibration Cooking; or, The Travel Notes of a Geechee Girl* (Garden City: Doubleday, 1970). Subsequent editions of *Vibration Cooking* were issued in 1986 and 1992. See also Witt, *Black Hunger*, ch. 6.

51. Denise Gee, "The Gospel of Great Southern Food," *Southern Living* 31 (June 1996): 128.

52. Edna Lewis, *The Taste of Country Cooking* (New York: Borzoi-Knopf, 1977).

53. The story is reprinted in McPherson's short story collection *Elbow Room* (New York: Fawcett Crest, 1979), 9–31.

54. For specific citations for these general references see Witt, *Black Hunger*, 223–28. The widow of co-bibliographer David Lupton donated his extensive collection of African American cookbooks to the University of Alabama. The collection contains many hard-to-find community cookbooks not listed in *Black Hunger*.

55. Pearl Bailey, *Pearl's Kitchen: An Extraordinary Cookbook* (New York: Harcourt, 1973); Mahalia Jackson, *Mahalia Jackson Cooks Soul* (Nashville: Aurora, 1970); Bobby Seale, *Barbeque'n with Bobby: Righteous, Down-Home Barbeque Recipes* (Berkeley: Ten Speed, 1988); George Foreman and Cherrie Calbom, *George Foreman's Knock-Out-the-Fat Barbeque and Grilling Cookbook* (New York: Villard-Random, 1996).

56. Leah Chase, *The Dooky Chase Cookbook* (Gretna, La.: Pelican, 1990); Sylvia Woods and Christopher Styler, *Sylvia's Soul Food: Recipes from Harlem's World-Famous Restaurant* (New York: Hearst-Morrow, 1992); Mildred Council, *Mama Dip's Kitchen* (Chapel Hill: University of North Carolina Press, 1999).

57. Dori Sanders, *Dori Sanders' Country Cooking: Recipes and Stories from the Family Farm Stand* (Chapel Hill: Algonquin Books, 1995); Ntozake Shange, *If I Can Cook, You Know God Can* (Boston: Beacon Press, 1998).

58. Paul Gilroy, *Against Race: Imagining Political Culture Beyond the Color Line* (Cambridge: Harvard University Press, 2000).

59. George Ritzer has explicated the concept of "McDonaldization" as "'the process by which the principles of the fast-food restaurant are coming to dominate more and more sectors of American society as well as of the rest of the world.'" Ritzer, *The McDon-*

aldization of Society: An Investigation into the Changing Character of Contemporary Social Life (Thousand Oaks, Calif.: Pine Forge Press, 2000), 1.

60. Bebe Moore Campbell, *Brothers and Sisters* (New York: Putnam, 1994), 337.

61. For information about the lawsuit filed by Bronx resident Caesar Barbar, see, for example, "Fat Americans Sue Fast Food Firms," BBC News, World, Americas, July 25, 2002, at http://news.bbc.co.uk/1/h:/world/americas/2151754.stm.

62. Gayl Jones, *Mosquito* (Boston: Beacon Press, 1999), 44.

63. Jones, *Mosquito*, 44.

64. Ibid., 44–45.

5

Chickens and Chains: Using African American Foodways to Understand Black Identities

Psyche Williams-Forson

Shackles on my feet, won't let me dance,
Shackles on my feet won't let me stand,
Turn up the music that has a nice beat,
Turn it up loud and take these shackles off my feet.
—R.J.'s Latest Arrival, 1984

Back in those days, coming from every part of the country . . . from Southern places and things, it wasn't nothing to see mockery. Black folks was always mocked. You know you would see "Little Daisy and Sambo" on the lawn with the water bucket. Those days, we went on to work. Now, I would be upset if somebody call [*sic*] me a Coon.
—Roy Hawkins, former waiter, Coon Chicken Inn

In his film *Black Is, Black Ain't,* which was completed after his death, the award-winning filmmaker Marlon Riggs calls into question black people's definitions of identity.[1] Using his grandmother's gumbo as a metaphor, he challenges the perception that "black" is a monolithic concept.[2] He furthers his challenge by exposing the diverse and complex identities among black people of all age groups. In one segment of the documentary, for example, a conversation takes place at the Youth Achievement Center in Los Angeles between a young black woman and two young black men. She desperately tries to convince her male counterparts that in order to better understand who they are in American society (and the world) they need a sense of their history. "History is more than chains on your ankle," she implores, "and knowing this black leader and knowing that black leader. There is much more to history than that. I mean, the thing with black people is, if you are going to be black, you don't want to know your black history? You wanna forget about your black history?"

The memory of this scene has lingered with me through countless viewings of the documentary for class preparations, and it returns when I see students' blank reactions to discussions of African American historical and contemporary issues. That impassiveness is particularly acute in classes in which I teach the topic of food and food culture. In general, people tend to rely upon very narrow versions of group identity when food is the topic of conversation. But food and the meanings assigned to it, whether cognitive, oral, or visual, also have an infinitely greater value—the ability to reveal embedded associations that deeply affect individual and group identities. In this way, food can serve as a locus of oppression and liberation. For many African Americans, chicken—whether fried, baked, or broiled or appearing in literature or on film—is one such object. Building on Riggs's gumbo metaphor, this essay offers an analysis of African American associations with chicken to further illustrate the variations of black identity and build an appreciation for the level of analysis that food studies can offer.

Foods are cultural products that invoke a range of individual and collective memories. They reveal cultural traditions and culturally transmitted values that govern societies far and wide. Food events, with specific delicacies, have tremendous power to define social organization as well as cultural and social identities. For this and other reasons then, food is particularly evocative for the study of memory, politics, and identity. In seeking to detail how a food such as chicken has sometimes had a central yet complex role in African American lives, an interdisciplinary perspective is recommended. For the larger study from which this work derives I drew upon material and visual culture studies and literary theory, history, black women's studies, popular culture, and personal narratives. Visual and material culture (postcards, advertisements, greeting cards, photographs, and sheet music), literature, oral history, and stand-up comedy, among other genres, were explored. The broad examination allows disclosure of the myriad ways in which black people, using chicken as one object of choice, come to realizations about themselves and the world.[3]

The historical relationship between chicken and black people was one of the many linchpins of white racist propaganda that claimed black inferiority. A culture of avoidance has surrounded a study of that relationship, which has been deemed either insignificant or unimportant. Most likely, the discomfort that racial stereotyping of the past causes has kept researchers from discussing the topic. I have found few articles on the topic even though popular culture of the last century is full of food imagery that appears in photographs, literature, sheet music, post cards, and advertisements.

All in all, the imagery, whether of African American men, women, or children in compromising positions with chickens, is perversely overwhelming. During the not-so-distant past these images helped create stereotypes about African Americans, and the stereotypes endure and continue to shape public opinion. As Stephanie Moser has written, "The visual mode of communication . . . becomes key in the production of meanings about our past, present, and future."[4] Consequently, it is necessary that such images be considered for the power inherent in them and, by association, their ability to yield tangible effects.

A Look Back . . .

Zip Coon or "the Dandy" (no matter what name he might be given in a particular artifact) was a popular stereotype—an overzealous, "dandified" black man (figure 1). He was described as being fashionably dressed with the intention of trying to make himself better than other blacks. He was the white man's competitor. Much as he tried, however, he could never achieve that status because he was a buffoon, "a stumbling and stuttering idiot." He was lazy, unreliable, and an all-around piece of work.[5] The name *coon* implied his tendency to steal chickens and other animals—just like a raccoon. It was a supercilious image that portrayed blacks in the worst ways imaginable. Even black male children were subjected to ridicule (figure 2).

Portrayals relied heavily upon a series of signifiers, signifieds, and linguistic messages to convey slanderous ideologies as natural. They also reaffirmed the notion of blacks as being on the bottom of the social ladder at a time when war, Reconstruction, and immigration put the concept of national identity in question. Meanwhile, technological advances in printing and distribution at the turn of the twentieth century helped fuel the spread of various forms of popular and mass culture, contributing to a network of the mainstream culture's power. Although the association of black people with chicken began long before the post–Civil War era, it is particularly important to the Reconstruction era for its political and economic implications.[6]

Figure 1. Sheet music for Ashley Ballou's "Chicken Charlie," 1905. Author's collection.

With the ending of the Civil War came freedom for most African Americans, many of whom began the long journey to other states and regions. People were galvanized; some moved westward in search of new beginnings, whereas the majority began to migrate to the North. Inasmuch as there was already a steady but small presence of African American people in the western region

Right here's where I'se
SORELY TEMPTED

Figure 2. Postcard, no date.
Author's collection.

during the mid-nineteenth century, racially based economic and political disparities were in place similar to those of other locales. Reconstruction's steady
stream of industrial advancements did little to diminish the anti-black senti-
ments in existence throughout much of the United States. In fact, in some
instances Emancipation fueled these emotions. Chicken, which black men
had been frequently accused of stealing, was handy in that it could be used as
a social, political, and emotional weapon and was a prime object for waging
ideological warfare.

White racial and class animus resulted in hatred directed specifically toward black men, and the image of Zip Coon made a mockery out of those who
had any kind of aspirations, whether economic, political, social, or cultural. As
Eric Lott explains, "The black dandy literally embodied the amalgamationist
threat of abolitionism, and allegorically represented the class threat of those
who were advocating it; amalgamation itself, we might even say, was a partial
figuration of class aspiration."[7] These types of images (and perceptions) speak

Figure 3. Postcard, 1902. Author's collection.

to how power can be present in even the most mundane objects. Chickens were certainly not the sole source of grist for the stereotype mill, but in using a food object to project cultural stereotypes whites were able to capitalize on a truth: Black people raised, ate, and sometimes stole chickens. Through advertising trade cards, sheet music, children's books, cartoons, and postcards, the stereotype became a pervasive means of describing African American people and their association with a food only marginally part of their cuisine.[8]

Chickens are considered to be low on the evolutionary food chain and also one of the cockiest of animals. This is not insignificant considering the metaphorical associations. In "Deep Play: Notes on the Balinese Cockfight," Clifford Geertz says the word *cock* is also used to mean "hero" or "dandy," both of which suggest the cock as a symbol of virility.[9] Cocks were considered to be sexually potent and virile, and chicken keepers were viewed as people of importance. Figure 3 illustrates the distortions that led to cocks (i.e., any kind of bird or fowl) being seen as potentially symbolizing both the sexual prowess and confidence of black men.

Self-assured black men caused anxiety among the white men of the South because their self-confidence suggested a capacity to rise above the station permitted them by white society. To overcome such psychological intimidation it was necessary to reduce black men to a stereotype. Visual emasculation enabled white society to see black men—and, by extension, black people—as slaves rather than rivals. The happy-go-lucky image was needed to reassure northerners that the South was "in control," a viewpoint bolstered by illustrations of black men stealing chickens. Black people thus became the butt of jokes that offered comic relief to white America. Despite these assaults on their image and being, however, and despite less-than-favorable material conditions, what was paramount for black people was progress—familial, social, economic, and political.

My intention in this essay is to illustrate the inherent power of objects to manipulate and to be manipulated and point out the "heterogeneous" and pervasive nature of power, its elusiveness, and its ability to be present in such ordinary objects as food.[10] The images on which I focus suggest that food serves more than its intended function to nourish and satiate. Material culture objects such as food have the power to evoke a series of interpretations, meanings, and misinterpretations. As Ian Hodder suggests, "Most material symbols do not work through rules of representation, using a language-like syntax. Rather, they work through the evocation of sets of practices within individual experience[;] . . . they come to have abstract meaning through association and practice."[11] In this instance the meanings are complex, and social and historical contexts fuel the representations. Chicken does not "mean" at any straightforward level, nor does it have the symbolic representation it is supposed to have, that of a food source. Instead, chicken can be considered to be embedded in a pattern of power and domination that has come to mean, among other things, predatory and slothful behavior by black men.

Many caricatures and images have helped to shape the most basic ideologies and worldviews about race. Black people had been freed, which in many white people aroused deep-seated fears of black political and economic advancement. Even though twentieth-century caricatures of Mammy, Sambo, Zip Coon, Jezebel, and the Pickininny were consistently used in popular and mass culture to reinforce the idea of African Americans as inferior and deviant, many African American people saw themselves very differently and persevered despite the negative images. One example is a man named Roy Hawkins, who served as the headwaiter at a restaurant that was part of a then-well-known chain of establishments named the Coon Chicken Inn. Diners entered the restaurants through a doorway surrounded by thick, red, open lips—a grinning black man's face (a "coon head") topped with a tilted cap.

Hawkins was one of the African Americans who migrated to the West during World War II. Many of these migrants came as soldiers or porters, and some, like Hawkins, found employment in the service industry at establish-ments like the Coon Chicken Inn.[12] M. Lester Graham had founded the chain in 1925; his first restaurant was located in Salt Lake City, and two others fol-lowed, one in Seattle in 1929 and one in Portland in 1931.[13] There is no extant documentation to explain why the restaurateurs chose to use the "coon" image or the "Coon Chicken" name, but it must have been effective. Hawkins recalls people waiting for hours on end to get chicken, and the restaurants were in full swing for almost twenty years.

Despite knowing the secrets to cooking the chicken and other food served at the Coon Chicken Inn, Hawkins was a waiter and as such endured a number of insults. Like many African Americans of the time, however, he accepted insults in exchange for a decent living wage. Hawkins could capitalize on the ignorance of customers and make, he said, up to $200 in tips a night. Inasmuch as many of his friends and acquaintances were making only as much as $5, he was able to laugh in the face of adversity.[14] Sometimes Hawkins and the other wait staff would preserve dignity in more surreptitious ways, such as forgetting to bring food to customers, spilling their drinks, or laughingly correcting them when they were called demeaning names. These measures were not extraordi-nary in themselves but rather examples of everyday acts of survival, resistance, and agency. Such everyday life acts helped people minimize the denuncia-tion directed toward them and, although usually writ small, kept them sane. Hawkins's life narrative is but one example of that dynamic.

Here, we see how food images and encounters exemplify the various ways that power operates in our lives. Food is subtle and unexpected because it is not seen as a tool of opposition but as a necessary substance. Chicken could be more than sustenance for black people. The customers at the Coon Chicken Inn valued the restaurant for its menu, but Hawkins saw that menu as a source of capital. He did not work at the restaurant specifically to rebuke the racism that confronted him, yet the Coon Chicken Inn became a locus for social and political activism on an almost daily basis. Hawkins was fully aware of the racial implications levied against him by virtue of where he was employed, and by all accounts he was noticeably prepared to fight back, using verbal jabs, quick wit, and anything else at his disposal.

Based on such insights into the examples of racist imagery and the lives of men like Roy Hawkins, it is important to stress that there is great advantage to studying how food operates in people's lives. To understand how foods have meaning is to begin to appreciate the connections people have to those foods. It also becomes possible to grasp how a food as insignificant as chicken offers evidence of the ways in which black people disrupted the hegemonic cultural assumptions that tried to define them.

A Look at the Present

> Young black male #1: "I'm just sayin', I hate history, period. Because I don't like studyin' on things that people did before. You know it's just all about what's goin' on now. What people got to do now. They can't keep looking back on things that happened a long time ago."
> Young black male #2: "It's all right to know who Martin Luther King and Harriet Tubman is [sic] you know . . . know what they've done, and all that. But like you said, history: ain't no need for that! Better be looking for the future. Study the future. Computers and technology and all that stuff. Umm, chains tied on your ankles and stuff, that ain't gonna help you. You better learn that IBM computer or something."
> —Riggs, *Black Is, Black Ain't*

Although the young men from Riggs's documentary might believe that the past holds no relevance, a look at the present might indicate just the opposite. Roy Hawkins was not the only African American male to "laugh all the way to the bank" by capitalizing on the ignorance of popular culture consumption. Many of today's young music artists argue that they are doing the same under the guise of the brawny phrase "keepin' it real." In his 2001 release *Thugs Are Us* the hip-hop artist Trick Daddy is the quintessential bad boy who "wouldn't change for the world." In fact, he is so bad that in the video "I'm a Thug" he urinates on a lawn, shames his "middle/upper-class" girlfriend and her parents by consuming a bucket of fried chicken at an upscale restaurant, and horrifies them by using his ring-clad pinky finger to pick his teeth after tossing chicken bones into their glasses of fine champagne.[15] What Trick Daddy may not know, or may not care to know, are the ways in which such images reinforce the notion of black people, particularly black men, as being barbarian and brutish, uncouth and lewd. The images also reify perceptions of blacks as salacious lovers of chicken. Current artists might be laughing all the way to the bank, but what they do, in effect, degrades all black bodies, not just those displayed on television.

Studying a food in this context forces the recognition that black people speak in different voices. To be sure, not everyone challenges normative perceptions in the same way as Hawkins. In the present, those who might want to be perceived as offering a form of resistance walk a gossamer-thin line of perpetuating the ills of the past. We cannot be sure of the intent of an artist like Trick Daddy. Is it resistance or perpetuation? The answer may not fall clearly into one of those dichotomous categories but is likely composed of a complicated mélange that involves imagery, historicity, politics, gender, race, and, yes, even food.

It is interesting that popular hip-hop artists who are "all about the Benjamins" are not the only ones who perpetuate harmful stereotypes. In Riggs's documentary *Ethnic Notions* Barbara Christian observes, "I have students, both black and white, who believe these images because it has become a thread throughout major fiction, film, popular culture, the songs, [and] even the jokes black people make about themselves. It is become a part of our psyche. It's a real indication that one of the best ways of maintaining a system of oppression has to do with the psychological control of people."[16]

The study of African American foods can take, and has taken, many forms. It is interesting to note, for example, the representations found in archeological texts and the abundance of cookbooks that represent cultural sites where food and memory intersect.[17] These cultural documents, which have inextricable links to the African Diaspora, shed some light on African American people and how food factors into the process of identity formation.[18] Not to be dismissed, some of the cookbooks place African American culinary habits within a political and social history context. In doing so they share the experiences, realities, and variety of ways in which African American foods connect to their African, Brazilian, and Caribbean influences.

It is also interesting to examine the kinds of foods that African Americans consume and otherwise use.[19] It is equally compelling, however, to study food representations for what they teach about material culture, power, gender, race, and class in past and present forms. That requires a different understanding of food, particularly given the long history of visual and material racist misreadings. In the case of African American foodways, a food like chicken has been associated with black people in a way overdetermined by race. But the study of African American foodways also requires consideration and recognition of the methods of survival in a dialectic relationship to the often-static and stereotypical representations of black life. Stories, memories, and interviews tease out the ways in which personal identities emerge, and food helps privilege the voices and discussions of African Americans from all walks of life. It is thus possible to understand the ways in which food has been a tool of self-expression, self-actualization, resistance, and even accommodation and power. Perhaps more important, the study of foodways also makes it possible to respond to the young woman in Riggs's documentary who insisted that to be black is to know "your black history." It is, as she wisely argued, more than "knowing this black leader and that black leader." Rather, it is about knowing that the future has a past.

NOTES

This essay owes much in the way of thanks to Eva George, who read repeated drafts. Her comments and insights are reflected here, but any errors in interpretation are solely my own. The epigraphs are taken from R. J.'s Latest Arrival, *Shackles*, ARS Records, 1984, and my interview with Roy Hawkins.

1. Marlon Riggs, *Black Is, Black Ain't* (California Newsreel, 1995), VHS.
2. This essay uses "black" and "African American" interchangeably to both capture the essence of Riggs's argument and illuminate the complexities surrounding racial and ethnic identity in American society.
3. This essay is derived from my book *Building Houses Out of Chicken Legs: Black Women, Food, and Power* (Chapel Hill: University of North Carolina Press, 2006). Employing "close readings" of various texts borrows heavily from black literary criticism. As Henry Louis Gates has noted, "Learning to decipher complex codes is just about the blackest aspect of the black tradition." For further clarification on close readings see Gates, "Introduction: Criticism in De Jungle," *Black American Literature Forum* 15 (Winter 1981): 123–27.
4. Stephanie Moser, "Archaeological Representation: The Visual Conventions for Constructing Knowledge about the Past," in *Archaeological Theory Today*, edited by Ian Hodder (Cambridge: Polity Press, 2001), 267.
5. I borrow the notion of the Dandy and Zip Coon from three sources: Kenneth Goings's *Mammy and Uncle Mose* (Bloomington: Indiana University Press, 1994), which offers an excellent context for the emergence of the image; Eric Lott's *Love and Theft* (New York: Oxford University Press, 1993), which presents a compelling discussion of the Dandy as he relates to issues of minstrelsy, abolition, and class (131–35); and Donald Bogle's, *Toms, Coons, Mulattoes, Mammies, and Bucks*, 4th ed. (New York: Continuum, 2001), 7–9, which also provides a succinct context for the coon image. Bogle puts the image in dialog not only with the Pickanniny, Tragic Mulatto, and Mammy but also within the coon genre itself to compose a triumvirate: Rastus, Stepin Fetchit, and Uncle Remus. To further make this connection, Bogle discusses some of the "chicken films" of this genre, *How Rastus Got His Turkey*, *Rastus and Chicken*, and *Chicken Thief*, which appeared in the early twentieth century.
6. Elsewhere, I offer a more historical overview of Africans, African Americans, and chicken: Psyche Williams-Forson, "'Suckin' the Chicken Bone Dry': African American Women, Fried Chicken, and the Power of a National Narrative," in *Cooking Lessons: The Politics of Gender and Food*, edited by Sherrie Inness (Lanham, Md.: Rowman and Littlefield, 2001), 169–91, and "Building Houses Out of Chicken Legs: African American Women, Material Culture, and the Powers of Self-Definition" (Ph.D. diss., University of Maryland College Park, 2002), ch. 3. Additional historical context may be gleaned from Alex Lichtenstein, "'That Disposition to Theft, with which They Have Been Branded': Moral Economy, Slave Management and the Law," *Journal of Social History* 21 (1989): 413–40; Roderick A. McDonald, *The Economy and Material Culture*

of Slaves (Baton Rouge: Louisiana State University Press, 1993); Philip D. Morgan, "Economic Exchanges Between Blacks and Whites," in *Slave Counterpoint: Black Culture in the Eighteenth-Century Chesapeake and Lowcountry* (Chapel Hill: University of North Carolina Press for the Omohundro Institute of Early American History and Culture, Williamsburg, Virginia, 1998), 318–76; Anne E. Yentsch, *A Chesapeake Family and Their Slaves* (New York: Cambridge University Press, 1994), 239–55; Ira Berlin and Philip D. Morgan, eds., *The Slaves' Economy: Independent Production by Slaves in the Americas* (Portland, Ore.: Frank Cass, 1991); and Charles Ball, *Fifty Years in Chains* (New York: Dover Publications, 1970), 203–32.

7. Lott, *Love and Theft*, 134.

8. There has been disagreement over the point of African American's consumption of chicken during the era of enslavement. It is now believed that some, depending on region and circumstance, consumed quite a bit of barnyard fowl. Even so, I am primarily referring to what Tony Whitehead has called "low status" chicken—the necks, feet, giblets, and back. I have elsewhere referred to the richness of chicken fat as a source of cooking oil and chicken bones for seasoning and eating (Williams-Forson, "'Suckin' the Chicken Bone Dry'"). Another source on this point is Anne E. Yentsch, "Hot, Nourishing, and Culturally Potent: The Transfer of West African Cooking Traditions to the Chesapeake," *Sage* 9 (Summer 1995): 15–29.

9. Clifford Geertz, "Deep Play: Notes on the Balinese Cockfight," in *The Interpretation of Cultures* (New York: Basic Books, 1973), 412–53.

10. Robert Paynter and Randall McGuire suggest the notion of the "heterogeneity of power" as being multifaceted and devoid of one single source or structure as its base. That concept greatly expands the realm of social activities that are laden with power. Paynter and Randall, eds., *The Archaeology of Inequality* (Oxford: Basil Blackwell, 1991), 1.

11. Ian Hodder, "The Interpretation of Documents and Material Culture," in *Collecting and Interpreting Qualitative Materials*, edited by Norman K. Denzin and Yvonna Lincoln (Thousand Oaks, Calif.: Sage Publications, 1998), 110–29.

12. While reading an article from the *Salt Lake Tribune*, I came across the name of Roy Hawkins, one of the only black people employed by the Coon Chicken Inn. A telephone interview was conducted with the former headwaiter on August 1, 2001.

13. For additional information on the Coon Chicken Inn see Kenneth Goings, *Mammy and Uncle Mose: Black Collectibles and American Stereotyping* (Bloomington: Indiana University Press, 1994), 47–49, and http://www.ferris.edu/htmls/news/jimcrow/links/chicken/.

14. Interview with Roy Hawkins. For more on the experiences of Hawkins, see Steve Griffin, "Black Pioneers Blazed Their Own Utah Trails," *Salt Lake Tribune*, Feb. 15, 1998, A1, and Elaine Jarvick, "Good Food, but an Offensive Name," *Deseret News* (Salt Lake City), Feb. 26–27, 1987, sec. 1.

15. Trick Daddy, "I'm a Thug," *Thugs Are Us*, Atlantic Records, B00005A8MT, 2001.

16. Barbara Christian in Marlon Riggs's documentary film *Ethnic Notions*, California Newsreel, 1987, available on VHS and DVD.

17. Anthropologists and archeologists have greatly contributed to discussions of food that black people consumed during enslavement. Among them are Sam Hilliard, *Hogmeat and Hoecake: Food Supply in the Old South* (Carbondale: Southern Illinois Uni-

versity Press, 1972); James Deetz, *In Small Things Forgotten* (New York: Anchor Books, 1977); Joe Gray Taylor, *Eating, Drinking, and Visiting in the South* (Baton Rouge: Louisiana State University Press, 1982); Charles Joyner, *Down by the Riverside: A South Carolina Slave Community* (Urbana: University of Illinois Press, 1984); Theresa Singleton, *The Archaeology of Slavery and Plantation Life* (Orlando: Academic Press, 1985); Tony Whitehead, "In Search of Soul Food and Meaning: Culture, Food, and Health," in *African Americans in the South: Issues of Race, Class, and Gender,* edited by Hans A. Baer and Yvonne Jones (Athens: University of Georgia Press, 1992), 94–110; Anne E. Yentsch, "Gudgeons, Mullet, and Proud Pigs: Historicity, Black Fishing, and Southern Myth," in *The Art and Mystery of Historical Archaeology,* edited by Mary Beaudry and Anne E. Yentsch (Boca Raton: CRC Press, 1992), 283–314; Larry McKee, "Food Supply and Plantation Social Order: An Archaeological Perspective," in *"I, Too, Am America":* *Archaeological Studies of African-American Life,* edited by Teresa Singleton (Charlottesville: University Press of Virginia, 1999), 218–39; Leland Ferguson, *Uncommon Ground* (Washington: Smithsonian Institution Press, 1992); and Mark Warner, "Ham Hocks: Examining the Role of Food in African American Identity," *Archaeology* 54 (Nov.–Dec. 2001): 48–52. For a related discussion pertaining to Caribbean blacks see Lydia Mihelic Pulsipher, "'They Have Saturdays and Sundays to Feed Themselves: Slave Gardens in the Caribbean," *Expedition* 32, no. 1 (1990): 24–33.

18. Doris Witt in consultation with David Lupton has compiled a thorough chronological bibliography of African American cookbooks in *Black Hunger: Food and the Politics of U.S. Identity* (New York: Oxford University Press, 1999), 221–28. Jessica Harris should be noted for the brief introductory histories she includes in her cookbooks, especially *Iron Pots and Wooden Spoons* (New York: Athenaeum, 1989) and *The Welcome Table* (New York: Simon and Schuster, 1995).

19. See, for example, Tony Whitehead, "In Search of Soul Food and Meaning: Culture, Food, and Health," in *African Americans in the South: Issues of Race, Class, and Gender,* edited by Hans A. Baer and Yvonne Jones (Athens: University of Georgia Press, 1992), 94–110. A wealth of information is included in *The Encyclopedia of Food and Culture,* edited by Solomon Katz and William Woys Weaver (New York: Charles Scribner Sons, 2003), 425–37, particularly "United States: African American Foodways" by Whitehead and Williams-Forson. For a discussion of how food is used not only as a source of nutrition but also for income, sacred rituals and ceremonies, and its connections to cultural traditions and heritage, see Jualynne Dodson and Cheryl Townsend Gilkes, "There's Nothing Like Church Food: Food and the U.S. Afro-Christian Tradition," *Journal of the American Academy of Religion* 63, no. 3 (1995): 519–39.

6

Recipes for Respect: Black Hospitality
Entrepreneurs before World War I

Rafia Zafar

"Why, then, should not the hair-dresser write, as well as the physician and the clergyman? She will tell her story in simpler language; but it will be none the less truthful, none the less strange."[1] The African American entrepreneur Eliza Potter wrote these words on the eve of the Civil War. Her allusion to the possibilities of confidences revealed and mysteries unveiled speaks not only to her own anonymously published tell-all of Cincinnati and Saratoga Springs society life but also to the best-selling *Behind the Scenes at the White House* by one Elizabeth Keckley, modiste and confidante to Mary Todd Lincoln.[2]

Beginning in the early nineteenth century, a number of African Americans published works about their experiences serving the white world. Although the two earliest known volumes, Robert Roberts's *The House Servant's Directory* (1827) and Tunis Campbell's *Hotel Keepers, Head Waiters, and Housekeepers' Guide* (1848), may be described most aptly as housekeeping manuals, cookbooks and other related manuals began appearing by the mid-nineteenth century.[3] Three later volumes of this type, *What Mrs. Fisher Knows about Old Southern Cooking* by Abby Fisher, *The Ideal Bartender* by Tom Bullock, and

Good Things to Eat by Rufus Estes, offered tips for a wide range of items from infant pap to mint juleps and eclairs.[4] Their books help us to write the history of a nascent black middle-class cohort of hospitality entrepreneurs.[5]

Fisher, Bullock, and Estes promised to reveal backstage scandals or gossip as gathered from a behind-the-scenes vantage point, as had their predecessors Eliza Potter and Elizabeth Keckley. These African American authors of the later nineteenth century, however, gave evidence of the invisible labor, the "black back regions," that made a certain kind of lifestyle possible for unthinking generations of European Americans.[6] Although none of the three were slaves at the time they published their volumes, Estes's prefatory life story is framed within the tradition of the slave narrative, Fisher was almost surely born into slavery, and Bullock began his life in a south yet smoldering from the war. All worked in the culinary service sector within a nineteenth- and early-twentieth-century American economy that offered precious few career options for an ambitious black person. Their publications were thus extensions of their careers. Such books should be treasured not only as gastronomic social history but also for their authors' display of business acumen and social mobility.

Despite what is now a nearly ineradicable association in the collective national unconscious of black women with cookery, early black books containing recipes were as likely to be written by men as by women.[7] The first two such works could not, in truth, even be strictly classified as cookbooks. Written by former or current domestic male servants, they were early entries in the realm of "domestic economy" or housekeeping. Robert Roberts published his *House Servant's Directory; or, A Monitor for Private Families* in 1827, before the publications of either of the much better known doyennes of domestic economy, Catherine Beecher and Lydia Maria Child.[8] Roberts's guide includes some 105 "receipts" for everything from "a most delicious salad sauce" (item 36) to "a cheap and wholesome beer" (item 99). In addition to comestibles, he also provides directions "to prevent the breath from smelling, after liquor" (item 90) and to compound "Italian polish to give furniture a brilliant luster" (item 6). By means of coded instructions on surviving as a free black in a white-dominated world Roberts offered in his introduction suggestions for smooth employee-employer relations. Although he urged readers to get along with their employers, Roberts, a "delegate to the Second National Convention of Free People of Color in the 1830s," found no difficulty speaking out publicly against racist practices.[9]

If, on the one hand, Roberts, in *The House Servant's Directory*, seemed to preach a career doctrine of individual submissiveness, on the other hand the former butler to Governor Gore spoke out publicly against those whites who would try to remove native-born Americans to a strange land. Patterns of deference between working and bourgeois classes would be difficult to avoid, much less dislodge, especially for a black man. Yet keeping one's pride was possible. As Graham Russell Hodges points out, "Roberts's insights into the personality of the head servant created a black persona capable of remaining calm and professional under very trying circumstances. . . . [We need to recognize] black men whose work mandated external deference but who conducted themselves with dignity and skill."[10] Here lay the quandary facing entrepreneurial African Americans: To secure independent livelihoods they had to adhere to (or at least pay lip service to) the prevailing hierarchical pattern of white master–black servant.

When some decades later the southern-born Abby Fisher began a new life in California, she, too, would learn to parlay her expertise as a domestic worker into entrepreneurial success and the higher-status role of author. Fisher's preface reveals the balancing act performed by black Americans dependent on white patronage for social mobility:

> The publication of a book on my knowledge and experience of Southern Cooking, Pickle and Jelly Making, has been frequently asked of me by my lady friends and patrons in Francisco and Oakland, and also by ladies of Sacramento during the State Fair in 1879. Not being able to read or write myself, and my husband also having been without the advantages of an education—upon whom would devolve the writing of the book at my dictation—caused me to doubt whether I would be able to present a work that would give perfect satisfaction. But, after due consideration, I concluded to bring forward a book of my knowledge—based on an experience of upwards of thirty-five years—in the art of cooking.[11]

In 1881 Fisher became the fourth African American to publish a book containing recipes and the second black American woman; Malinda Russell was the first to have published a cookbook.[12] Fisher's book does not explicitly take up the matter of slavery, sexual oppression, and racial discrimination although her predecessor, Russell, explicitly addresses her former status as a slave.[13] Abby Fisher's instructions to readers allude to a lifestyle defined by entertaining not servitude. Were she to dwell on her early years in service, years perhaps spent as a slave, readers might be less willing to accept her authority as an expert. Furthermore, black authors during the latter part of the nineteenth century may have sensed that white Americans, with the Civil War over and the Gilded Age begun, were less concerned with the struggles of the formerly enslaved.[14]

In such a climate, then, *What Mrs. Fisher Knows about Old Southern Cooking*—the "complete instructor" to prospective readers seeking the right way to pickle or to form a croquette—offers the barest glimpse of the private life of its entrepreneurial author. Her experiences as a black woman nevertheless shaped, faintly but distinctly, her contribution to American cookery.

Career options were extremely limited for black women who came of age before the Civil War. When she was young, laws and local custom prevented Fisher from even the most basic of educations; later on and after the war's end, earning a living must have taken precedence over literacy. The antebellum attitude legally or informally denying citizenship to those of African descent also kept thousands upon thousands from knowledge of their families or even their beginnings. As Frederick Douglass once observed, plantation slaves knew "as little of their age as horses know of theirs."[15]

It is not surprising, therefore, that little factual evidence has been uncovered on Abby Fisher's early life. Initially, she was not even identified as a black woman because she did not so identify herself within the pages of her book. That omission could have stemmed from the desire to appear foremost as a chef-caterer rather than a member of an oppressed group seeking patronage. That she published her book under the auspices of a woman's publishing cooperative could indicate that her sponsors knew her origins and so she did not feel the need to include references to her African ancestry. Much of what is now known about Fisher is due to the efforts of the culinary historian Karen Hess, editor of the modern edition of *What Mrs. Fisher Knows about Old Southern Cooking*, and her librarian colleague Dan Strehl. Hess notes that the author was born about 1832 in South Carolina, married to an Alexander C. Fisher, himself born in Alabama, and was listed in a San Francisco city directory of 1880 as a manufacturer of pickles.[16] To ascertain more we must turn to Fisher's own words.

Something of Abby Fisher's personality can be surmised from her "Preface and Apology." The standard rhetorical move in which an author admits frailty with letters is not guided here by false modesty. The cook's educational disability leads to initial hesitation: "Not being able to read or write myself . . . caused me to doubt whether I would be able to present a book." Yet her self-possession and years as a sought-after caterer convinced Fisher to pursue her goal of authorship. Her customers valued her culinary skills, and the chef correctly saw her talents as bankable. Her confidence led her to attest that anyone following her instructions could duplicate her successes. Indeed, she seems almost dismissive when she appears to imply that if a "child" can follow her instructions, then an inept white middle-class reader can do so as well.[17] Ending the introductory note, Fisher lists a variety of the well-off San Francisco customers on whose patronage she could depend.[18]

Before her renown as a Bay Area chef and caterer, Abby Fisher lived in the Deep South. Brief references to this previous life, and possibly to her place within a plantation slavery system, appear within the context of only three recipes: one for hoe cake, another for a health tonic, and a third for infant food (recipes 9, 102, and 160).[19] The first, "Plantation Corn Bread or Hoe Cake," does not necessarily indicate a black or even southern-born author, for compilers of the day regularly borrowed recipes from other texts. Because whites and blacks alike considered corn bread a staple, this item alone does not indicate her former status. Fisher's instructions, furthermore, do not refer to the slave's practice of baking a meal in the field, on the flat side of a heated hoe; she says only to bake the mixture on a hot griddle. The second recipe might suggest more of an insider's knowledge, because instructions for the folk remedy, blackberry syrup, include a comment with the daily dosage: "This is an old Southern plantation remedy among colored people." Still, the recipe could have been borrowed or written from other than firsthand knowledge.[20]

The third and final reference, the last recipe in Fisher's book, reveals the most about its author and elliptically gestures toward her southern, black origins. In fewer than two dozen words the self-possession evident in the book's opening paragraph returns when, at the end of "Pap for Infant Diet" Fisher concludes, "I have given birth to eleven children and raised them all." Such a revelation resoundingly endorses this specie of baby food. Any prior reticence about her past—a hesitation that led to the nearly complete lack of overt references to her southern, black origin—is subordinated to insuppressible pride in her success as a black mother. The significance of her racialized maternal identity is something that readers more than a hundred years later can acknowledge with admiration.

It's not that Fisher and her readers did not know the odds against any woman giving birth to and raising eleven children in the nineteenth century. Even among well-to-do whites the infant mortality rate made early motherhood an uneasy waiting game.[21] What makes the achievement extraordinary in Fisher's case is that she was black and perhaps even a former slave.[22] Giving birth many times over isn't what was remarkable but rather that Abby Fisher could say that she saw all those children grow up.[23] Her quiet affirmation constitutes an open secret, a hidden-in-plain-view boast.

Karen Hess has surmised that Fisher's birth in the slave-owning South supports the conclusion that the cook-author had herself been in bondage. Yet those nearly dozen children reared by a loving and proud mother complicate the statement that Fisher had been a slave. When her history as a mother is viewed in the context of the racial category assigned to her (in the U.S. Census of 1880 she is counted as a "mulatto"), I conclude that Fisher was likely to have been a favored slave. Self-identified as the offspring of a French father and possibly light-skinned (another path to middle-class status due to the racism that skewed the hiring decisions of white employers), Fisher could boast of her maternity because her status was out of the ordinary. If she were indeed like many fair-skinned African American children of planters she may have received a better deal. Such slaves could be the targets of jealous mistresses, but the luckiest individuals were sometimes given favors like the sanctity of having nuclear families of their own or manumission at adulthood. Fisher's anomalous slave-era motherhood could have been the result of a white progenitor's favor. It could have also been sheer, delirious fortune.

Fisher's seemingly offhand remark, coming at the close of her one hundred and sixtieth recipe, celebrates the unusual nature of her endeavors. Yet her achievements, almost buried among the varied culinary tasks that she elucidates, can go unremarked. Like many of the era's striving black women who committed themselves to a "politics of respectability" meant to expunge centuries of black female stereotyping, Fisher might well have tended toward giving less information about her private life rather than more. To be a black woman in the pre-Emancipation era and well beyond meant to be considered no more enterprising than livestock, to be thought an entity who could be sexually assaulted with impunity, and to be destined to motherhood without the secure knowledge that one could love and raise one's children. As a cookbook author, Fisher's relative silence on these subjects hardly surprises; her volume is not, after all, an autobiography or slave narrative. Perhaps unconsciously, perhaps not, the few facts of Abby Fisher's life break through the lines of her treatise on "Old Southern Cooking."[24] Who are we to say that she did not deliberately salt some recipes with well-earned pride?

Within a few decades of Fisher's book two others by black hospitality entrepreneurs appeared. In 1911 Rufus Estes self-published *Good Things to Eat, as Suggested by Rufus,* and six years later Tom Bullock brought out *The Ideal Bartender* under his own imprimatur. That each volume was privately published may point to the difficulty that black authors who ventured beyond the familiar genre of the slave narrative then had securing the sponsorship of a regional or national publisher.[25] (Few would now have access to these two intriguing windows onto black middle-class life before the Great War were it not for the interest of the publisher of one small press.[26])

Like Fisher, Estes and Bullock used their talents in domestic service to rise up and away from their slavery-shadowed beginnings, for a chef or country club butler could and often would be counted as part of the black middle class.[27] One would proudly recount his Booker T. Washingtonian–like rise in status, and the other would simply present his recipes, leaving the commentary to a powerful white friend.

Rufus Estes wanted to be known as an accomplished chef *and* a former slave. To do both would be to demonstrate the professional heights to which he had climbed from the lowliest of beginnings. *Good Things to Eat, as Suggested by Rufus: A Collection of Practical Recipes for Preparing Meats, Game, Fowl, Fish, Puddings, Pastries, Etc.* begins with a foreword and proceeds to a "Sketch of My Life." In the foreword's opening paragraphs Estes agrees with the vernacular wisdom that parents frequently overlook the faults of their children, be the offspring flesh and blood or paper. Estes avers, however, that he "has honestly striven to avoid this common prejudice . . . [and] frankly admits [that his book] is not without its faults"; nevertheless, *Good Things to Eat* "will serve in a humble way some useful purpose." Like Fisher three decades earlier, Estes offers the expected topos of modesty while simultaneously proclaiming the worthiness of his project. All the recipes within were written down during moments "snatched" from daily duties. The railway chef took time to make up this compendium because some of the powerful patrons he served, "some of whom have now become his stanchest [*sic*] friends," urged him again and again to write a cookbook. Generously if not diplomatically, Estes dedicated the volume to those white friends and patrons who encouraged him and added the occupation "author" to his resume.

A chief difference between the Estes volume and Fisher's and Bullock's guides is the slave narrative with which the author self-authenticates his text. Beginning, as do countless other such narratives, with the incantation "I was born," Estes's "Sketch of My Life" briefly outlines the earliest years of the former slave who could later list his address as in care of the Appomattox Club, a place harboring "every [black] man in Chicago who holds any kind of responsible position or occupies a big place politically." He came into the world the supposed possession of one D. J. Estes in Murray County, Tennessee and was his mother's ninth and youngest child. The coming of the Civil War to his home county led to all male slaves of sufficient age joining the Union forces. The little Rufus thereafter became one of the children left behind "to carry water from the spring . . . drive the cows . . . mind the calves . . . gather chips, etc."[28]

When Estes was about ten, he and his mother moved to Nashville, where he attended school for a single term. Although now legal for blacks, education still had to give way before the exigencies of gaining a livelihood. In that and other ways black life after the war would not have been much different than in the years before it. The "brief sketch" of Estes's life connects him generically and historically with antebellum autobiographers such as Frederick Douglass, who also described his first jobs for wages and his lack of formal schooling, and Reconstruction-era coevals like Booker T. Washington.[29]

From early on a culinary career seemed to have been forecast for Estes. One job he undertook in Nashville was to tote meals to workers in the field. For doing so he earned a quarter from each man per month, although "all this, of course, went to my mother." From sixteen to twenty-one years of age he was employed at a restaurant, and not long after that he went north to Chicago. What might be called his big break came in 1883 when he was hired by the Pullman service and subsequently "selected to handle all special parties." Clients would include presidents Grover Cleveland and William Henry Harrison, the noted musicians Ignacy Paderewski and Adelina Patti, and Princess Eulalie of Spain. In the mid-1880s Estes sailed to Japan in private service, and by the end of the century he was settled into his career as chef, first on a private railway car and later "for the subsidiary companies of the United States Steel Corporation in Chicago."[30]

Perhaps so that his recipes appear unencumbered, perhaps to authenticate his status as an expert with years of experience, Estes places his biography at the beginning of the book. After a brief version of his personal life he directly moves to the primary goal: a compilation of "good things to eat." Directions for such dishes as "Mushrooms in Cream" and "Fried Hamburg Steak, with Russian Sauce" are thorough and clearly written. Rarely does an authorial persona intrude, although occasionally Estes's professional self cannot resist an aside, as when he indicates in "Broiling Steak" that "my own preference" in steak is for one not "burned to a cinder, but slightly scorched over a very hot fire."[31] "Hints to Kitchen Maids" shares tips with less-experienced workers, suggesting, for example, how much in the way of breakfast one should serve to "a person employed indoors." Estes does not set himself up as a kitchen autocrat, however, and closes his advice column with the remark that "the above [ideas] are merely suggestions that have been of material assistance to me."[32] Unlike Robert Roberts a century earlier, who felt it necessary to advise inexperienced domestic servants, Estes's remarks are less avuncular and more distanced.

Estes states that he includes no "delicacies that would awaken the jaded appetite of the gourmet." Despite this stated desire to avoid haute cuisine, he points out that the meals readers could now duplicate could serve for either "the home table or banquet board." Rarefied items like "Crystallized Cowslips . . . a prized English confection" could be reproduced with Estes's assistance even though more usual are instructions for solid, tasty fare, as with directions for steak, "Scalloped Shrimps," "Glazed Carrots with Peas," "Whole Wheat Bread," and "Fresh Raspberry Pie."[33] If Estes reveals anything personal within his recipes it may be a powerful sweet tooth. The "Beef, Veal, and Pork" chapter, the only one dedicated to meat, contains fifty recipes, and a chapter each is devoted to poultry and game. Yet such sturdy provender is overshadowed by dozens upon dozens of recipes in four chapters for "Pies and Pastries," "Cakes, Crullers, and Eclairs," "Candies," and "Ice Cream and Sherbets [*sic*]." The chapter on "Preserves, Pickles, and Relish" is followed with a final exegesis, "Desserts." More psychoanalytic readers may wonder whether the abundance of sweets was intended as compensation for black America's bitter travails, for Estes published his book during the violent years of the nadir, the era of the worst race relations. Perhaps we should just say, to paraphrase Freudian apocrypha, that sometimes an eclair is just an eclair.[34]

The last and most elusive of the three authors I am discussing, Tom Bullock, author of *The Ideal Bartender*, was born in Louisville, Kentucky, around 1872. His mother had almost certainly been a slave; his father, a furniture drayman, was a former Union soldier who apparently adopted his wife's surname. In his twenties Bullock worked as a bellboy, but within a few years he was working as a bartender, first in Louisville and then on a railroad club car. He cared for his mother after his parents separated and at one time maintained a household that included his brother, sister-in-law, and their child. Around the beginning of the twentieth century Bullock settled in St. Louis. Like his parents, he married and had a child, but the relationship did not last. Within a few years of his book's publication Bullock disappeared from St. Louis directories.[35] Prohibition foreclosed the position of bartender to the wealthy, and Bullock may have moved elsewhere in search of employment.

Bullock's talents behind the bar were highly regarded, first in his position as bartender for the Pendennis Club of Louisville and then at the elite St. Louis Country Club. Inadvertently, Bullock's prodigious skills as a "mixologist" led him to a moment on the national stage. That time in the spotlight is memorialized in *The Ideal Bartender*'s preface, which is an "authenticating document" by George Herbert Walker, a wealthy and influential white man, in much the same way as other white men had introduced many a slave narrative.[36] Walker, who would become the grandfather and great-grandfather of two U.S. presidents, memorializes the occasion when the St. Louis bartender crossed paths with Theodore Roosevelt. Perhaps Walker, who wrote that "it is a genuine privilege to be permitted to testify to his qualifications," suggested Bullock include the editorial from the St. Louis *Post-Dispatch* that pointed to the supposedly temperate presidential candidate only drinking part of one of Bullock's famed mint juleps. The editor scoffed at Roosevelt's equivocation, writing that for a "red-blooded man, and a true Colonel at that," not to drain to the dregs a julep mixed by Mr. Bullock "strain[s] credulity too far."[37] What Bullock thought of his ancillary part in a presidential candidate's public relations debacle he never says. With only the briefest comment the editorial is reproduced as "a testimonial" to his genuinely intoxicating touch.

Bullock's brush with the national stage, however, remained just that. His book, unlike that of Mary Todd Lincoln's dress designer Elizabeth Keckley, did not "tell-all" about his experiences among the politically well-connected. Like the best barkeeps today, Bullock spread no tales. The book includes no reminiscences of conversations overheard or advice humbly given along with the dozens of drink recipes, including a few free of alcohol. As could be expected from one born in horse racing country, Bullock includes not one but two julep receipes. One for "Mint Julep — Kentucky Style" calls for a silver mug, a lump of sugar, water, ice, "Old Bourbon Whiskey," and mint, and a second, for "Overall Julep — St. Louis Style," strays far from the julep formula by omitting the bourbon and using rye whiskey, "Gordon Gin," grenadine, lemon, lime and "Imported Club Soda."[38]

None of the recipes even fleetingly refer to the author's life. His personal history remains off-limits behind the welcoming yet reserved demeanor presented in the volume's photographic frontispiece. To regard Bullock's tuxedo-clad image, his face offering the barest of smiles, is to call to mind once more Graham Russell Hodges's remark about the all-too-frequent necessity for a black man to perform service work under trying conditions that may have nothing to do with the physical state of his kitchen and everything to do with his clientele. If at times he was confronted with belligerent racism or drunken ignorance there is no hint of that from either text or photograph. An exemplary, professional host, Bullock presents his time-tested and renowned decoctions with nary a glimpse of the man within.

Early cookbooks and bartenders' guides offer valuable if somewhat incomplete insights into the rise of the black middle class. Although socially disadvantaged, some African Americans were able to turn the skills learned in slavery or domestic service into successful entrepreneurial, even political, careers.[39] By gathering the results, tangible and otherwise, of a life in service, black Americans could transform a life of manual labor into something more self-affirming if something less than ease. In writing and publishing their books, black butlers, cooks, and bartenders propounded racial self-worth, individual achievement, and economic self-sufficiency. Theirs were indeed recipes for respect.

NOTES

1. [Eliza Potter], *A Hairdresser's Experience in High Life* (1859, repr. New York: Oxford University Press, 1988), iv. This essay is adapted from a chapter of my work in progress, "And Called It Macaroni." I thank Warren Belasco, Susan Strasser, Anne L. Bower, Dianne Seay, and Doris Witt, along with Washington University's English department and the American Antiquarian Society, for feedback, encouragement, and support.

2. Elizabeth Keckley, *Behind the Scenes: Thirty Years a Slave and Four in the White House* (1868, repr. New York: Oxford University Press, 1988).

3. Tunis G. Campbell, *Hotel Keepers, Head Waiters, and Housekeepers' Guide* (1848, repr. as *Never Let People Be Kept Waiting: A Textbook on Hotel Management* [Raleigh, N.C.: Graphic, 1973]); Robert Roberts, *The House Servant's Directory; or, A Monitor for Private Families: Comprising Hints on the Arrangement and Performance of Servants' Work . . . and Upwards of One Hundred Various and Useful Receipts, Chiefly Compiled for the Use of House Servants* (1827, repr. Bedford, Mass.: Applewood Books, 1993). I discuss Roberts and Campbell at greater length in "And Called It Macaroni."

4. Abby Fisher, *What Mrs. Fisher Knows about Old Southern Cooking, Soups, Pickles, Preserves, Etc.* (1881, repr. [edited by Karen L. Hess], Bedford, Mass.: Applewood Books, 1995); Tom Bullock, *The Ideal Bartender* (St. Louis: Published by the author, 1917); Rufus Estes, *Good Things to Eat, as Suggested by Rufus: A Collection of Practical Recipes for Preparing Meats, Game, Fowl, Fish, Puddings, Pastries, Etc.* (Chicago: Franklin, 1911). Fisher's book, like those of Estes and Bullock, was published noncommercially, in her case by the Women's Co-Operative Printing Office of San Francisco.

5. After reading an earlier version of this essay, Susan Strasser suggested that the phrase *home economist*, which I had been using, was anachronistic. Although I believe the phrase, with its connotation of "managing" the domestic sphere, describes the labor that Fisher and others performed, I now use the term *hospitality entrepreneur*, a helpful locution suggested by the work of Doris King, a historian of "public hospitality."

6. The term *black back regions* is a multiple pun, the provenance of which must be attributed to P. Gabrielle Foreman. See Foreman, "Manifest in Signs: The Politics of Sex and Representation in *Incidents in the Life of a Slave Girl*," in *Harriet Jacobs and Incidents in the Life of a Slave Girl: New Critical Essays*, edited by D. Garfield and Rafia Zafar (New York: Cambridge University Press, 1996), 76–99, well as Karen Halttunen's *Confidence Men and Painted Women: A Study of Middle-Class Culture in America, 1830–1879* (New Haven: Yale University Press, 1982), on status anxiety in antebellum America. See also Patricia Yaeger, "Edible Labor," *Southern Quarterly* 30 (Winter–Spring 1992): 150–59; and Rafia Zafar, "Dressing Up and Dressing Down" in

We Wear the Mask: African Americans Write American Literature, 1760–1870 (New York: Columbia University Press, 1997).

7. See Doris Witt and David Lupton's bibliography of cookbooks written by black authors before 1914 in Witt, *Black Hunger: Food and the Politics of U.S. Identity* (New York: Oxford University Press, 1999), 221–28. Malinda Russell was the first black woman to publish a cookbook, *A Domestic Cook Book: Containing a Careful Selection of Useful Receipts for the Kitchen* (Paw Paw, Mich.: Published for the author by T. G. Ward, 1866); see also Jan Longone, "Early Black-Authored Cookbooks," *Gastronomica* 1 (Feb. 2001): 96–99.

8. Catherine Beecher's *A Treatise on Domestic Economy: For the Use of Young Ladies at Home, and at School* was first published in 1841 and went through numerous editions; Lydia Maria Child's *The Frugal Housewife: Dedicated to Those Who Are Not Ashamed of Economy* appeared in 1829.

9. James Oliver Horton and Lois E. Horton, *Black Bostonians: Family Life and Community Struggle in the Antebellum North* (New York: Holmes and Meier, 1979), 25.

10. Graham Russell Hodges, Introduction to reprint edition of *The House Servant's Directory* (Armonk: M. E. Sharpe, 1998), xxxvi.

11. Fisher, *What Mrs. Fisher Knows*, n.p.

12. I have read the only known extant copy of Malinda Russell's work at the Clements Library at the University of Michigan but have yet to make an extensive study of it. The study of black cookbooks and instruction books is a relatively recent field, and new scholarship will be necessary as texts are uncovered.

13. Published before the end of the Civil War, Russell's book would have been unusual had it not addressed the subject of slavery, yet she wrote of it in rather veiled terms. Evelyn Brooks-Higginbotham's phrase "the politics of respectability" would apply to the self-protective strategy among black women writers like Russell. Brooks-Higginbotham, *Righteous Discontent: The Women's Movement in the Black Baptist Church, 1880–1920* (Cambridge: Harvard University Press, 1993), 14–15.

14. William L. Andrews has remarked on this rhetorical strategy among postbellum African American authors. Andrews, "Reunion in the Postbellum Slave Narrative: Frederick Douglass and Elizabeth Keckley," *Black American Literature Forum* 23 (Spring 1989): 5–16.

15. Frederick Douglass, *Narrative of the Life of Frederick Douglass* (1845, repr. New York: Bedford Books, 1993), 39.

16. Hess's persistence, and Strehl's sleuthing, led to the positive identification of Fisher as an African American, for Hess "had read [somewhere] that Abby Fisher was an ex-slave." See the afterword in *What Mrs. Fisher Knows*, 76–78, for biographical information on Fisher and how Hess gathered it.

17. Susan Strasser has noted the crisis among middle-class Americans when hiring "help" in the late nineteenth century; many domestic economy manuals and cookbooks of the era, in spelling out the way to run a home or cook a meal, may have had as one goal reassuring bourgeois women that their households could be well run even without domestic servants. Strasser, *Never Done: A History of American Housework* (New York: Pantheon Books, 1982), especially the chapter "Mistress and Maid," 162–79.

18. Hess notes that these women and men included "a stockbroker . . . a manager of . . . Pacific Mutual Life Insurance . . . [an] attorney and school director" and so

on. Fisher, *What Mrs. Fisher Knows*, 92n1. The listing also brings to mind the dozen Colonial-era men whose prefatory signatures confirmed that Phillis Wheatley had indeed written *Poems on Various Subjects, Religious and Moral* (1773). That poet's favored-slave status in some ways anticipated the white patronage on which some later enterprising African Americans would find themselves dependent.

19. Further discussion of Fisher's identification with southern food traditions (and a description of her hoe cake recipe) appears in Mark Zanger, *The American History Cookbook* (Westport: Greenwood Press, 2003), 122–23.

20. Fisher, *What Mrs. Fisher Knows*, 11, 50.

21. Joan Hedrick has called infant mortality "one of the most common and profound events of nineteenth-century family life," and she cites Kenneth Stampp, who estimated that slave women lost children at more than double the rate of white women. Hedrick, *Harriet Beecher Stowe: A Life* (New York: Oxford University Press, 1994), 191, 434n30.

22. For a discussion of motherhood within the enslaved black American community see Deborah Gray White, *Ar'n't I a Woman? Female Slaves in the Plantation South* (1985, repr. New York: W. W. Norton, 1999), esp. 99–114.

23. Sojourner's Truth's most recent biographer, Nell Irvin Painter, notes that although Truth bore five children she could only take one of them when she escaped to freedom. By the time she was ten, Truth had lost both parents and ten siblings to death and sale. Painter, *Sojourner Truth: A Life, a Symbol* (New York: W. W. Norton, 1996), passim.

24. Playing with the literary concept of an unreliable narrator, the critic Robert Stepto has observed that "the African American discourse of distrust assumes many narrative forms and infiltrates many literary genres." In other words, it is the reader who can't be trusted. Stepto, "Afterword: Distrust of the Reader in Afro-American Narratives," in *From Behind the Veil: A Study of Afro-American Narrative*, 2d. ed. (Urbana: University of Illinois Press, 1991), 199.

25. A number of scholars have pointed to the difficulty that African American authors had in finding national publishers. Carla Peterson, *"Doers of the Word": African American Women Speakers and Writers in the North (1830–1880)* (1995, repr. New Brunswick: Rutgers University Press, 1999), 150. Although now enshrined in Oxford University Press's series of nineteenth-century black women writers, Pauline Hopkins brought out her novel *Contending Forces* with the Colored Co-Operative Publishing Company in 1900.

26. Dianna Seay edited and reprinted both the Rufus Estes and the Tom Bullock volumes; her later editorial additions to Bullock's book were necessary when she discovered the participation of one D. J. Frienz. The more recent reprint of Bullock's *The Ideal Bartender* is entitled *173 Pre-Prohibition Cocktails: Potations So Good They Scandalized a President* (Jenks, Okla.: Howling at the Moon Press, 2001). Dianna Seay's generosity with her research enabled me to fill in some authorial omissions, and I am grateful for her assistance.

27. Earl Lewis has observed that what might be considered lower-middle-class positions in white communities could be parlayed into middle-class or better status in the African American community. Lewis, *In Their Own Interests: Race, Class, and Power in Twentieth-Century Norfolk* (Berkeley: University of California Press, 1991), 14–15.

28. Estes, *Good Things to Eat*, 7. I am indebted here, as with the biographical information on Tom Bullock, to the investigative labors of Dianna Seay (Introduction in *Good Things to Eat*), who also shared additional research on Estes's life (Dianna Seay

to author, July 16 2002). For the quotation from the *Chicago Whip* on the Appomattox Club, see Allan H. Spear, *Black Chicago: The Making of a Negro Ghetto 1890–1920* (Chicago: University of Chicago Press, 1967), 109.

29. Houghton-Mifflin published Washington's autobiography *Up from Slavery* in 1901.

30. Estes, *Good Things to Eat*, 7.

31. Ibid., 28.

32. Ibid., 8.

33. Ibid., 5, 6, 103, 20, 68, 84, 88.

34. Anne Bower points out that many early American cookbooks contained a "preponderance of sweets recipes," suggesting that home cooks would need more assistance with such fancy items.

35. Even in his former hometown of St. Louis, information about Bullock is scarce; the Missouri Historical Society does not even own a copy of his book. As she had with Rufus Estes, Dianna Seay provided me with whatever biographical information she was able to obtain, including material from city directories and census records. Dianna Seay to author, July 16, 2002.

36. On authenticating documents, see Stepto, *Beyond the Veil*, 3–6.

37. Bullock, *The Ideal Bartender*, 5, 3.

38. Ibid., 43.

39. Tunis Campbell became a successful politician in Reconstruction-era Georgia and also a minister.

7

Recipes for History: The National Council
of Negro Women's Five Historical Cookbooks

Anne L. Bower

In 1958 the National Council of Negro Women (NCNW) published its first
fund-raising cookbook, *The Historical Cookbook of the American Negro*. That
unusual collection of recipes emphasized history as much as food, eschewed
conventional chapter categories, denied readers a full contents page or index,
and made no attempt to standardize recipe formats or the types of foods included. Many people urged the book's editor, Sue Bailey Thurman, to use
a more traditional format, but Thurman, a journalist and historian by training, insisted on the original design, what she termed a "culinary approach
to Negro history."[1] Recipes celebrating famous African American events and
people (along with a few whites such as Abraham Lincoln and Harriet Beecher
Stowe) were arranged in calendar order. Thus, the book begins in January, celebrating both New Year's and the Emancipation Proclamation with an "Emancipation Proclamation Breakfast Cake" recipe and carries through to three
recipes selected to mark the December 14 birthday of John Mercer Langston.[2]
Historical information is set off from recipes by italics and may include facts
about particular figures, events, and the recipe's donor—whether an individual

NCNW member, a chapter, or an affiliated group—and why the donor picked one or more particular recipes.

In spite of the book's success, the NCNW did not publish another cookbook until *The Black Family Reunion Cookbook* in 1991. Then, in 1993, 1994, and 1998 it issued three more: *The Black Family Dinner Quilt Cookbook, Celebrating Our Mothers' Kitchens,* and *Mother Africa's Table.* Each looks more like a traditional cookbook than does the 1958 book and includes a contents page, main chapters organized by food categories, and an index. In addition, the more recent cookbooks standardize recipe formats and often detach recipes from donors, perhaps to give the books a more commercial or professional quality. Finally, each book from the 1990s was produced by cookbook professionals, whereas the 1958 book was compiled and edited by NCNW staff under Thurman's leadership.[3] As different from the "parent" text as the four 1990s' texts may be, there is one thing they all share with the 1958 book. In each, some form of history is central to the text.

The National Council of Negro Women continues to stress history in its cookbooks because it has always seen African American women as central figures in forging history through direct action and the production of various programs and texts. From its founding in 1935, the council, under the initial guidance of its founder, Mary McLeod Bethune, worked to "educate, encourage and effect the participation of Negro women in civic, political, economic, and educational activities and institutions" and "plan, initiate and carry out projects which develop, benefit and integrate the Negro and the nation."[4] By the 1950s the organization had fought for fair labor policies, improved education and health care for African Americans, and civil rights. It published the *AfraAmerican Women's Journal* from 1940 (later changing the name to *Women United*), which Sue Bailey Thurman edited. And it supported the formation of the United Nations and arranged to have an NCNW official observer at all U.N. proceedings. From its inception the organization's encouragement of black women activists and its integrationist stance put it in opposition to mainstream America's vision of who made, studied, and wrote history. In the 1990s the same ethos continued to underscore women's capacity to make and tell history, but it included exploration of additional ways to protect traditions as well as work for change.

The historian John Hope Franklin considers the 1958 cookbook to be an important educational tool, one sorely needed, in its time. What was taught during the 1950s and earlier, when people who would have bought the 1958 book were being educated, was dictated by white-dominated school boards. African American educators such as Carter Woodson created and distributed curricula about black history, but it was often, as Franklin has explained, "snuck in via the bottom drawer" in segregated or even integrated schools. Teachers would fit such history into classes as they were able to do so without being accused by supervisors of deviating from the approved curriculum. Although a certain amount of black history was passed along through the oral traditions of home and church, Franklin maintains that many people knew very little of it and that although advances have been made, there are African Americans who still do not understand "how we got from there to here."[5]

Following the model established by The Historical Cookbook of the American Negro in 1958, the four later NCNW cookbooks demonstrate enduring conviction that just as African American women have kept alive their culture through sharing recipes and family stories, they also can, and should, be responsible for passing along their history. Only by becoming historians can they present their understanding of that history. Darlene Clark Hine puts the issue bluntly: "Historians shape, make, or construct history" and for a very long time they left out black women. Of her own undergraduate and graduate education in the 1960s and 1970s, Hine, a historian, reports that it completely excluded the community-making, political, and leadership roles of black women. Central to her work is a concept, the "culture of dissemblance," which she explains as "the behavior and attitudes of Black women that created the appearance of openness and disclosure but actually shielded the truth of their inner lives and selves from their oppressors."[6]

Hine writes of women in slavery times and through the early part of the twentieth century who had to use subterfuge to achieve goals, whether for unionization, voting, or housing. That concept of dissemblance can amplify understanding of the four cookbooks. Although each has the unassuming "face" of a cookbook, each also includes information and formatting that advance goals beyond ways in which to fix food. Each promotes a different vision of history and women's roles in making it, and each relays a somewhat different concept of the relationship between women's public and private spheres.

Beginning with The Historical Cookbook of the American Negro, consider the difficulties involved in an African American woman publishing a history book during the 1950s. Indeed, it was almost impossible. Sue Bailey Thurman's Pioneers of Negro Origin in California appeared in 1952. But that was unusual. In America during the 1950s history was still largely the province of white men.[7] Black men were often left out, and, as Hine writes, the absence of black women was almost total.[8] If Thurman and her collaborators had only written about black history, how many people would have bought and read their boook? The members of the NCNW who created *The Historical Cookbook of the American Negro* thus also practiced a "culture of dissemblance." Their book seemed to be a cookbook, but as they admit in the preface, what they created was a "palatable history" that focuses on black leaders—politicians, doctors, educators, and other professionals, artists, writers, musicians, and clubwomen, some famous and others barely known.

Historical material occupies a smaller share of each of the 1990s' cookbooks yet plays a major role. The non-recipe items in *The Black Family Reunion Cookbook* (1991) have two goals: to honor Bethune and to honor families and family connections. The history being valued is personal and familial, and the text is full of sidebar narratives about individual memories of and relationships to relatives. *The Black Family Dinner Quilt Cookbook* of 1993 celebrates the work of Dorothy Height and again honors Bethune. The majority of sidebars center on the work of Height and her colleagues, whether strengthening the United Nations, participating in the civil rights movement, promoting the education of black women, or influencing governmental policy about women in the military.

Celebrating Our Mothers' Kitchens, which came out a year later, focuses on the maternal presence in the home and elevates black women's importance as keepers of tradition and guardians of family unity and strength. In *Mother Africa's Table* (1998), it is African heritage that takes center stage along with a surprising narrative that emphasizes the "Voice of Mother Africa." Beginning with an introductory passage that bears that title and urges readers to "listen quietly and carefully with your innermost heart while Mother Africa speaks," the tone of the book is surprisingly personal. The voice seems nurturing, even maternal, as it provides information about West African customs and history, how to purchase and prepare unfamiliar ingredients, and dispenses cooking instructions and philosophical advice.

In the sections that follow, my intent is to analyze the nature of the history being told in each cookbook, the strategies used in each to tell that history, and the relationship between history and recipes. Of course, other community cookbooks also include historical information. The Junior League cookbooks, many of which are famous for lavish illustrations and well-tested recipes, sometimes include snippets of regional history; community cookbooks from ethnic or religious groups since the mid-1950s sometimes give historical information on life in the old country or explain the origins of certain holiday traditions; and cookbooks published to support arts institutions, schools, or historical organizations often describe details of the group's founding and development.[9]

Yet no other community cookbooks I have seen compare to the NCNW's in the intensity with which they emphasize history and the importance they attribute to women as historians.[10]

The Historical Cookbook of the American Negro

The women who compiled the 1958 text were creating their own version of national history. Their underlying message seems to be that all those honored in the book contributed to the nation and to the advancement of African Americans. In addition, of course, they assert their right and responsibility to tell that history.

The book's layout is unconventional. Chapter headings are the months of the year, and listings under each month indicate some of the people and events, and a few of the recipes, to be discussed within that particular month. Under "June," for example, the contents page lists Harriet Tubman, Iota Phi Lambda (an organization of business and professional women in Chicago), Charles Richard Drew, Howard Thurman, James Weldon Johnson, Juneteenth, and the Daughters of Elks organization. In two of these cases a particular food is mentioned. "June Commencement Soup" is linked with Howard Thurman's name, and a recipe for rock Cornish hens is with the Iota Phi Lambda group's section. Without browsing the chapter itself, there is no way to know that its nine pages include, in addition to the poultry recipe and Thurman's soup (a beef-, onion-, potato-based mixture, with Thurman providing a seasoning guideline that associates twenty-seven herbs with their symbolic values), recipes for "Pistachio Parfait"; a dinner of broiled steak, buttered baked potatoes, green beans, and hot rolls ("A Favorite Meal of Charles Richard Drew"); watermelon-rind pickle; artichoke soup; honey-orange bread; barbecued veal roast; green beans, hot mustard sauce; "Texas Tongue"; home-made chili sauce; "Watermelon Sherbet"; and "Crab Meat Delight."

The June chapter honors three black women (Harriet Tubman, Maggie L. Walker, and Emma V. Kelley) and three black men (James Weldon Johnson, Charles Richard Drew, and Howard Thurman), a break-down that holds true throughout the book; four white men and three white women are also celebrated. Who is celebrated reveals a great deal about the role of the NCNW book compilers as "national" historians. Of the three men featured, the best known nationally was likely Johnson (1871–1936), a founder and secretary of the NAACP, an educator, a Tin Pan Alley songwriter (with his brother), and, perhaps most famously, a poet and author. Among his works are *The Autobi-*

ography of an Ex-Coloured Man (1912), poetry collections, and three ground-breaking anthologies of African American poetry published during the 1920s. Drew taught at Howard University Medical School and was surgeon-in-chief of Freedman's Hospital. His research into blood preservation was critical to the success of the Red Cross in supplying blood to the Armed Forces during World War II. Thurman, a noted theological writer and religious leader, served as dean of Marsh Chapel at Boston University at the time of *The Historical Cookbook of the American Negro*'s publication.

These three men contributed not only to African American history but also to the nation's. The women discussed are not all as easy to categorize that way. The chapter begins, as do they all, with a photograph. Oddly enough, in this case it's of a ship. The caption explains, "The S.S. Harriet Tubman: Launched at South Portland, Maine, June 3, 1944." The message is that mainstream America has already recognized and honored Tubman. Although female and black, she was an established national hero of such stature in the 1940s that her name could be attached to a naval vessel. Elsewhere in the cookbook (the March chapter) Tubman is recognized more personally with historical text and recipes, but at this point the compilers featured her in another way.

The other two women would probably have been as unknown to many of the cookbook's readers as they are to most people today, and yet Thurman and her colleagues found them worthy of inclusion. Walker was selected by Iota Phi Lambda as an honoree because she was a noted Chicago philanthropist and president of the Saint Luke Penny Savings Bank of Richmond when it opened in 1903. Thus she was the "first woman in America to become the executive of a bank."[11] In the history of women's achievements, as well as those of African Americans, she is singled out for attention. Kelley founded the Grand Temple, Daughter of Elks in 1902, an organization that was a national affiliate of the NCNW and promoted education. Tubman's, Kelley's, and Walker's achievements take their place beside those of Johnson, Drew, and Thurman, and history is expanded to include women as well as men, which rarely happened in earlier books. Without articulating it as a goal, and within their national history, the NCNW compilers launched a feminist, or proto-womanist initiative.[12]

Thus Thurman and the cookbook committee of the NCNW took charge of and changed the nature of history—with a cookbook! Like black women historians who would follow them (e.g., Paula Giddings with *When and Where I Enter: the Impact of Black Women on Race and Sex in America* [1984]), or black literary women who recovered "lost" figures, as Alice Walker did for Zora

Neale Hurston in the 1960s, the women of the NCNW reshaped the nature of what counted as history and who could tell it.

The recipes in the June chapter were typical of those in the rest of the book. Few African American cookbooks of any kind were published before 1970, and the concept of "soul food" associated with the African American culinary heritage did not exist until the late 1960s. Typical of community (or fund-raising) cookbooks, *The Historical Cookbook of the American Negro* is intended for middle-class African Americans, and its compilers sought to maintain certain values of mainstream society, particularly upward mobility and propriety.

To return to the concept of "dissemblance," many recipes in the book draw on distinctly African American foodways and use foods and methods deriving directly from an African heritage, but the rhetoric of the cookbook never dwells on that history. Indeed, the foods presented are eclectic, and discursive material seldom focuses on food itself. The impression created is that, to a large extent, the food that the NCNW contributors prepare and eat is part of mainstream cuisine. Although they no doubt sensed a long affiliation to the foods that were part of their cultural heritage, the compilers chose not to discuss that topic. They knew, however, that a great deal of "southern" cooking was based on the traditions and innovations of black cooks, and that yams, peanuts, black-eyed peas, greens, and hot peppers were African favorites long before they were part of southern or African American cookery.

Only part of the decision not to discuss those culinary roots may reside in philosophical or critical issues. In the 1950s, scholarship on the national and regional derivations of African American cuisine was not widely available, and food history as a field was still in its infancy. Thus it is not surprising that *The Historical Cookbook of the American Negro* contains so little background on the African derivations of foods. Still, based on which recipes are included and which are excluded we learn a little more about how the cookbook promotes the NCNW's integrationist stance while focussing on history.

Consider for a moment "A Favorite Meal of Charles Richard Drew," which consists of food typically associated with "American men" regardless of ethnicity or other grouping: broiled steak, buttered baked potatoes, green beans (made from frozen beans at that, with the simple addition of sliced sautéed mushrooms), hot yeast rolls. Elsewhere, other foods that have little or nothing to do with African roots are included—artichokes, in this case in a soup, and veal in the form of an oven-barbecued roast. Veal is seldom used in the West African countries that were the ancestral homes of most American blacks; barbecue, however, has deep African roots.[13] Yet in *The Historical Cookbook of the*

American Negro barbecuing is brought indoors and applied to a "non-African" meat, veal.

Aside from that barbecue recipe, only one other is mentioned in the June section, and it alludes to the usual outdoor nature of barbecuing. As part of the historical explanation about Juneteenth, readers are told, "The finest 'barbecues', picnics and outings of [Oklahoma and Texas] take place on 'Juneteenth.'"[14] That dissembling statement is interesting because nowhere in the cookbook is there a recipe for barbecuing outdoors. Perhaps the NCNW compilers considered that food tradition, except when linked to particular holidays, to have too many associations to working-class life and outdoor rowdiness. Similarly, the book eliminates a group of foods long part of African American cookery—pig feet, pig tails, and chitterlings (which only appear as a minor and optional ingredient for a Creole gumbo). Evidently, backyard barbecues, chitterlings, and certain other items did not fit into the middle-class lifestyle that the NCNW cookbook creators valued, not only because of class associations but also, especially in the case of chitterlings, because of the connotations of "blackness, "filth," and sexuality.[15]

Consider also what happens to watermelon, that food so stereotyped as part of black culture that to this day some African Americans will not eat it in public. The June chapter mentions watermelon twice, but in neither recipe would the raw fruit be eaten by hand. One recipe is for pickled watermelon rind, and in the other the watermelon is diced and combined with sugar, egg white, lemon juice, and gelatin to produce a sherbet that can be eaten, delicately, with a spoon.

Recipes for greens, black-eyed peas, okra, eggplant, and coconut are part of the cookbook. Certainly, some readers may have known about their African origins, but the compilers do not discuss that fact. Africa enters the discussion only to honor a particular country (as is the case with the stewed beef or chicken selected to mark Ghana's independence day on March 6) or a particular person, such as the Liberian ambassador's wife or the wife of the education attaché to the Ghanian embassy. The food affiliations mentioned are primarily regional. Many foods are described as "southern," a word that, for the compilers, may have been a code for "black" or attributed to various countries, as in the section of recipes that celebrate the United Nations. Overall, the selection of foods is eclectic, ranging from fancy (lobster is in more than one dish) to humble (more than one recipe for corn bread is included), from southern (southern fried chicken) to northern (cranberries), and from simple (frozen green beans) to elaborate (Howard Thurman's "June Commencement Soup" calls for many herbs).

In each case, the recipes were included because various NCNW chapters and members selected them to honor figures and events the compilers considered to be of national importance. Sometimes the tie between food and historical figure is direct and obvious, building on something we know of the individual. "Cherry Torte Ice Cream," for example, is linked to George Washington. Sometimes the pairing becomes obvious after reading the historical background on a person. Two recipes for Indian curry, for example, are paired with the information on Juliette Dericotte, who frequently traveled to India when a member of the World Student Christian Federation. Dericotte later became dean of women at Fisk University. At other times what links an individual and a food is the person donating the recipe. Vivian Carter Mason, for example, a leading member of the NCNW, contributed "Aunt Harriet's Favorite Dish" (corn bread). According to the accompanying story, when Harriet Tubman visited Mason's mother she was served the corn bread and found it delicious.

I have pointed out some of the ways that the foods selected for this book indicate its authors' cultural attitudes and historical knowledge, but it is important to remember that what we now call soul food should not be seen as somehow the authentic culinary marker of black experience, with other foods then located in some less authentic space. It is just as inappropriate to stereotype people by their food as by any other aspect of their lives. Bell Hooks maintains that in most cases, "Our concept of black experience has been too narrow and constricting."[16]

Part of what the collective authors of *The Historical Cookbook of the American Negro* managed by means of inclusive history and an eclectic group of recipes was to expand the sense of what black experience encompassed. While shunning certain food customs as too laden with negative class associations (chitterlings and pig's feet) the compilers managed to create subtextual messages of great importance: Don't stereotype black women, don't stereotype black history, and don't stereotype black food. Through the book, black women assert the right to claim their place in history and narrate that history in a way that includes food, customs, and figures well known or less recognized.

The Black Family Reunion Cookbook: Recipes and Food Memories from the National Council of Negro Women, Inc.

Under the leadership of Dorothy I. Height, the NCNW began Black Family Reunion Celebration programs across the nation in 1986 to foster "new community energy and . . . self-help approaches to many contemporary concerns" and work to advance "the values, traditions and historic strengths of the African-American family."[17] The organization dedicated its 1991 cookbook to Bethune, and Janet Cheatham Bell, a professional editor and book publisher, compiled the volume. Libby Clark, food editor of the *Los Angeles Sentinel*, and Jessica Harris, a professor of French and English who is also well known for the African American cookbooks she has produced, provided considerable background on food origins. The book focuses on family history, "family" referring to individual families as well as the "family" of the NCNW, as Height explains in her introduction.

The Black Family Reunion Cookbook contrasts with the 1958 book by being a much more standardized collection of recipes. Its main chapters cover breads, soups and salads, vegetables and side dishes, main-meal dishes, and family desserts. In addition to Height's introduction, a publisher's note about Height, a dedication to Bethune, and the "Black Family Reunion Pledge" written by Maya Angelou for the NCNW's May 14, 1986, Black Family Reunion Celebration precede the recipes. At the end of the book is an "African-American Heritage" section. Each of the six food chapters begins with special pages that carry a portion of "The Legacy of Mary McLeod Bethune" along with an image of a West African textile and a brief explanation of the textile's origin, how it was made, and the significance of its pattern.[18]

The recipes in *The Black Family Reunion Cookbook* consistently call for standard measurements and follow a rigorous format: a list of ingredients, a bit of space, and then a numbered series of instructions. Occasionally, a tip, or variations, or a note follow; the number of servings per recipe is always given. The only names attached to recipes are those of certain prominent contributors, whether entertainers, executive chefs, officers of major black service organizations, or journalists. A list of all recipe donors, however, is included at the back of the cookbook, just before the index. A special icon and the words *Heritage Recipe* accompany certain recipes to indicate these foods as having African or traditional soul food origins. The term is also used for certain recipes taken from the 1958 cookbook.

"Party Pigs Feet," "Navy Beans and Pig Tails," "Chitlins à la California," "Chicken Feet Stew," and "Ham Hocks and Red Beans"—dishes that would never be found in the earlier *Historical Cookbook of the American Negro*— proudly share space with a standing rib roast, "Deep Fried Maryland Crab Cakes," roast turkey, and baked ham. When it comes to recipes for barbecue, *The Black Family Reunion Cookbook* provides "Southern Style Barbecued Pigs

Feet," three pork rib variations (two cooked on the grill, one in the oven), and "Sweet and Spicy Barbecued Grilled Chicken."

How the books present their first recipe, "Emancipation Proclamation Breakfast Cake," provides a sense of how the volumes differ. The recipe begins the earlier book, which is arranged in calendar order, because it is associated with New Year's Day and the Emancipation Proclamation. In the later book, the first food category is "Bread Specialities," and the breakfast cake is listed first because it is considered a Heritage Recipe within that category.

The only changes in the 1991 version of the recipe are that Crisco replaces butter and frozen blueberries are given as an option for fresh ones. Measurements are also more exact. The earlier book asks for one to two cups of blueberries, whereas the 1991 publication calls for 1½ cups; the earlier recipe lists "½ cup (more or less) milk," and the later book requires exactly a third of a cup. Preparation directions for the earlier recipe are somewhat unclear. The cook is instructed to "cut [the batter] with a biscuit cutter and arrange in greased pie pan in tilted fashion." *The Black Family Reunion Cookbook*, by contrast, provides more information: "Cut into nine three-inch rounds. Place one in center of pie plate. Arrange eight, tilted and overlapping, around center dough circle."

"The Emancipation Proclamation New Years' Day, 1863, is celebrated in all parts of the United States. The Council recipes assembled from the six geographical regions have been taken from the oldest files of Negro families" appears in italics at the foot of the first page of the 1958 book to begin a section that contains five recipes in addition to "Emancipation Proclamation Breakfast Cake." The words demonstrate the "national history" attitude of Thurman and her collaborators. In the 1991 cookbook we find something quite different. The cake recipe begins a section on breads and is unrelated to other New Year's or Emancipation Proclamation traditions. It is followed by a sesame seed cracker recipe and ones for biscuits and rolls. The historical information linked to the breakfast cake no longer explains what the Emancipation Proclamation is but rather relates history in terms of family and regional traditions. As part of her sidebar to the cake recipe, Mayme L. Brown of Williamsburg, Virginia, writes, "In my home state we have commemorated the Emancipation Proclamation on the 8th of August, or the closest weekend to that date, with basket dinners. Former slaves and descendants of slaves would come from around the country for this grand day of celebration."[19]

In the case of "Texas Tongue," another recipe from the earlier book that appears as a Heritage Recipe in the later book, there are a few differences. Aside from standardized format of the recipe itself, the only ingredient change is substitution of Crisco for olive oil.[20] The earlier book makes clear that this recipe is traditionally associated with "Juneteenth," but the 1991 text has no such information, nor does it include Juneteenth in the section toward the end, where menus are given for Kwanza, the Fourth of July, graduation, New Year's Eve, Thanksgiving and Christmas, a Martin Luther King breakfast celebration, a family reunion picnic, and a Friday night fish fry.

Given its emphasis on family history, it is not surprising that this recipe collection has room for chitterlings (one recipe), a "Chicken Feet Stew," ham hocks, "Hog Head Souse," pig tails, and three recipes for pig's feet. The book also includes recipes for foods that can be costly, such as shrimp and a standing-rib beef roast. The implication is that black families can eat food that is expensive and food that is not, mainstream dishes, and traditional ones. Although *The Black Family Reunion Cookbook* presents a somewhat standardized format and regularized recipes, its text as a whole provides a diversified, complex portrait of black experience and history and the ways in which women, within families and communities, carry on that history.

The Black Family Dinner Quilt Cookbook: Health Conscious Recipes and Food Memories

Conceptually, this book presents a coherent depiction of communal female action within which strong individual women serve as leaders. "Mealtime Dialogue," a quilt, is reproduced on the front of the book. Created by textile artist Faith Ringgold, the work depicts Bethune and Height sharing lunch and notes; the women are surrounded by quiltmakers, children who are reading, and women hanging quilts. A quotation from Bethune is part of the quilt's border: "I leave you love. I leave you hope. I leave you the challenge of developing confidence in one another. I leave you a thirst for education. I leave you responsibility for the use of power. I leave you faith. I leave you racial dignity. I leave you a desire to live harmoniously with your fellow man. I leave you responsibility to our young people." The quilt on the back of the book features a strong individual of the past, Harriet Tubman, and text explaining that the quilt was made during the 1920s by a collective, the History Quilt Club of Sausalito and Morin City, California. The history in this book could be termed womanist-organizational, for it stresses the capacity of generations of women to work together in accomplishing important goals.

The balance between individual women and collective action continues with a dedication by Alice Walker, who describes women of her mother's generation as "Headragged Generals" who battled to create better lives for their daughters. They "booby-trapped / Kitchens / To discover books / Desks / A place for us."[21] In emphasizing the soldierlike strength of her maternal ancestors and evoking the plotting and manipulations women underwent to advance opportunities for their daughters, Walker's poem recalls the direct actions and the "culture of dissemblance" approach that black women have employed to improve life for themselves and their people. The unattributed prose passage that follows the poem extends the concept of strong women coming together to make a better world. Among them are generations of women of many skin tones, those who survived slavery, European immigrants, and "the patrician women, the American aristocrats by virtue of their birth or their own accomplishments." Then a formal introduction recalls Bethune's words and actions and emphasizes Height's leadership, all the while strengthening the ideal of group action. The introduction ends with a return to the idea of "quilting as a metaphor for communication, fellowship and the richness of sharing between women of all races."[22]

This "health conscious" book was created by a team of five: an artist, a writer, a nutritionist, a quilting consultant, and a book designer. The team approach to recipes echoes the notion that many quilts are created by groups and much history comes from group action. Recipes use Crisco shortening or oil rather than butter or lard; often feature turkey or another low-fat alternative to pork; and include calorie, fat, carbohydrate, protein, cholesterol, and sodium content. For the most part, recipe sources are not given, although well-known donors are acknowledged, as with "Favorite Cajun Catfish" adapted from a recipe of Alvin F. Poussaint or "Melba's Collard Greens and Turkey Wings" from the entertainer Melba Moore. There is no list of donors in the book.

As in its 1991 predecessor, some dishes in the 1993 publication are labeled "Heritage Recipes." Ones for barbecueing a number of foods are included (pork, chicken, and fish), but there are no recipes for ham hocks, jowls, or chitterlings, presumably for health reasons although that is not made explicit. Food is crafted to be healthy to strengthen those who consume it so they can continue the important work of education, leadership, and achievement modeled by the NCNW.

In conjunction with the healthier eating promoted by *The Black Family Dinner Quilt Cookbook* is the moral and social health information offered through sidebars about women leaders and collectives of women; many feature Dorothy Height. In one such passage, for example, Lauren Cooper tells of meeting Height at a conference and learning about her experiences in Pennsylvania, where none of Height's teachers was black yet she still learned and grew. In another sidebar Wilma Harvey describes a typical NCNW staff meeting and stresses that the meetings covered inspirational material and global concerns. Height made sure that each meeting took "place over a meal," whether "Chinese food, deli sandwiches or a soul food feast."[23] Sally Shigley observes that "through its narratives, its 'food memories,' and its connecting of domestic and public worlds, it [the cookbook] offers hope and a sense of continuity to a wide spectrum of women."[24]

The 1993 cookbook, like its NCNW predecessors, refuses to reside neatly within the category *cookbook*. As Shigley points out, the book is not just a cookbook although it contains many recipes, it is not just a story although it contains narratives, and its intent is not just rhetorical although it "has a persuasive intent to raise money." As it crosses genre boundaries it also breaks down the "hierarchical disjunction between 'domestic' and 'professional' women, or between public and private spheres."[25] Thus, although there is still some dissembling, the book—which, after all, is titled a cookbook and positions women as the traditional guardians of family health and domestic well-being—takes advantage of every representational mode to undo its dissemblance. Scientists helped formulate these recipes, artists of repute supplied the book's illustrations, accomplished public leaders provided stories, and food is seen as part of public life as well as something to nourish each separate family. Once again an NCNW cookbook positioned women to represent and shape history and a worldview.

Celebrating Our Mothers' Kitchens: Treasured Memories and Tested Recipes

Responding perhaps to actual and perceived social threats to family, the NCNW produced its fourth cookbook under the dual leadership of Jessica Harris, who served as editorial consultant, and Cheryl Whiteman-Brooks, Kraft General Food's manager of ethnic marketing. Many of the recipes use Kraft products, and the desire to feature some of those products seems to have influenced the book's overall collection of recipes although the long list of recipe contributors provided on pages 215 and 216 include Rosa Parks, Patti LaBelle, Dorothy I. Height, Coretta Scott King, and Carol Moseley-Braun. With its emphasis on convenience, a standardized format, and a wide variety of dishes, however, the cookbook can be very serviceable. What is noteworthy, as the volume's title reveals, is the emphasis on mothers. Readers sense a maternal presence, whether from Height, who dedicates the book to her mother; Bethune, the organization's "mother"; the "Mothers of the Women of Distinction"; or the many NCNW members who provided their mothers' sayings and phrases featured in attractively bordered boxes at the bottoms of many, many pages. These featured phrases all begin with "my mother [name of person] said" and then reproduce a piece of advice or a proverblike sentence. The use of past tense creates a memorializing tone that seems to emphasize the mothers' absence. In her introduction, Harris, too, indicates longing for the missing mother. She admits that society's difficulties cannot be solved by a home-cooked meal from mother in the kitchen, but she still has great nostalgia for "the timeless, sustaining warmth of our Mother's [*sic*] kitchen."[26]

As in so many other community cookbooks regardless of their creators' race or ethnic heritage, responsibility for the well-being of the family is delineated as the mother's role. Very occasionally a father is mentioned, as in a recipe for black bean fritters, but that is rare. Here, history starts with the mother and the responsibility she takes to create her family's strength. That strength derives in part from heritage (there is a section of Heritage Recipes annotated by Harris) and in part from wisdom accrued and passed on to daughters. They, in turn, listen to that wisdom and may also pass it along.

The mothers and daughters (and editors) who collected recipes for *Celebrating Our Mothers' Kitchens* enjoy a wide variety of foods, from chitterlings to *fuul medames* (made with red beans rather than the traditional fava beans), spinach artichoke casserole to "Cassava Mojo," and "Kente Cloth Cake" to *arroz con dulce*. Recipes for corn bread, greens, barbecue (pork ribs, beef, and meatballs), macaroni and cheese, and other homey soul food dishes abound. The mothers responsible for such food are inventive in creating new variations on old standards and in using mixes and prepared items to shorten preparation time. Their personal lives and those of their daughters, however, are seldom featured. We sense a variety of cultural forces at work, shaping the lives of the women who created the recipes, but must interact imaginatively with the text in order to begin to fully realize those complexities. Of course, that is the nature of most cookbooks. Even as one measures and stirs, following instructions for a cake or casserole, one may mentally mix and meld hints in the text to realize experiences that have shaped the women who contributed to *Celebrating Our Mothers' Kitchens*.[27] In that sense the book, although it does not provide a concept, theory, or full statement about the maternal as a source of history, does imply that individuals, communities, and societies depend on maternal forces.

Mother Africa's Table: A Collection of West African and African American Recipes and Cultural Traditions

The National Council's fifth cookbook takes and shapes history in a way that perhaps had to wait until the end of the twentieth century, when cultural studies, black studies, women's studies, and even food studies became integral to understanding history. Since the 1960s, popular and scholarly histories have explored the West African background of those who came to the United States in chains. *Roots* is but one example in popular culture. In food studies, scholars and cookbook authors began to explore soul food and its West African traditions. Only since the 1980s, however, has intensive food history about West Africa been widely published. At the same time, recent years have seen Americans import and use more "foreign" or exotic foods. In addition, there has been greater promotion of food as a cultural expression, and increased publication of cookbooks that encourage cooking authentic food of other countries whether or not such food is part of the cook's own ancestry. A pursuit of ancestral history is what is valued in *Mother Africa's Table*.

This cookbook, compiled by Cassandra Hughes Webster but crediting a list of nearly thirty contributors, "speaks" maternally. Webster opens with the "Voice of Mother Africa," a short passage that depicts Mother Africa weeping and mourning a past when so many of her children were stolen. Yet Mother Africa is said to have "imparted pearls of wisdom" to those leaving her shores, giving them forever "proverbs . . . songs . . . the story of a people's past."

In that imagined monologue, Webster's mother figure imbues proverbs, songs, and story with wisdom about "family, faith, tradition, memory, respect, dignity, empathy, and knowledge." Those eight categories are paired with food categories for the food chapters, so, by implication, Mother Africa somehow transmits values through food. A short introduction by Jessica Harris again depicts Mother Africa crying for her children but whispering "into their ear the very food that was to enable them to survive." Harris blurs the line between the nourishment provided by a sense of the past and one's ancestry and that provided by food rooted in that past and ancestry. Chapter 1 provides "Menus for African Ceremonies," and chapter 2 features menus for "African American Celebrations." The following seven chapters supply recipes within food categories such as "Salads, Soups, and Breads" and "Rice, Legumes, Porridges, Dumplings, and Starchy Vegetables." Chapter 10 concentrates on "West African Food, Culture, and History at a Glance," and the epilogue, written by Dorothy Height, stresses the synergy produced when "Mother Africa's people—old and new, near and far" gather and share food, work, and concern for their own people and others. For Height, the epitome of that synergistic process is the National Council of Women.

In providing a cookbook based on ancestral history the NCNW seems to advance the message that African Americans are now free to explore the authentic foods and customs of their ancestors. They can celebrate Kwanzaa and/or Christmas, and they can eat Nigerian "Moi-Moi (Steamed Black-Eyed Pea Pudding)" and/or African American black-eyed peas and ham hocks. The book includes food commonly found in other African American cookbooks (e.g., corn bread and fried chicken). What is special here is an elaboration of background material on African ingredients, cooking methods, and food customs and recipes for dishes unique to the countries of West Africa, from Ghana to Nigeria and Liberia to Côte D'Ivoire.

The presentation of the cookbook is cohesive; recipes and discursive texts blend with decorative elements to conceptualize a cultural tradition that offers ethical depth and gustatory choice. In a way, it's as if the book's creators imagined that time before cookbooks when daughters could learn wisdom and cooking through working with mothers at hearths or stoves, the traditions passed down orally. In slavery times, that close mother-daughter relationship was frequently broken when the mother was separated from her children. At another level the mother-child relationship was ruptured because so many people were separated from their mother country. Because many social and economic factors still deter the traditional oral transmission of wisdom across generations—wisdom the creators of the book think it necessary to know— *Mother Africa's Table* attempts an overt connection between the written tradition of a cookbook and the oral traditions of earlier times.

Although I have stressed this book's orality, the "voice" of Mother Africa is not chatty or colloquial. In fact, it is quite formal. In the passage about knowledge that opens chapter 3, "Beverages and Openers," for example, we are told: "One good way to really get to know and connect with someone is to invite him or her to dinner." Sometimes the voice uses proverbs and old sayings to make its points ("Knowledge is like the communal cup of palm wine. Hoarded it turns into vinegar; shared, it is the nectar of the gods").[28] Within recipes the voice provides information about ingredients that might not be familiar. In "Watermelon-Ginger Refresher," as in the other recipes, a standard presentation lists the ingredients first, followed by the instructions for combining them. In this recipe and in many others, however, two more paragraphs follow. The first begins "HINT: To grate the ginger." It is as if an instructress was standing beside the cook and discussing how to do something that many readers may not have seen.[29] The second paragraph describes what to look for when buying ginger. In the past, one would have learned how to select and grate ginger through shopping and cooking with a person—most likely, one's mother. In this book, that absent person, that mother, is replaced by words that represent her presence.[30]

As an idealized mother-text the 1998 cookbook has a quiet presence although it comes dressed brightly. The book's boards are red, and its jacket illustration, four adults and three children during meal preparation in an African village, is multicolored and dramatic. The book is printed in brown ink on off-white paper and has light-brown border decorations, a different pattern for each chapter. Each chapter begins with a page of wisdom that includes an anecdote, direct address, and abstract speculation. Thus, chapter 6 on fish, seafood, poultry, and meat begins with a section entitled "Dignity." It sketches out a television news segment that shows poor African villagers as dignified even though they struggle against many troubles. "When the world seems to be crashing down all around you and you can still walk with your head held high," the narrative voice observes, "that is dignity." It continues with similar phrases and then states that "the dignity of a people is rooted in self-love and self-knowledge." These, in turn, depend upon an authentic sense of identity. Identity and authenticity are linked to creativity and finally to food. "Where else but from dignity could a really good jambalaya spring?" Mother Africa asks.[31] In creating another conceptually unusual cookbook the NCNW has continued to put forth the role of women in guarding and shaping history and culture.

The motherly tone of the text mixes instruction about exotic foods with the usual recipe form, often allowing readers to expand their knowledge of African folk traditions as well. A passage at the end of the "Callaloo Soup" recipe explains that the term *callaloo* is given "to many of the popular green-leafed vegetables" in Caribbean cooking, deriving from West African cuisine. *Efo* is the word usually used in Nigeria for the edible leaves of root vegetables, and "silver beets" is a name for spinach greens in many parts of Africa. Likewise, in a recipe for *bajia* (a sauce made of coconut milk, tomatoes, chilis, and beer), readers are told, "In Kenya, this sauce is made with coconut alcohol." A note at the beginning of the recipe for Ghanian "Banku (Corn Dumplings)" explains, "Traditionally, banku is made with fermented corn (maize) and/or cassava dough. These traditional dumplings are generally made without spices or herbs and served in a spicy sauce or savory stews. This modern variation uses cornmeal and spices."[32]

Conclusion

The five cookbooks published by the National Council of Negro Women each have different objectives but share an enduring dedication to black women's capacities and responsibilities as guardians of history and culture and as people who can provide effective self-representation to their own people and a wider readership as well. As Marvalene H. Hughes has noted, in order to find "missing pieces of our life's puzzles" we delve into "ancestral cultures and genetic roots." Implying that what she has found to be true is relevant, albeit with different patterns of emphasis, for others who search the past to understand the present and future, she adds, "As a Black woman, some pieces of my puzzle will relate to my African ancestry; some pieces will relate to the Black struggle in U.S. history; and other pieces will relate to my female identity."[33] Each piece of the puzzle is touched upon by the NCNW cookbooks, whether the national history in *The Historical Cookbook of the American Negro*, the family history in *The Black Family Reunion Cookbook*, the womanist-organizational history in *The Black Family Dinner Quilt Cookbook*, the implied maternal-as-part-of-history in *Celebrating Our Mothers' Kitchens*, or the ancestral history in *Mother Africa's Table*.

The NCNW has used cookbooks to unfold various versions of history, and compilers, editors, and collaborators have also enabled the books to transcend genre boundaries and assert creative, womanist approaches to history. The books give voice to all the silenced mothers and grandmothers of Alice Walker's "In Search of Our Mothers' Gardens," women "driven to a numb and bleeding madness by the springs of creativity in them for which there was no release."[34] It is clear that cookbooks remain useful to the National Council as a means of presenting "palatable history" even as the focus of such work changes. Whether trying to maintain a sense of their place in national history in the 1950s or to preserve family identity, maternal identity, womanist-organizational power, or ancestral heritage in the 1990s, NCNW members have found, in cookbooks, a way to transport history to a wide audience and position themselves as creative historians.

NOTES

1. Dorothy Height, the former president of the National Council of Negro Women and a member of the advisory committee for the 1958 cookbook, recalls Thurman using this phrase. Height was unsure of Thurman's motivation but agreed that the result of her decision is that anyone looking for a specific recipe is forced to browse through the

cookbook in search of it and is consequently exposed to a great deal of history. Telephone interview with Dorothy Height, April 6, 2000.

2. The Emancipation Proclamation was drawn up in September 1862 but withheld until after the Union won the Battle of Antietam. As *The Historical Cookbook of the American Negro* explains, June 19 is commonly used as the date to celebrate the Emancipation Proclamation in the South "in preference to the official Emancipation Proclamation Day, January 1. It was not until June of 1863 that recognition was given and action taken regarding the White House Proclamation" (58). Langston was born a slave but went on to obtain a law degree and be vice president of Howard University, secretary of the District of Columbia, president of Virginia State College in Petersburg, and U.S. consul-general in Haiti. In 1888 he was elected to the U.S. Congress. These recipes end the calendar cycle but are followed by a section entitled "Favorite Family recipes of Charter Members and Past and Present Officers of The National Council of Negro Women."

3. *The Black Family Reunion Cookbook* was produced by Tradery House in 1991 and then reprinted by Fireside, a subsidiary of Simon and Schuster. *The Black Family Dinner Quilt Cookbook* (1993) was published by the Wimmer Companies "in corporate sponsorship with the Crisco Division of Procter and Gamble." *Celebrating Our Mothers' Kitchens* (1994), also published by Wimmer, was produced in corporate partnership with Kraft General Foods. Ellen Rolphe, a professional book packager, took the lead in seeing *Mother Africa's Table* to press, and it was published in 1998 by Doubleday under their Main Street Book division. *The Historical Cookbook of the American Negro* was printed by the Corporate Press, but Sue Bailey Thurman, founding editor of the NCNW's *AfraAmerican Women's Journal* and the NCNW Cookbook Advisory Committee, researched, compiled, and edited the book. The original plates of the book have been lost. The reprinted edition (Beacon Press, 2000) was made from a copy of the original book.

4. Tracey A. Fitzgerald, *The National Council of Negro Women and the Feminist Movement, 1935–1975* (Washington, D.C.: Georgetown University Press, 1985), 13.

5. John Hope Franklin, author of *From Slavery to Freedom: A History of African-Americans* (New York: A. A. Knopf, 1947), a civil rights activist, and noted teacher, owns a copy of *The Historical Cookbook of the American Negro* and appreciates it for its role as a tool of history education. Author interview with John Hope Franklin, Aug. 1, 1999.

6. Dorothy Clark Hine, *Hine Sight: Black Women and the Re-Construction of American History* (Brooklyn: Carlson, 1994), xxviii.

7. For a sense of this distribution see the bibliographies of two mid-century history books, Lerone Bennett Jr., *Before the Mayflower: A History of the Negro in America, 1619–1962* (Chicago: Johnson Publishing, 1962), and J. Saunders Redding, *They Came in Chains: Americans from Africa* (Philadelphia: J. Lippincott, 1950).

8. Hine, *Hine Sight*, 20.

9. For background on community cookbooks see Anne Bower, "Cooking Up Stories: Narrative Elements in Community Cookbooks" in *Recipes for Reading: Community Cookbooks, Stories, Histories*, edited by Bower (Amherst: University of Massachusetts Press, 1997), 29–50.

10. One delightful exception is *Canyon Cookery: A Gathering of Recipes and Recollections from Montana's Scenic Bridger Canyon*, which was produced by the Bridger

Canyon Women's Club of Bozeman, Montana, in 1978. This informally published, eight-and-a-half-by-eleven-inch, paperbound volume of somewhat more than 150 pages brings together history, geology, photographs, drawings, personal recollections, and recipes. In *Canyon Cookery*, women have created their own compendious notion of history.

11. Thurman, ed. and comp., *The Historical Cookbook of the American Negro*, 51.

12. The term *womanist*, used to heighten awareness that black feminists did not necessarily fit into patterns delineated by white feminists of the 1960s and 1970s, was unavailable to the compilers of *The Historical Cookbook of the American Negro*. I am therefore calling their implied attitudes "proto-womanist." Their implicit philosophy and social stance is very much within the concept of womanist as provided by Alice Walker at the beginning of *In Search of Our Mothers' Gardens: Womanist Prose* (San Diego: Harvest-Harcourt Brace Jovanovich, 1984), xi. The definition reads, in part, "Womanist: A black feminist or feminist of color. . . . Usually referring to outrageous, audacious, courageous, or *willful* behavior. . . . Responsible. In charge. *Serious.*"

13. Thurman, ed. and comp., *The Historical Cookbook of the American Negro*, 52–53. In *Soul and Spice: African Cooking in the Americas* (San Francisco: Chronicle Books, 1995), Heidi Cusick traces barbecue back thirty thousand years in Africa; see also Helen Mendes, *The African Heritage Cookbook* (New York: Macmillan, 1971).

14. Thurman, ed. and comp., *The Historical Cookbook of the American Negro*, 58.

15. For a discussion of the relationship between chitterlings, blackness, and "filth" along with sexuality, see Doris Witt, "Soul Food: Where the Chitterling Hits the (Primal) Pan," in *Eating Culture*, edited by Ron Scapp and Brian Seitz (Albany: State University of New York Press, 1998), 258–87.

16. Bell Hooks, *Yearning: Race, Gender, and Cultural Politics* (Boston: South End Press, 1990), 38.

17. Natonal Council of Negro Women, *The Black Family Reunion Cookbook: Recipes and Food Memories from the National Council of Negro Women, Inc.* (Memphis: Tradery House, 1991), iii, 202.

18. Shortly before her death Bethune dictated what has come to be known as the "Bethune Legacy" to the editor of *Ebony* magazine. Her words are inscribed on the base of Bethune's bronze memorial in Washington, D.C.'s Lincoln Park. *The Black Family Reunion Cookbook*, v.

19. Because communications were slow at best and often interrupted during the Civil War, news of the Emancipation Proclamation reached various parts of the South and the West at different times. The date for celebrating this event is still not uniform around the United States, although in the years since publication of *The Historical Cookbook of the American Negro* it seems that more and more people use "Juneteenth" (usually June 19) as the somewhat official celebration date. Mayme Brown's explanation occurs on page 3 of *The Black Family Reunion Cookbook*.

20. Nothing in the frontmatter of the book indicates sponsorship by Procter and Gamble, the maker of Crisco, but they were likely a silent partner, for Crisco is specified in almost all cases that require shortening or oil. (In contrast, the copyright pages of the 1993 and 1994 NCNW cookbooks carry specific corporate partnership information.) The original recipe, which calls for olive oil, is probably healthier than the 1991 version that specifies Crisco oil.

21. As it appears on page 5 of *The Black Family Dinner Quilt Cookbook,* the poem follows the word "Dedication," without a separate title although a footnote gives the original title as "Women" and credits its publication in Alice Walker's *Revolutionary Petunias and Other Poems* (New York: Harcourt Brace Jovanovich, 1973).

22. *The Black Family Dinner Quilt Cookbook,* 9.

23. Cooper's story appears on pages 44–45 of *The Black Family Dinner Quilt Cookbook;* Harvey's is on page 141.

24. Sally Shigley, "Empathy, Energy, and Eating: Politics and Power in *The Black Family Dinner Quilt Cookbook,*" in *Recipes for Reading,* edited by Anne L. Bower (Amherst: University of Massachusetts Press, 1997), 118–31.

25. Shigley, "Empathy, Energy, and Eating," 124, 125.

26. *Celebrating Our Mothers' Kitchens,* 6.

27. For fine examples of how imagination can interact with cookbook texts to re-create the cookbook authors, see Janet Theophano, *Eat My Words: Reading Women's Lives Through the Cookbooks They Wrote* (New York: Palgrave, 2002).

28. *Mother Africa's Table,* 18.

29. Ibid., 20.

30. While I was first writing this essay I was also, quite by chance, rereading Toni Morrison's novel *Jazz* and was fascinated to see how that novel, like *Mother Africa's Table,* centers around a missing mother. Most of the central characters—Joe and Violet Trace, Dorcas (the young girl with whom Joe has an affair), Felice (the young girl who at first seems like she'll be another Dorcas but becomes a healing force for Joe and Violet)—are motherless.

31. *Mother Africa's Table,* 82.

32. Ibid., 45, 141.

33. Marvalene H. Hughes, "Soul, Black Women, and Food," in *Food and Culture: A Reader,* edited by Carole Counihan and Penny Van Esterik (New York: Routledge, 1997), 273.

34. Walker, *In Search of Our Mothers' Gardens,* 233.

Contributors

ANNE L. BOWER, retired from her position as associate professor of English at the Ohio State University–Marion, is the author of *Epistolary Responses: The Letter in Twentieth-Century American Fiction and Criticism;* the editor of (and a contributor to) *Recipes for Reading: Community Cookbooks, Stories, Histories;* the concept editor for the reprinted edition of *The Historical Cookbook of the American Negro,* originally published in 1958 by the National Council of Negro Women; and editor of *Reel Food: Essays on Food and Film.* She also serves on the editorial board of *Food and Foodways.*

ROBERT L. HALL is an associate professor of African American studies and history at Northeastern University and has also taught at Tallahassee Community College, Florida State University, the University of West Florida, Rice University, the University of Maryland–Baltimore County, George Mason University, and Yale University. He is the author of numerous articles, essays, and reviews and editor of *Viewpoints on the African American Past: From the Middle Passage to* Plessy v. Ferguson (1995) and *Making a Living: Work Experience of African Americans in New England* (1995). He coedited, with Carol B. Stack, *Holding on to the Land and the Lord: Kinship, Land Tenure, and Social Policy in the Rural South* (1982). He has received fellowships from the Whitney M. Young Memorial Foundation, Duke University's Center for the Study of Civil Rights and Race Relations, the Smithsonian Institution, and the American Council of Learned Societies.

WILLIAM C. WHIT, retired from his position as associate professor of sociology at Grand Valley State University, is the author of *Food and Society: A Sociological Approach* (1995). Among his numerous articles is "World Hunger," which appeared in *A Sociology of Food and Nutrition* (2005). He is a co-founder of the Association for the Study of Food and Society.

PSYCHE WILLIAMS-FORSON, an assistant professor of American studies at the University of Maryland College Park, is the author of *Building Houses Out of Chicken Legs: Black Women, Food, and Power* (2006). During 2005–6 she served as a Ford Fellow at the National Museum of American History at the Smithsonian Institution.

DORIS WITT is an associate professor of English at the University of Iowa, where she teaches primarily post–World War II literary and cultural studies. She is the author of

Black Hunger: Soul Food and America (2004). Having completed a J.D. at the University of Iowa College of Law in May 2007, she is pursuing research in food, cultural, and legal studies.

ANNE YENTSCH is a professor of anthropology and teaches in the biology department of Armstrong Atlantic State University. She is the author of *A Chesapeake Family and Their Slaves* and at work on a project about the archaeology of recipes.

RAFIA ZAFAR is a professor of English, African and African American, and American culture studies at Washington University in St. Louis. She is the author of *We Wear the Mask: African Americans Write American Literature, 1760–1870* and coeditor of *God Made Man, Man Made the Slave: The Autobiography of George Teamoh* and *Harriet Jacobs and Incidents in the Life of a Slave Girl: New Critical Essays.* Her book-in-progress is entitled "And Called It Macaroni." She also serves on the editorial board of *Food and Foodways.*

Index

Adanson, Michel, 22, 39n22

African American culture: food in, 1, 6–10, 12n12, 35, 44nn66–67, 46–47, 50, 53–56, 57n3, 59–60, 102, 114, 117–19, 127, 135, 161–64; and southern (white) culture, 9, 18, 36n3, 56–57n11, 71, 74, 85, 93nn50–52, 107, 122n21; women's role in, 1–7, 12nn5–6, 12n8, 36n3, 154–58, 166–67, 170–71, 172n4

African American entrepreneurship, 3, 9, 46, 69–70, 71–75, 79, 84, 86, 93n46, 93nn51–53, 94n58, 94n60, 94n64, 94n68, 97n115, 98n120, 105, 139–42, 149, 149n5, 151n18

African ancestry and heritage, 5–9, 17–19, 24, 31, 32nd, 46–47, 52–53, 62, 74, 142, 156, 159, 162, 168–71, 174n33

Alagoa, E. J., 28, 40n34, 42n 45, 42n48

Al-Mas'udi, 26, 41n37

Angelou, Maya, 59, 82, 87n3, 97n105, 162

Armstrong, Louis, 103, 121n8

ash baking, 49, 52, 62, 77, 95n84

Atlantic slave trade, 9, 17–18, 23–24, 28, 32–33, 35, 36n2, 36n5, 42nn50–51, 106. *See also* Middle Passage

Aunt Jemima stereotype, 3–4, 12n5, 119–20

Ayensu, Edward S., 31, 43n59, 44n64

Bailey, Pearl, 117, 124n55

Baker, H. G., 22, 38n16

Baker, Huston, 101, 120n1, 123n30

banana: cultivation in Central Africa, 21–22, 39n21; introduction into Africa, 17, 21, 25–26, 41nn36–38; introduction into Western hemisphere, 26, 41n38, 47; as luxury for sharecroppers, 78; origin and name 26, 41n36; in parts of American south, 81; pudding, 59

Baraka, Amiri (Leroi Jones), 114, 124n45

barbecue, 69–70, 85, 92n43, 103, 157, 159–60, 162–63, 165, 167 173n13

Barbot, James, 21, 38n14

Barbot, John, 28, 42n48

Barth, Heinrich, 31, 43m59

Beoku-Betts, Josephine, 40n27, 53, 57n20, 90n33

Birmingham, David, 26–27, 41nn40–41

biscuit, 1, 12n5, 30, 51, 54, 59, 62, 67, 69, 79, 115, 118, 163

Bivins, S. Thomas, 108, 122n25

blackeyed peas, 2, 8, 17–18, 31–33, 47, 52 , 82, 159–60, 169. *See also* cow peas

black power, 102, 109, 111–12, 114, 116

Black, Sandra A., 4, 12nn8–9

Bowditch, Thomas Edward, 19, 37n8

Brand, Joseph C., 35, 44n66

Brown, Mayme L., 163, 173n19

Bullock, Tom, 139–40, 144, 147–48, 149n4, 152n35, 152nn37- 38

Burns, Effie, 77, 81, 95n85, 96n101

Burton, Annie, 66, 89n23

Butler, Octavia, 104, 121n11

Caillié, René, 21, 38n15

cake: and church suppers, 82; introduction into black families, 82; as symbol of affluence, 75–76, 79–80

Campbell, Bebe Moore, 118, 125n60

Campbell, Robert, 20, 37n11

Campbell, Tunis G., 105–6, 121nn14–15, 139, 149n3, 152n39

Carney, Judith A., 23, 31, 33, 39n25, 47–49, 57n6, 57n11

Carver, George Washington, 110–12, 123n34

cassava (manioc): on African plantations, 21; introduction into Africa, 25–28, 40n33–34, 41n39, 42nn44–45, 42nn48–49; name, 28, 42n48; and slave trade, 28–29, 35, 42n50, 47; yield per acre, 19

celebratory meals: barbecue, 69, 92n43; church social, 54, 58n24, 78, 82, 86, 104, 97nn104–5; 121n12, 138n19; family reunion, 12n7, 117, 161–64; seasonal celebrations, 49, 63, 80, 96n98, 117, 153, 157, 160, 163–64, 168–69, 173n19. *See also* Sunday dinner

cereals: African varieties, 21–22, 38nn16–18;

The Food Series

A History of Cooking   *Michael Symons*
Peanuts: The Illustrious History of the Goober Pea   *Andrew F. Smith*
Marketing Nutrition: Soy, Functional Foods, Biotechnology, and Obesity
   Brian Wansink
The Banquet: Dining in the Great Courts of Late Renaissance Europe   *Ken Albala*
The Turkey: An American Story   *Andrew F. Smith*
The Herbalist in the Kitchen   *Gary Allen*
African American Foodways: Explorations of History and Culture   *Edited by*
   Anne L. Bower

The University of Illinois Press
is a founding member of the
Association of American University Presses.

Composed in 10/13.5 Electra
with Type Embellishments display
by Type One, LLC
for the University of Illinois Press
Designed by Paula Newcomb
Manufactured by Thomson-Shore, Inc.

University of Illinois Press
1325 South Oak Street
Champaign, IL 61820-6903
www.press.uillinois.edu